WHEN PROLIFERATION CAUSES PEACE

WHEN PROLIFERATION CAUSES PEACE

THE PSYCHOLOGY OF NUCLEAR CRISES

MICHAEL D. COHEN

Georgetown University Press / Washington, DC

The publisher is not responsible for third-party websites or their content. URL links were active at time of publication.

Library of Congress Cataloging-in-Publication Data

Names: Cohen, Michael D., PhD, author.
Title: When Proliferation Causes Peace : The Psychology of Nuclear Crises / Michael D. Cohen.
Description: Washington, D.C. : Georgetown University Press, 2017. | Includes bibliographical references and index.
Identifiers: LCCN 2017002309 (print) | LCCN 2017008144 (ebook) | ISBN 9781626164949 (hc : alk. paper) | ISBN 9781626164956 (pb : alk. paper) | ISBN 9781626164963 (eb)
Subjects: LCSH: Nuclear crisis control. | Nuclear weapons--Government policy. | Nuclear nonproliferation. | International relations.
Classification: LCC JZ5675 .C62 2017 (print) | LCC JZ5675 (ebook) | DDC 327.1/747—dc23
LC record available at https://lccn.loc.gov/2017002309

♾ This book is printed on acid-free paper meeting the requirements of the American National Standard for Permanence in Paper for Printed Library Materials.

18 17   9 8 7 6 5 4 3 2 First printing

Printed in the United States of America

Cover design by 4 Eyes Design

CONTENTS

ILLUSTRATIONS

Figure

Tables

ACKNOWLEDGMENTS

I HAVE PUZZLED at the strikingly different effects that nuclear weapons have exerted on state foreign policy and international politics since my undergraduate days. How are the weapons that sometimes threaten interstate adversaries and their regions with imminent destruction able to at other times act as the apparent source of geopolitical stability? This book argues that nuclear proliferation is dangerous when leaders learn that "nuclear assertion" is safe but also that it can become safer when they learn that nuclear assertion is dangerous. I have accumulated many debts along the way. John Hobson and Jason Sharman, then at the University of Sydney, consolidated my interest in international politics. In an introductory undergraduate class on international relations theory in 2000, and during an honors thesis year in 2003, when I somehow ended up exploring the psychological sources of sixteenth-century Spanish imperial conquests, John probably unwittingly pushed me onto this career path. Jason has been a more recent source of encouragement and feedback, and I will miss him as he heads to the University of Cambridge.

I have been very fortunate to receive guidance and support from Dick Price, Alan Jacobs, and Patrick Morgan at the University of British Columbia. Dick permitted me to follow my curiosity while ensuring that I maintained a focus on the broader international relations landscape. Pat Morgan continues to amaze me with his knowledge of nuclear weapons and deterrence and was a great initial sounding board for many of the ideas developed here. Alan Jacobs ensured that the research design and methodological choices were held to (his own) very high standards. I am thankful for these three fine scholars' commitment to my own intellectual development. I am also thankful to Nathan Allen, Adam Bower, Arjun Chowdhury, Fred Cutler, Nic Dragojlovic, Wade Huntley, Brian Job, John McAndrews, Ben Nyblade, and John Voortman, all at UBC, for their constant source of encouragement and feedback. I am grateful to P. R. Chari at the Institute of Peace and Conflict Studies in

Delhi for hosting me for a month and for offering many helpful introductions. Also worthy of special mention is John M. Owen, who during his annual summer sojourns to Vancouver was kind enough to share his reactions to my ideas and his swimming pool—sometimes at the same time—on many occasions.

My debts have continued to mount since leaving Vancouver. I owe a special debt of gratitude to Sten Rynning at the University of Southern Denmark for offering what became my first academic position. Most of this book was written there, and I am especially thankful to Sten as well as to Erik Albaek, Arjen van Dalen, Peter Viggo Jakobsen, Bob Klemmensen, Paul Marx, Asbjorn Norgaard, Niels Bjerre Poulsen, and Casper Sylvest for providing such a wonderful academic environment. I am deeply grateful to Soren and Lisbeth Hesseldahl for welcoming my family and I to Denmark with such great hospitality and good humor.

My greatest academic thanks go to Robert Jervis. He invited me to spend the fall of 2014 at Columbia University to complete this book. Upon arriving and having my first meeting with Bob, I presented a long and detailed reviewer's memo that had generated some reactions on my part and had led to further questions that I was keen to discuss. He smiled and informed me that he had written the memo. Bob's knowledge about history, international relations, nuclear weapons, and political psychology continues to astound me. I could not have asked for a better mentor, and this book is far better as a result of his critical input over several often-lengthy discussions. I am thankful for a mini workshop Bob hosted on an article-length start of this book, and I appreciate the comments of Peter Clement, Mike Horowitz, Jack Levy, Peter Liberman, Kimberly Marten, Jack Snyder, and Keren Yarhi-Milo. Further afield, I am grateful to Debbie Larson, Paul MacDonald, Jonathan Mercer, and Todd Sechser, all of whom offered detailed and helpful comments on multiple chapters even in the face of their own research commitments. For other helpful insights on the psychological sources of foreign policies and nuclear weapons–related issues I benefited from discussions or correspondence with Taylor Fravel, Frank Gavin, Jacques Hymans, Tim Naftali, Vipin Narang, and Brian Rathbun. I am also very grateful for very helpful feedback by the external reviewers. In 2015 an opportunity arose to relocate to my hometown of Sydney, and I am thankful to Natalie Klein and Ben Schreer at the Department of Security Studies and Criminology at Macquarie University for a rewarding first year. Last, but not least, I thank Don Jacobs at Georgetown University Press for guiding me through the editorial process. I am astounded at the immense capacity of all those that have helped me write this book, and I am thankful to everyone. I apologize if I have missed anyone.

My sources of scholarly support pale in comparison to that provided by my loving and supportive family. My mother has encouraged my pursuit of scholarship for as long as I can remember, and I am deeply thankful for her support throughout my life in Sydney, Vancouver, Denmark, and now Sydney again. My father encouraged me to pursue my dreams, and I was lost for words when he passed away two weeks after I returned to Sydney. My sons, Samuel and Robbie, were born during graduate school years and have provided an endless source of love, joy, and engagement; they always find a way to force on me the need to spend some time away from writing. My newborn daughter, Sofia, has enriched my life in all sorts of ways. My parents-in-law, Tim and Georgina, have frequently asked about this book and have been great sources of encouragement and stimulation along the way.

My greatest debt of gratitude goes to my wife, Anna. She said "I do" and two months later followed me to Vancouver, where she knew no one. She was later willing to leave Vancouver for Denmark and then leave Denmark for Sydney. She has sat through too many discussions about nuclear weapons and foreign policy and has been an unparalleled model of commitment. I could not have asked for a more loving, caring, and supportive wife, and I dedicate this book to her.

Nuclear Weapons: Cause of Conflict or Principle of Peace?

NUCLEAR PROLIFERATION threatens international peace and security. The development of nuclear weapons can lead states to pursue dangerous foreign policies that they will otherwise usually avoid. Since the dawn of the nuclear age, policymakers and scholars have grappled with stopping the international spread of nuclear weapons and ensuring that those few states that develop nuclear weapons adopt safe and desirable policies. Nuclear powers can engage in conventional and subconventional aggression if their nuclear arsenals deter their adversaries from some types of retaliation and can complicate if not evade others' coercive diplomacy, issue military threats themselves, and deter others' military intervention. Nuclear powers can also undermine their adversaries' alliances by challenging them to uphold their commitments to others in the face of the high costs of nuclear escalation. They can consolidate their own alliances by exporting sensitive nuclear materials that assist their own allies in developing the bomb. All of this can cause still others to develop nuclear weapons. In short, nuclear proliferation currently is considered by many scholars and policymakers to be the greatest challenge to the stability of the international system.[1]

However, what new nuclear powers might actually do with their nuclear weapons remains unclear. US strategy toward nuclear proliferation in recent decades has been founded on the assumption that nuclear weapons will embolden new nuclear powers to challenge their regional orders and cause conflict. These countries are determined to revise the status quo but are unable to do so; nuclear weapons would, according to conventional wisdom, embolden US adversaries to revise their regional orders and threaten defiance or retaliation with nuclear escalation. Because these states' more powerful adversaries cannot easily deter this, nuclear proliferation by states such as North Korea and Iran is usually considered a very serious threat to regional stability and international security.

President Barack Obama's director of national intelligence, James Clapper, recently argued that "nuclear proliferation poses one of the greatest threats to US national security."[2] Former undersecretary of state for arms control and international security Robert Joseph claimed that an Iranian bomb "could embolden the leadership in Tehran to advance its aggressive ambitions in and outside of the region, both directly and through the terrorists it supports."[3] Former US ambassador to the United Nations Susan Rice claimed that "North Korea with nuclear weapons adds to the larger proliferation risk."[4] When he was president, George W. Bush claimed that "adversaries such as Iran, Iraq and North Korea would be able to 'blackmail' the United States if they obtained nuclear weapons."[5] Former secretary of state Hillary Clinton claimed that "a nuclear-weapons armed Iran . . . is a direct threat to the lives and the livelihoods and the stability not only of the region but beyond."[6] Former US secretary of defense Robert Gates said that "with the North Koreans' continuing development of nuclear weapons, and their development of intercontinental ballistic missiles, North Korea is becoming a direct threat to the United States."[7] Scholar Barry Posen notes that policymakers fear that an Iranian nuclear arsenal could "embolden Tehran to undertake aggressive, even reckless, actions."[8] As scholar Scott Sagan claims, "we should worry that Iranian leaders with nuclear weapons will see them as a shield behind which they can more safely engage in aggression against neighbors and the United States."[9]

These many expressed concerns are not new nor the totality of comments. After only weeks into his presidency, George H. W. Bush began a national security review by asking how "acquisition by Libya, Iraq or others of long-range weapons, chemical, biological, and nuclear warheads and other advanced systems affect the prospect that countries would threaten or attack U.S. interests, U.S. friends and allies or other nations."[10] Even as far back as 1965, the Gilpatric Committee declared that "the spread of nuclear weapons poses an increasingly grave threat to the security of the United States."[11]

One can make theoretically plausible and empirically supported claims that nuclear weapons do not cause conflict. After all, most nuclear powers most of the time authorize more-desirable foreign policies. This begs a question: Under what conditions do nuclear powers typically authorize dangerous and aggressive foreign policies, and under what conditions do they authorize restraint? The argument here is that nuclear proliferation is dangerous when leaders believe that nuclear assertion is safe, but proliferation becomes safer when leaders learn that nuclear assertion is dangerous. If the leaders of future new nuclear powers such as North Korea and Iran develop nuclear weapons and behave aggressively, the United States and its allies will need to ensure that they experience fear of imminent nuclear war and also believe that they have control over escalation. If US policymakers are able to strike this balance, brazen new nuclear powers will exhibit the same restraint that most experienced nuclear powers do already.

The basic question of how nuclear weapons influence new nuclear powers' foreign policies remains unaddressed. Scholarly attention has focused largely on why states develop nuclear weapons and how others can influence these states' policies. However, we presently have a poor understanding of when and how nuclear weapons might cause new nuclear powers to authorize aggressive foreign policies. Were North Korea to acquire the capability to target South Korea or the United States with nuclear weapons, whether and how North Korea's foreign policy would change is open to debate. If Iran were to successfully acquire nuclear weapons, whether and how that country would be emboldened to pursue greater regional ambitions through dangerous coercive threats remains unclear. And it is uncertain how Israel, Iran's regional nuclear adversary, and other potential nuclear powers such as Saudi Arabia might respond. What foreign policy choices will these new nuclear powers make? How will these foreign policy decisions affect regional stability and conflict?

Examining the foreign policy decisions that established nuclear powers have made in the past will help answer these questions, as well as others of importance, such as why some nuclear powers are more prone to conflict than others. For systematic and predictable reasons, *new* nuclear powers make clearly identifiable strategic gambles that greatly influence regional and global peace and stability. As *experienced* nuclear powers, however, they tend to adopt markedly different foreign policies that have different effects.

The foreign policy choices made by nuclear powers in the past can provide valuable insight into today's crucial challenges of nuclear proliferation and international stability, particularly in the context of new powers appearing. The analysis herein thus will focus on the overlooked causes of new nuclear power foreign policy choices and concentrate on answering three primary questions: What major strategic and foreign policy choices do new nuclear powers make, and why? What choices do experienced nuclear powers make, and why? What is the impact of these choices on interstate conflict? This focus helps resolve three outstanding puzzles: First, why are some nuclear powers more conflict prone than others? Second, why do recent nuclear powers such as India and Pakistan seem to have learned little from the experiences of the superpowers about the political limits and opportunities of nuclear weapons? Third, why do some new nuclear powers push so dangerously hard to resolve unfavorable disputes but then accept the status quo when the underlying diplomatic issues remain unchanged? Robert Jervis notes that the question of "*when* and *how* states adjust to an unacceptable situation remains a yawning gap in our knowledge" (emphasis added).[12]

New Nuclear Power's Foreign Policy Choices

Despite having lived with nuclear weapons for over seven decades, we presently have scant knowledge about the foreign policy decisions of new nuclear powers.[13] Analysis has tended to focus on *why* they have developed nuclear weapons.[14] Little comparative thought has been given to the ensuing foreign policies. The scholarly literature on the consequences of nuclear proliferation and deterrence assumes that how long a state has had nuclear weapons is irrelevant. This literature offers two positions. One argues that, according to the emboldenment logic combined with the challenges associated with maintaining an operational nuclear deterrent, the spread of nuclear weapons will increase the probability of aggressive foreign policies and interstate conflict.[15] The other argues that the high costs of nuclear war deter most nuclear and conventional aggression most of the time.[16] But these are both incomplete.[17]

The fact is, how long a state has possessed nuclear weapons does profoundly and systematically influence its foreign policy decisions and the likelihood of that state being in conflict or at war.[18] In light of accepted wisdom, the actual experiences of nuclear powers present a striking picture. The historical record does not show consistent emboldenment or moderation; rather, there is significant *temporal variation* in the conflict propensity of nuclear powers. Soviet policies in Berlin and Cuba from 1958 through 1962, immediately after Moscow developed the capability to target the United States with nuclear weapons, caused the most dangerous years of the Cold War. But Soviet policies in Berlin and Cuba were safer after 1963. Pakistani policies in Kashmir from 1990 through 2002 caused the 1999 Kargil War and the ten-month nuclear crisis in 2001–2002. But Pakistani policy in Kashmir after 2003 has been significantly less dangerous and by 2012 fatalities in Kashmir had dropped down to near the 1989 level. Chinese forces engaged in several skirmishes with Soviet troops around Zhenbao Island in 1969, five years after China developed nuclear weapons. But Chinese troops have not engaged in conflict with the Soviet Union since 1970. Israel fought an average of one war every two years with its Arab adversaries immediately after developing nuclear weapons in 1967; in the forty years after the 1973 Yom Kippur War it fought a war only once every eight years.

New nuclear powers, in fact, tend to behave in ways that cause conflict and increase the likelihood of nuclear war. Their policies look very different from the policies chosen by the same *experienced* nuclear powers. Yet the foreign policies of new nuclear powers that are most relevant to the emerging geopolitical environment in East Asia and elsewhere have been largely ignored. Scholarship must address *how* nuclear proliferation can cause and prevent conflict and *when* these different outcomes occur. At present, scholars and policymakers lack an analytical lens to use in understanding the core strategic foreign policy choices of new nuclear powers.

In their magisterial work, *The Spread of Nuclear Weapons: An Enduring Debate*, Scott Sagan and Kenneth Waltz show how nuclear weapons have caused and prevented interstate conflict. But we lack an understanding of when these different outcomes are likely to occur. As a result, policymakers and scholars have cherry-picked particular episodes to support prior contentions about the dangers associated with the spread of nuclear weapons. This is an unfortunate state of the field. We need a dynamic theory about nuclear weapons and state foreign policies to better specify the conditions within which nuclear weapons are likely to cause or prevent aggressive foreign policies and interstate conflict, and when proliferation optimists and pessimists are likely to be correct.

A few studies have touched on the issue of new nuclear powers' foreign policies. Vipin Narang developed the first comparative theory of nuclear doctrine, specifying the conditions when states are likely to select three distinct nuclear postures that result in very different deterrent effects.[19] But posture is not policy, and Narang's important book does not address the link between nuclear weapons and foreign policy. Why, for example, did Pakistan's assertiveness in Kashmir increase after it developed what Narang calls an asymmetric escalation doctrine in 1998, but then decrease after 2003? His otherwise important book provides no answers to this question. Jeffrey Knopf has argued that the stability that proliferation optimists expect is not automatic but requires leader learning about the dangers of nuclear weapons.[20] This book builds on this argument through developing and testing a theory to specify the conditions when leaders learn what lessons about nuclear weapons, the effects of this learning on their foreign policy, and the effects of this foreign policy on interstate conflict. The learning that teaches leaders about the dangers of nuclear weapons and actually changes state foreign policy is not only cognitive but also deeply emotional. Russell Leng has argued that in enduring rivalries, leader learning "most often encourage[s] behavior that reinforce[s] the hostility between the rival states and fuel[s] the escalation of subsequent crises."[21] But Leng's model does not address how nuclear weapons influence the variation in escalation dynamics, and the lack of escalation that followed the Cuban Missile Crisis—and to which we must add the decline in violence in Kashmir since 2003, which occurred after Leng's book was published—contradicts Leng's thesis. Leng noted that "a different kind of learning occurred as the Cuban Missile crisis escalated."[22] The sources of this learning and why it caused the changes in US and Soviet policies remain unclear. Indeed, Leng's core finding—that "the lessons that key policymakers in each state drew from their recurring crises were all within the bounds of realpolitik"—says little about significant variation in these choices.[23] Why, for example, did Khrushchev approach his revisionist goals in West Berlin so differently after the Cuban Missile Crisis? The discussion that follows incorporates nuclear weapons and human psychology into a framework that explains foreign policy choices and escalation patterns between nuclear-armed rivals.

More will be said about why new nuclear powers are highly prone to authorizing aggressive foreign policies that cause interstate conflict but are not once those same states gain experience. This variation will be explained with reference to leaders: the psychological biases that pervade their thinking and the approaches they take to key strategic choices regarding nuclear weapons and foreign policy. International relations specialists often assume that leaders are severely constrained by factors beyond their control, such as the balance of power, international institutions, and global norms. According to this view, leaders merely respond to environmental pressures and their roles are not important.[24] Those that study the role of leaders often focus on their strategic brilliance or constraints within powerful domestic institutions.[25]

Despite the influential scholarship of the late 1970s and 1980s that addressed how psychological biases influence deterrence, recent studies that attribute leader behavior to psychological factors usually apply prospect theory, which focuses on whether leaders believe that they are recovering losses or making gains.[26] Leaders do indeed often matter. The focus here will be on the sources of fundamental strategic foreign policy choices, and leaders' preferences and state policy are used interchangeably. As Barton Bernstein has argued, "crises fix attention and make the government leader the central decisionmaker . . . fundamentally, *the president decides*."[27] Thus John Kennedy ignored the advice of his executive committee and kept his colleagues in the dark about his decision to tell the Soviet ambassador, through Kennedy's brother, that he was willing to remove the Turkish Jupiter missiles. Leaders' foreign policies are fundamentally influenced by the psychological boost of developing their own nuclear weapons and the fear of imminent nuclear war.[28]

Leaders' behaviors in nuclear crises, as elsewhere, are likely to be influenced by the way they perceive and process information. Different beliefs lead to different policies. However, impersonal theories of nuclear behavior dominate the field: in the conventional wisdom, all leaders should exhibit near-equal policies conditional on the balance of power, information, and resolve.[29] A different approach will be taken here. The basic insight that fuels this analysis is that different personal experiences tend to cause people to develop unique beliefs and thus behave in strikingly different ways. This insight is at the core of what psychologists call the "availability heuristic," and it is one of the key findings from decades of psychological research. For example, consider people who have friends who have divorced: if those friends subsequently experienced temporary happiness, then these people are more likely to get divorced themselves, even though divorce generally causes long-term unhappiness. Or people in power with direct military combat experience are less likely to authorize the use of military force than those with military but no combat experience.[30]

The tendency for people to be profoundly influenced by their personal experiences while ignoring important information about events they have not personally experienced also leads to stereotyping and the perseverance of discredited beliefs. In all of these cases, variation in attention, perception, and information processing causes variation in policy preferences and behavior. This stands in contrast to theories that assume that people have near optimal attention and information-processing capabilities such that all tend to behave fundamentally similarly in the face of external constraints.

It is not clear why, from a strictly rational perspective, the experience of fear should influence behavior any more than a sense of danger short of fear. Recent advances in cognitive neuroscience (described in chapter 2) show that the experience of fear profoundly influences behavior. People with damage to the amygdala region of the brain—the part responsible for processing fear—tend to engage in all sorts of dangerous behaviors, from carelessly handling dangerous snakes to returning to places where their lives were threatened. Leaders willing to authorize risky foreign policies involving nuclear weapons tend to alter their behavior not after experiencing danger but rather following an incident of fear of imminent nuclear destruction. Contrary to rational expectations, behavior changes even when incentives and information do not. Rather than assume that people will behave in ways that computers might predict they would, the discussion will show how international politics are profoundly influenced by the limitations of the human mind and the dangers posed by nuclear weapons.

Fear has a long pedigree in the study of international relations: scholars as far back as Thucydides made explicit reference to it.[31] Kenneth Waltz argues that "deterrence does not depend on rationality but fear."[32] Robert Jervis argues that the fear of being exploited exacerbates the security dilemma.[33] For John Mearsheimer, acknowledging that "great powers fear each other is a central aspect of life in the international system: anarchy and uncertainty about other states' intentions creates an irreducible level of fear among states that leads to power maximizing behavior."[34] However, when fear has what effects is less clear.

Fear does not always deter aggressive nuclear powers, and it's unclear when and how it exacerbates or moderates international tensions. Of critical interest to this analysis is *not* determining how sensitive leaders are to the general costs and dangers associated with the development, maintenance, and operational planning associated with nuclear weapons. Rather, in this context "fear" refers to the situation when a leader stumbles into a nuclear crisis and genuinely expects nuclear escalation and massive destruction within hours or days. This fear has caused some of the most important foreign policy turnarounds of the nuclear era. The critical variable is not the possession of nuclear weapons nor a specific nuclear doctrine but whether a leader has personally experienced the imminent prospect of total destruction that nuclear weapons ultimately promise. This deeply emotional reaction influences fundamental variation in the foreign policies of nuclear powers.

Particular nuclear postures, defined as "a state's peacetime nuclear orientation and procedures for deployment and signaling during crises," will not be considered.[35] Rather, a differentiation will be made between two basic types of foreign *policies* that reflects the fundamental dilemma associated with nuclear weapons. On the one hand, leaders of new nuclear powers might believe that, given the high costs of nuclear war, their interests are best served by maintaining the status quo. This strategy usually proscribes force as a method of deterrence and sees a greater role for diplomacy and confidence-building measures. This generic strategy can be called *foreign policy restraint*. On the other hand, leaders who face threatening and dangerous security environments might believe that the simple fact of their nuclear weapons will deter retaliation, even in light of their own attempts to revise important parts of the status quo through coercive threats, territory grabs, displays and deployments of force, or support for insurgencies. This generic strategy is called *foreign policy assertion*. Undoubtedly, a leader can authorize foreign policy assertion to one state and foreign policy restraint to another. The discussion here focuses on foreign policies used in the context of the most menacing security threat, which is usually a nuclear-armed adversary.

Experienced nuclear powers facing assertive new nuclear powers have a similar dilemma. Such leaders might adopt foreign policy restraint, ranging from inaction and cheap talk to mobilizations suited to defending the status quo. Or they might authorize assertive foreign policies, especially if restrained policies have not reined in an adversary's assertive behavior. The discussion of the strategic choices and foreign policies of new and experienced nuclear powers will not explicitly address nuclear postures, the number and types of warheads, or the delivery vehicles that a state builds, although these choices and policies will tend to be different given geographic and other variables.

Nuclear weapons present leaders with a fundamental trade-off: nuclear assertion may lead to long-elusive geopolitical gains, but it also might risk conflict and escalation; nuclear restraint may minimize current risk but also lead to the tacit acceptance of an unbearable status quo. Leaders facing assertive nuclear powers might authorize restrained policies in the hope that either the adversary's nuclear assertion will be short-lived or that restraint will reduce the probability of conflict and escalation. But leaders who face an assertive nuclear power for long enough might also be willing to accept the risks of their own assertion in order to pressure the adversary to authorize restraint. They may reason that restrained foreign policies have proved insufficient in stopping the adversary's assertions or that the adversary's nuclear assertion did not precipitate a nuclear crisis, so theirs may not either.

Leaders' approach to this critical trade-off has driven the patterns in conflict and peace that nuclear weapons present. And variation in leaders' responses to this dilemma of nuclear assertion both drove the dangers and opportunities experienced during the Cold War and will continue to drive the creation of new dangers and opportunities in South Asia, East Asia, and the Middle East today. But why are some nuclear powers more conflict prone than others? Why are some nuclear powers willing to accept so much risk in order to revise an intolerable situation but then unwilling to accept it when the balance of power and the situation itself has not changed?

Despite much attention being paid to why states develop nuclear weapons, how they can be prevented from doing so, and how they can be deterred if they do develop them, little attention has been paid to the amount of experience a leader or state has with nuclear weapons because it is assumed that this experience is not relevant. This assumption is deleterious to understanding the sources of nuclear power foreign policy. Some nuclear powers are more conflict prone than others, and most new nuclear powers have authorized aggressive foreign policies early on but shown restraint once they have gained experience. Why has this occurred? Fear matters for international conflict and stability, particularly among adversaries with the potential to destroy each other within minutes. Variation in the strategic choices and foreign policies made by the same state, which has thus far been overlooked as a subject for study, is a striking puzzle. Attention to this variation greatly enhances our understanding of the causal explanations of nuclear powers' foreign policies and conflict behavior, and it promises to enrich the policies used with states such as North Korea and Iran. There is scant evidence that the recognition of the danger that nuclear weapons pose systematically influences nuclear powers' orientation to the fundamental dilemma of nuclear assertion. Rather, leaders' experience of fear of imminent nuclear war—whether or not nuclear war is in fact imminent—determines critical patterns of conflict and peace in the nuclear age.

The Argument in Brief

Despite an obsession with nuclear proliferation among the policymaking and scholarly communities, the fact that new nuclear states tend to adopt different and more dangerous foreign policies than experienced ones, at least toward their principal adversaries, has been almost totally neglected. This variation matters greatly to international conflict and stability. The psychological bias known as the availability heuristic tends to make leaders in new nuclear powers authorize assertive foreign policies. This focus on the availability heuristic builds on decades of research in psychology and international relations, which has produced a vast body of literature demonstrating the impact of how people's brains work in a wide variety of domains. The goal here is to show how the availability heuristic also influences the core direction of nuclear powers' foreign policies.

The availability heuristic causes people to mentally focus on data points that are more "available" to them and neglect those that are not. Nuclear weapons require large financial, technological, bureaucratic, and political investments. Nuclear weapons programs usually attract sustained international efforts to roll them back, and nuclear tests usually cause negative international reactions that are hard to miss. The psychological power of nuclear weapons is usually quite cognitively available to the leaders of new nuclear powers. When those leaders confront the nuclear assertion dilemma and the subsequent trade-offs, the high investment in their nuclear programs and attention of the world that their nuclear efforts generate are likely to loom large. Then, because their experience in nuclear weapon acquisition is largely positive, they will view the weapons' coercive possibilities in a similarly optimistic vein. They will tend to believe that because nuclear weapons have cost so much, they must be important tools for influencing international politics. They may not consider the experiences of other leaders who had confronted the nuclear assertion dilemma in the past, despite the high incentives to learn from others in similar situations. The experiences of others are not as cognitively accessible as a leader's own experiences with nuclear weapons. Leaders of new nuclear powers tend to authorize assertive foreign policies and accept the risk of nuclear escalation until those leaders experience fear of imminent nuclear war themselves. They will experience fear of imminent nuclear war only after their principal adversary authorizes an assertive foreign policy, whether that takes months or years.

Unfortunately, threats and use of force matched with demands for concessions will eventually yield not concessions but similar assertive behavior. Nuclear powers that receive assertive nuclear threats from others may respond with restrained foreign policies. But if a nuclear power leader is sufficiently resolved to authorize assertive policies, cheap talk and passive defenses may sustain the status quo but likely will not stop the nuclear assertion.[36]

Retaliatory nuclear assertion—threats to destroy troops or capture territory from the coercer, made credible by military mobilizations suited to offensive purposes—may be necessary to end the immediate dispute. But this increases the probability of armed conflict and advertent or inadvertent nuclear escalation. After both states have authorized assertive policies, leaders of one or both states may experience fear of imminent nuclear war even in cases when nuclear war is not imminent. The experience of imminent destruction is cognitively very available to them, and leaders will likely learn the limits and dangers of nuclear assertion from it. This experience of fear of imminent nuclear war causes leaders to authorize restrained foreign policies, both toward those states that they earlier authorized assertive foreign policies toward and quite possibly toward those that they did not.

Fear reduces one's tolerance of risk. Recent waves of cognitive neuroscience research have found that fear causes risk aversion in many areas of people's lives. The goal here is to show how the association between the availability heuristic and fear strongly influences nuclear powers' foreign policies and, as a result, the dangers posed by the spread of nuclear weapons. Leaders who experience fear of imminent nuclear war themselves tend to authorize restrained foreign policies and avoid the escalatory risks associated with assertion.[37]

Leaders do not stay in office forever, and the experiences of leaders who succeed leaders who experienced fear is beyond the scope of this book. Nonetheless, it is likely that successors to leaders who experienced fear in nuclear crises will also have experienced fear, especially in cases of autocracies where leader turnover is slower and successors may have been closely involved with the policies that dragged the nation into a nuclear crisis. Later generations of leaders, however, may not have experienced fear in the earlier nuclear crisis, and this suggests intergenerational dynamics at work (see the conclusion).

This experience of fear of imminent nuclear war may not occur after the first assertive attempt because defenders may respond with cheaper restrained policies before risking nuclear assertion themselves. If nuclear assertion tends to not cause sustained revisions to the status quo, why wouldn't leaders learn from these cognitively available experiences of the limits of nuclear assertion and authorize restrained policies before experiencing fear at the nuclear brink? The availability of nuclear weapons is likely to loom large. Nuclear assertion that does not yield the desired concessions but which also does not cause a leader to reach the nuclear brink are often followed by more nuclear assertion. Unsuccessful nuclear assertion is unlikely to lead to nuclear restraint because failures tend to be attributed to bad luck or random situational factors. However, leaders who authorize nuclear assertion and experience fear usually abandon the strategy and authorize nuclear restraint, irrespective of their beliefs regarding its success.

The overall point is that nuclear proliferation becomes dangerous when leaders believe that nuclear assertion is safe, but nuclear proliferation is actually safer when leaders believe that nuclear assertion is dangerous. Current alternative theories that can explain a nuclear power's foreign policy and conflict propensity—including rational choice, structural realism, and domestic politics—are indeterminate and thus of limited help in predicting the choices that leaders will make.

The psychological learning theory described above—what here is called the ALF two-stage model of availability, learning, and fear—is based on the neoclassical realist tradition in international relations theory that emphasizes the importance of both the balance of power in the international system and other factors at work inside the state (in this case, leaders bucking these forces).[38] ALF explains why most new nuclear powers tend to authorize assertive foreign policies whereas most experienced nuclear powers tend toward restraint. It also offers a clear prediction for a state's approach to the fundamental dilemma of nuclear assertion, based on whether a leader has personally experienced fear of imminent nuclear war.

A review of past experiences during the Cold War and in South Asia and East Asia (chapters 3, 4, and 5) shows that the ALF theory provides the most applicable and falsifiable framework for specifying throughout the historical record the causal mechanism whereby the foreign policies of new nuclear powers are made and change. Insofar as nuclear assertion is harder to deter than nuclear restraint, the theory also contributes to debates about when the deterrence of nuclear powers is more or less likely to work.[39] This analysis resolves the three puzzles mentioned earlier: why some nuclear powers are more conflict prone than others, why some leaders of nuclear powers seem to not learn from history, and why some nuclear powers push so hard to revise a regional security architecture then later simply accept it. While the good news is that nuclear proliferation is not as dangerous over the long run as is commonly assumed, the bad news is that no amount of learning from history can tame the perils of inexperience facing new nuclear powers. There is no substitute for staring down the nuclear brink and experiencing fear of imminent nuclear war.

Case Selection

A heavy reliance on historical data that addresses causation—"process tracing" and "causal process observations"—is a natural methodological choice for examining leader learning about nuclear assertion.[40] The study of leader learning, especially about nuclear assertion, is not amenable to statistical analysis, because it is difficult to identify learning—as opposed to simple policy changes—without detailed causal process observations.[41] Thus, detailed studies of Nikita Khrushchev and Pervez Musharraf and shorter treatments of John Kennedy, Atal Bihari Vajpayee, Richard Nixon, and Mao Zedong are included. These leaders were selected not only because of their obvious historical importance but also for specific methodological reasons.

Five points need to be highlighted concerning methodology. First, because this analysis is the first attempt to assess the effect of fear and the availability heuristic on new nuclear power leaders' fundamental foreign policy choices, the focus on relatively dominant leaders helps simplify the process.[42] Occasionally authority over foreign policy is more fragmented, such as was found in the Soviet Union in 1965. But leaders' preferences usually exert a powerful influence on their countries' foreign policies, and these chosen leaders are no exception. It should be relatively easy to assess whether psychological biases actually mattered in the development of foreign policy in these selected countries.

Second, like most contemporary nuclear proliferation challenges, the chosen leaders faced intense geopolitical competition and had no superpower "patron." France, Britain, and Israel, on the other hand, had a formal or robust US commitment to their defense. While it is likely that availability influences the foreign policy choices of *all* leaders of nuclear powers, any resulting emboldenment is likely to be less assertive when a state can rely on a superpower patron's commitment to their security. Britain and France behaved more assertively after developing nuclear weapons: the British invaded Egypt in 1956 and France substantially withdrew from NATO ten years later. But these assertive acts, while dangerous, were less destabilizing than Khrushchev's Berlin ultimatums or Musharraf's Kashmir grab. The United States during its period of nuclear monopoly between 1945–1949 is also anomalous in the sense that unlike all nuclear powers since then Truman did not face a nuclear-powered strategic competitor and was generally advised that the first Soviet nuclear test would occur well after 1949.

The model developed here therefore applies to all nuclear powers but is likely to point to more destabilizing effects on international security when the nuclear power does not have a powerful ally. Indeed, findings regarding nuclear powers lacking allies would be relevant for states most likely to develop nuclear weapons today, such as North Korea and Iran.[43]

Table 1.1 provides a summary of the cases of nuclear assertion examined here. This group of cases differs in several ways from an influential recent analysis of nuclear compellence done by Todd Sechser and Matt Fuhrmann.[44] Sechser and Fuhrmann addressed whether nuclear weapons help make coercive threats effective. But properly addressing the sources and mechanisms of nuclear emboldenment also requires a review of the logics of coercion and military victory.

Sechser and Fuhrmann looked for coercive demands made by nuclear powers and found forty-eight cases total. Seventeen of those were the demands made of the Serbian, Iraqi, and Afghan regimes by the US, the British, and the French from 1994 through 2001; nuclear emboldenment likely played no role in those. Five of the cases were South Africa's 1985 demands against leaders in Zimbabwe, Mozambique, Zambia, Lesotho, and Zambia; those leaders may not have known that South Africa possessed a small nuclear arsenal. For a case to be defined as nuclear assertion here, historical evidence must show that nuclear weapons *caused* revisionist behavior and specifically that a leader issued threats or used force because, and only because, he had nuclear weapons at his disposal.

Twenty-eight cases in Sechser and Fuhrmann's data set—about 60 percent—were made by the United States, the Soviet Union, China, India, and Pakistan. Nuclear assertion is much rarer than nuclear powers issuing coercive threats. Only six cases and four episodes of nuclear assertion—

Table 1.1. Cases of Nuclear Assertion

Challenger	Target	Issue	Year	Fuhrmann and Sechser coding	Revised coding
Soviet Union	France	Suez Crisis	1956	Success	Failure
Soviet Union	Britain	Suez Crisis	1956	Success	Failure
Soviet Union	United States	Berlin Crisis	1958–59	–	Failure
Soviet Union	United States	Berlin Crisis	1961	–	Failure
Soviet Union	United States	Berlin/Cuba Crisis	1962	–	Failure
Soviet Union	China	Zhenbao Island Dispute	1969	Qualified Success	Success
United States	Soviet Union	Berlin Crisis	1961	–	Failure
United States	Soviet Union	Berlin/Cuba Crisis	1962	Success	Success
United States	Soviet Union	Vietnam War	1969	–	Failure
United States	Soviet Union	Middle East Crisis	1973	–	Failure
China	Soviet Union	Zhenbao Island Dispute	1969	–	Failure
Pakistan	India	Kashmir Conflict	1999	–	Failure
Pakistan	India	Kashmir Conflict	2001	–	Failure
Pakistan	India	Kashmir Conflict	2002	–	Failure
India	Pakistan	Terrorist organizations	2001	Failure	Failure
India	Pakistan	Terrorist organizations	2002	–	Success

Note: Hash mark indicates no coding is assigned.

Soviet threats in the 1956 Suez Crisis, US threats in the Cuban Missile Crisis, Indian threats in 2001, and Soviet threats to China in 1969—are also captured in the Sechser and Fuhrmann data set. They found ten cases of successful compellent threats made by nuclear-armed challengers. At most only three cases of successful nuclear assertion were made, all of which were authorized in order to stop an adversary's assertive behavior. The only case of successful nuclear compellence or assertion found both in the Fuhrmann and Sechser group and in the current analysis is John Kennedy's nuclear threats to Nikita Khrushchev during the Cuban Missile Crisis. Both Sechser and Fuhrmann and the analysis here find that nuclear weapons allow revisions to a status quo in about one-fifth of compellence/assertive episodes. However, the argument here is that this overstates the effectiveness of nuclear weapon–supported revisionism because the only status quo that nuclear assertion actually revised was an adversary's nuclear assertion. Nuclear assertion restored the pre-nuclear assertion status quo but did not in any other way revise it.

Third, comparing these leaders at different points in time allows for wide variation in the independent variable of interest—that is, the fear of imminent nuclear war. Khrushchev, Musharraf, and Mao authorized very different foreign policies after experiencing fear of imminent nuclear escalation even though the balance of power, domestic politics, and other variables had not changed.[45] The studies of Nixon and Kennedy show that leaders in experienced nuclear powers can also authorize nuclear assertion when a leader finds particular experiences with nuclear weapons cognitively accessible (Nixon) or received assertive threats (Kennedy) cognitively accessible. Nixon never reached the nuclear brink, and he returned to a coercive foreign policy throughout his presidency. Although Kennedy's assertive strategy during the Cuban Missile Crisis is atypical insofar as it worked, the fear he experienced during the crisis caused him to adopt a restrained foreign policy toward the Soviet Union and Cuba thereafter.

Fourth, contrary to many contemporary analyses, the impact of nuclear weapons on the foreign policies of the two main cases examined in this book is strikingly similar. Vipin Narang echoes conventional wisdom when he claims that "the superpower model of nuclear strategy and deterrence does not seem to be applicable . . . to India and Pakistan, which have small arsenals and where an active and enduring territorial rivalry is punctuated by repeated crises that openly risk nuclear war."[46] But this line of argument overlooks an important similarity between the Cold War and South Asia: like most contemporary potential new nuclear powers, Khrushchev and Musharraf deeply desired permanent revisions to the status quos (in Berlin and Kashmir) that they were unable to sustain with conventional military power. As will be shown, the ejection of NATO's and India's influence from West Berlin and Kashmir respectively were viewed as imperative for the viability and security of the Soviet and Pakistani states.

During the Cold War, NATO and the Warsaw Pact were roughly equals in terms of soldiers, guns, vehicles, and other forms of conventional military power. One important study of the Allies concluded that "in many respects, we were 'superior'; in some respects, they were."[47] Khrushchev himself confessed to his presidium colleagues on January 8, 1962, that "the enemy is strong and not weaker than we are."[48] Moreover, while the Soviet Union first tested a nuclear device in 1949, Khrushchev did not acquire the capability to reliably target the United States with intercontinental ballistic missiles until 1959, the start of the crisis years.[49] In South Asia, fatalities in the Kashmir insurgency substantially increased after Pakistan developed nuclear weapons in 1990. In short, it is difficult to argue that material power or domestic politics alone explain why the Soviet Union and Pakistan adopted assertive foreign policies after developing nuclear weapons capable of targeting their principal adversaries but then shifted to restrained foreign policies after Khrushchev and Musharraf experienced fear of imminent nuclear war.

Finally, while data on the beliefs, attention spans, and experiences of fear of leaders in new nuclear powers is elusive, there is much more information available about the Soviet Union and Pakistan than about Israel, which still denies having nuclear weapons, or South Africa, which eliminated its nuclear arsenal shortly after developing it. We can assess whether and how Khrushchev's (and to a lesser extent Musharraf's) availability biases and experiences of fear played a role in the making of their strategic assessments and foreign policy, and we can test predictions about foreign policy decisions and how these decisions were made.

The sources drawn on most heavily for this purpose are Timothy Naftali's translated stenographic notes of Soviet decision-making during the Cold War Crisis years; translated Soviet and Eastern European archival documents at the Cold War International History Project and National Security Archive; and the many secondary studies on Nikita Khrushchev and the Cold War years, including several written or edited by Khrushchev's son, Sergei, who observed his father during the decision-making episodes. The sources drawn on for Musharraf are an interview with the former president; the more than one hundred speeches Musharraf made in Pakistan, South Asia, and the world forum during the first five years of his presidency; and the extensive secondary literature on the South Asian crisis years. The sources used for Nixon, Kennedy, and Mao were the archival documents available online at the Cold War International History Project, the National Security Archive, and many secondary studies. For India's prime minister Atal Bihari Vajpayee, several anonymous interviews in Delhi were reviewed, along with much secondary literature. Exhaustive blow-by-blow accounts of these leaders' nuclear crises are not provided. Rather, the empirical evidence focuses on the psychological and rational variables of interest.

Case studies that address the psychological variables of interest resolve some of the most persistent anomalies of the nuclear age. Why, for example, did Nikita Khrushchev push so hard and risk so much to revise the status quo in Berlin and Cuba between 1958 and 1962 but then accept that same status quo thereafter when little had changed? The experience of fear of imminent nuclear war during the Cuban Missile Crisis—one Khrushchev associate claimed Khrushchev had "shit his pants"—but not earlier explains this fundamental turnaround in Soviet strategy. Khrushchev persisted with assertive foreign policies despite the failures of the 1958 and 1961 ultimatums because Kennedy did not authorize an assertive foreign policy in response and thus he hadn't experienced genuine fear of imminent nuclear war.

Why did Pervez Musharraf push so hard to revise the status quo in Kashmir between 1999 and 2002 but then pursue his revisionist plans through confidence-building measures and secret diplomacy thereafter, even though the status quo had remained inherently undesirable? Why does Musharraf seem to have learned so little about the coercive limits of nuclear weapons from the Cold War? As the psychological model developed here would predict, Musharraf learned much more from his personal experiences than from the more abstract but nonetheless highly relevant historical record. After India deployed its three offensive strike corps in Rajasthan in preparation for an invasion of Pakistan in the spring of 2002, Musharraf experienced fear of imminent nuclear war at the peak of the ten-month mobilized crisis that May. He apparently didn't sleep for several nights because he feared nuclear escalation. This deeply psychological but personal reaction caused a fundamental shift in Pakistani policy. Musharraf hadn't experienced fear of imminent nuclear escalation during either the 1999 Kargil War nor the November 2001 crisis. Vajpayee authorized a restrained policy in 1999, and his credible threat to take the battle inside Pakistani territory later caused Musharraf to reach the nuclear brink. The fear of imminent nuclear war was the difference.

Why did Mao Zedong ambush Soviet patrols on the disputed Sino-Soviet border in 1969 but then never again target Soviet troops there or elsewhere thereafter? Mao reached the nuclear brink in the winter of 1969–70. He worried that a Soviet delegation that was flying to Beijing for peace talks was a cover for a special operation designed to ambush the city, much like the 1968 Russian invasion of Czechoslovakia. The record clearly shows that he ordered major evacuations of senior Chinese leaders from the capital.

Why did Richard Nixon persist with dangerous assertive strategies despite little signs of its effectiveness? He learned from his cognitively accessible experiences in Korea as vice president that nuclear threats alone could turn the tide. Because Moscow never authorized an assertive foreign policy toward him, then, he never experienced fear of imminent nuclear war and thus persisted with nuclear assertion throughout his presidency. These counterintuitive insights are apparent through the attention to psychological dynamics that most theories of nuclear behavior ignore.

Overview of the Book

The analysis begins by explaining why processes of learning are central to leaders' strategic orientation to the nuclear assertion dilemma. The goal is to develop a useful and determinate framework for explaining and comparing the foreign policies of new and experienced nuclear powers that may also be applied to future nuclear proliferators. This psychological learning model developed—the ALF two-stage model of availability, learning, and fear—is based on key findings from decades of experimental research in psychology and political science. Examples show how it causes variation in foreign policy choices over time.

Because learning that is biased by the availability heuristic presupposes unbiased rational learning, unbiased rational learning and the foreign policy choices that it should tend to cause must be understood. There is some disagreement about what unbiased rational learning is, so two learning models—the Waltzian model and the rational-signaling model—are presented; they offer clear predictions regarding the strategic foreign policy choices of nuclear powers. The Waltzian model expects leaders to always prefer restrained foreign policies. The rational-signaling model expects leaders to authorize assertive foreign policies as a signal of their resolve to revise the status quo but also to authorize restraint when an adversary makes a public display of his or her own to stop the assertion. This latter move is widely referred to by political scientists as a costly signal.

The ALF model expects leaders in new nuclear powers to authorize assertive foreign policies until they experience fear of imminent nuclear war. It presumes that an adversary will also authorize an assertive foreign policy. The ALF model also predicts that leaders will authorize restrained nuclear strategies after reaching the nuclear brink. The key difference between the two models is that the ALF model expects the experience of fear of nuclear escalation will stop a nuclear power's assertion, whereas the rational-signaling model predicts that any costly signal will do this. From a theoretical perspective, the assessment provides the first comparative theory of nuclear power foreign policy.

In chapter 3 the three learning models are applied to Soviet foreign policy between 1956 and 1962 and show that the Waltzian model cannot explain Khrushchev's nuclear assertion. The rational-signaling model does explain some Soviet nuclear assertion but cannot explain its persistence after 1961, when President Kennedy produced a costly signal in the Berlin Crisis. The ALF model explains why Khrushchev accepted the risk of nuclear escalation and authorized an assertive nuclear strategy through 1962: he overestimated the political opportunities that nuclear weapons provide, based on his cognitively available experiences of the 1956 Suez Crisis. The ALF model also explains why Khrushchev's nuclear assertion continued into 1962 during the Cuban Missile Crisis yet stopped once Khrushchev (and presumably his successors) had reached the nuclear brink.

The same learning models are tested on Pakistani foreign policy between 1990 and 2002 (chapter 4). Pakistan's sponsorship of the Kashmir insurgency throughout the 1990s, culminating in the 1999 Kargil War and the subsequent 2001–2002 crisis, was nuclear assertion that the Waltzian model cannot explain. The rational-signaling model can explain Pakistani assertion throughout the 1990s but cannot explain Musharraf's persistence with nuclear assertion following the 1999 Kargil War in light of Vajpayee's costly signal to defend India's position. The rational-signaling model would expect Musharraf to have learned of Delhi's resolve to defend the Kashmir status quo and thus adopt a restrained foreign policy. But Musharraf authorized an assertive foreign policy in 2000 to compel Vajpayee to renegotiate the status of Kashmir. It is unclear whether Musharraf did authorize the attacks on civilians in Parliament and at the military camp in Jammu in 2001 and 2002, but, based on a later interview, Musharraf experienced fear of imminent nuclear war in late May 2002. The ALF model explains why Musharraf's assertive foreign policy in Kashmir gave way to restraint: India's assertive strategy eventually caused Musharraf to experience fear of imminent nuclear escalation.

The three learning models are tested on four additional cases in chapter 5. The results show that the rational-signaling model is indeterminate: it is unclear whether Nixon should have learned from the costly North Vietnamese signal of Moscow's unwillingness to settle the conflict on terms favorable to Washington. But the ALF model can explain Nixon's actions. In the case of Mao, the rational-signaling model cannot explain why Mao challenged the Soviet position even though Brezhnev had demonstrated his resolve to intervene in other communist states at will, as seen in the 1968 invasion of Czechoslovakia. But the ALF model explains the change in Chinese behavior toward the Soviet Union in 1970 after assertive behavior toward Soviet patrols at Zhenbao Island in 1969. Mao experienced fear of imminent nuclear war through the winter of 1969–70, when Brezhnev authorized harsh retaliation against the Chinese patrols. The Waltzian model explains neither Nixon's nor Mao's actions, because that model always expects leaders to authorize restrained foreign policies.

US nuclear assertion in 1962 to remove Soviet nuclear missiles from Cuba can be explained by both the rational-signaling and ALF models: Kennedy issued his threats in the midst of a crisis brought about by Khrushchev's nuclear assertion. But Kennedy's previous experience of fear of imminent nuclear war in the Cuban Missile Crisis caused him to never again authorize nuclear assertion despite his prevailing in Cuba— as only the ALF model can explain. While Indian assertion in 2001 and Delhi's desire to establish its resolve to not tolerate attacks by Pakistan-sponsored groups can be explained by the rational-signaling model, Indian assertion in 2002 cannot, because Musharraf authorized a costly signal after India's earlier threat.

Much of the conventional wisdom about nuclear proliferation is incorrect or incomplete. The summary in chapter 6 considers the broader implications of and questions related to the ALF model and proposes several distinct possible directions for future research, especially as they apply to North Korea and Iran. While leaders in Pyongyang and Tehran may develop nuclear weapons and authorize assertive foreign policies in the short term, this behavior is unlikely to continue over the long run. Nuclear assertion by North Korean and Iranian leaders will likely cause them to experience fear of imminent nuclear war because their adversaries will eventually authorize assertive responses. The historical record suggests that this will then cause the leaders of these new nuclear powers to authorize restrained foreign policies regarding the status quo, like most other experienced nuclear powers have done.

Notes

1. Jervis, "Unipolarity," 212.
2. James R. Clapper, "Worldwide Threat Assessment of the U.S. Intelligence Community," Statement for the Record, US Senate Select Committee on Intelligence, January 29, 2014, http://www.dni.gov/index .php/newsroom/testimonies/203-congressional-testimonies-2014/1005 -statement-for-the-record-worldwide-threat-assessment-of-the-us-intelli gence-community.
3. Robert G. Joseph, Under Secretary of State for Arms Control and International Security, "Address Before the House International Relations Committee," March 8, 2006, http://www.iranwatch.org/sites/default/files/us -hirc-joseph-prepared-testimony-030806.pdf.
4. "Rice Calls for International Action on North Korea," *PBS NewsHour*, April 6, 2009, http://www.pbs.org/newshour/bb/asia-jan-june09-rice_04–06/.
5. George W. Bush, "Address Before a Joint Session of Congress on the State of the Union," January 29, 2002, Washington, DC.
6. Matthew Kaminski, "The Hillary Doctrine: The Secretary of State Takes an Optimistic View of Human Nature, Not to Mention Vladimir Putin," *Wall Street Journal*, August 14, 2009, http://online.wsj.com/news/articles/SB10 00142405297020386320457434884358570617 8.
7. Robert M. Gates, "Media Roundtable with Secretary Gates from Beijing, China," news transcript, US Department of Defense, January 11, 2011, http://archive.defense.gov/Transcripts/Transcript.aspx?TranscriptID =4751.

8. Barry R. Posen, "We Can Live with a Nuclear Iran," *New York Times,* February 27, 2006.

9. Sagan, "Reasons to Worry," 210.

10. George H. W. Bush Presidential Library, *National Security Review* 12 (March 1989): 3.

11. Office of the Historian, *Foreign Relations of the United States,* hereafter referred to as *FRUS,* 1964–68, Vol. XI, Doc. 64; and Gavin, "Blasts from the Past," 100–135.

12. Jervis, "Kargil, Deterrence, and International Relations Theory," 383.

13. Feaver, "Optimists, Pessimists, and Theories," 769; Karl, "Proliferation Pessimism," 118–19; Montgomery and Sagan, "Perils of Predicting Proliferation," 321; and Jervis, "Unipolarity."

14. See, for example, Sagan, "Why Do States Build Nuclear Weapons?"; Paul, *Power versus Prudence*; Solingen, *Nuclear Logics*; Hymans, *Psychology of Nuclear Proliferation*; and Hymans, *Achieving Nuclear Ambitions.*

15. Sagan, "More Will Be Worse"; Sagan, *Limits of Safety*; Blair, *Logic of Accidental Nuclear War*; Blair, "Nuclear Inadvertence"; Feaver, *Guarding the Guardians*; Feaver, "Politics of Inadvertence"; Miller, "Case against a Ukrainian Nuclear Deterrent"; Lavoy, "Strategic Consequences of Nuclear Proliferation"; Feaver, "Neooptimists and the Enduring Problem"; and Kapur, "Revisionist Ambitions."

16. Waltz, "More May Be Better"; Mearsheimer, "Case for a Ukrainian Nuclear Deterrent"; Gaddis, "Long Peace"; Bueno de Mesquita and Riker, "Assessment of the Merits"; Karl, "Proliferation Pessimism"; Seng, "Less Is More"; Hagerty, *Consequences of Nuclear Proliferation*; and Jervis, *Meaning of the Nuclear Revolution.*

17. See, for example, Freedman, *Evolution of Nuclear Strategy*; Morgan, *Deterrence Now*; Gavin, *Nuclear Statecraft*; Jervis, *Meaning of the Nuclear Revolution*; Sagan, *Moving Targets*; Glaser, *Analyzing Strategic Nuclear Policy*; Eden and Miller, *Nuclear Arguments*; Schelling, *Arms and Influence*; Schelling, *Strategy of Conflict*; and Brodie, *Strategy in the Missile Age.*

18. Horowitz, "Spread of Nuclear Weapons"; and Gartzke and Dong, "Bargaining, Nuclear Proliferation."

19. Narang, *Nuclear Strategy in the Modern Era.*

20. Knopf, "Concept of Nuclear Learning."

21. Leng, *Bargaining and Learning,* 267.

22. Ibid., 13, 280, 293.

23. Ibid., 299.

24. Waltz, *Theory of International Politics.*

25. Byman and Pollack, "Let Us Now Praise Great Men"; Post, *Leaders and Their Followers*; Chiozza and Goemans, *Leaders and International Conflict*; Weeks, *Dictators at War and Peace*; and Croco, "Decider's Dilemma." For exceptions, see Saunders, *Leaders at War* and Yarhi-Milo, *Knowing the Adversary.*

26. For a review, see Levy, "Prospect Theory, Rational Choice." For exceptions, see Mercer, "Emotion and Strategy in the Korean War"; McDermott, "Feeling of Rationality"; and Kennedy, *International Ambitions of Mao and Nehru*.

27. Bernstein, "Understanding Decisionmaking," 162, italics in original.

28. Fear is defined as the dread of impending disaster that tends to cause intense urges to defend oneself by escaping a situation. It is differentiated from anxiety, which is an ineffable and unpleasant feeling of foreboding. See Öhman, "Fear and Anxiety," 710.

29. See, for example, Powell, *Nuclear Deterrence Theory*; Powell, "Crisis Bargaining"; Powell, "Nuclear Brinksmanship"; Kroenig, "Exporting the Bomb"; and Fuhrmann and Sechser, "Signaling Alliance Commitments." For an exception, see Hymans, *Psychology of Nuclear Proliferation*.

30. Horowitz and Stam, "How Prior Military Experience Influences."

31. For a succinct summary, see Tang, "Fear in International Politics," 452.

32. Waltz, "Waltz Responds to Sagan," 154.

33. Jervis, "Cooperation under the Security Dilemma," 172.

34. Mearsheimer, *Tragedy of Great Power Politics*, 42–43.

35. Narang, *Nuclear Strategy in the Modern Era*, 4.

36. Fearon, "Selection Effects and Deterrence."

37. This is not, strictly speaking, risk aversion since the leader's belief about the probability of nuclear escalation is constant throughout.

38. Lobell, Ripsman, and Taliaferro, *Neoclassical Realism*.

39. Narang, *Nuclear Strategy in the Modern Era*.

40. George and Bennett, *Case Studies and Theory Development*; and Brady and Collier, *Rethinking Social Inquiry*. For a criticism, see Beck, "Is Causal Process Observation an Oxymoron?"

41. Russell Leng defined learning as policy change in his statistical analysis of the Indo-Pakistani rivalry and offered the ambiguous conclusion that "whatever learning occurred remained within the bounds of realpolitik assumptions about inter-rivalry relations." See Leng, "Realpolitik and Learning in the India-Pakistan Rivalry," 103, 121. See also Leng, *Bargaining and Learning*.

42. Hermann et al., "Who Leads Matters."

43. Ukraine, Kazakhstan, and Belarus never had independent control over the nuclear weapons they inherited from and returned to Russia.

44. Sechser and Fuhrmann, "Crisis Bargaining and Nuclear Blackmail."

45. A "controlled comparison" result could be further approximated by addressing the beliefs of the associates of Khrushchev, Mao, and Musharraf when those nations became new nuclear powers. If availability and fear influenced their choices on nuclear weapons, their associates—who found different events cognitively available and who may not have experienced fear—should have developed different policy preferences. However, their associates'

beliefs about nuclear assertion tended to not be recorded. See George and Bennett, *Case Studies and Theory Development*, 151–79.

46. Narang, *Nuclear Strategy in the Modern Era*, 1.

47. Enthoven and Smith, *How Much Is Enough?*, 142. For similar claims, see Evangelista, "Stalin's Postwar Army Reappraised," 111; Posen, "Is NATO Decisively Outnumbered?," 189, 200; Posen, "Measuring the European Conventional Balance"; and Mearsheimer, "Numbers, Strategy, and the European Balance."

48. Fursenko and Naftali, *Khrushchev's Cold War*, 412.

49. Podvig, *Russian Strategic Nuclear Forces*, 181; Zaloga, *Kremlin's Nuclear Sword*, 232; S. Khrushchev, *Nikita Khrushchev*, 282–83; and Matthias Uhl and Vladimir I. Ivkin, "'Operation Atom': The Soviet Union's Stationing of Nuclear Missiles in the German Democratic Republic, 1959," *Cold War International History Project Bulletin* 12/13 (Winter–Spring 2001): 299–307.

2

Fear and Learning: Psychology, Nuclear Crises, and Foreign Policy

MANY OBSERVERS of international affairs assume that leaders possess little power in the face of international constraints, such as the balance of power or domestic political institutions. This assumption is a substantial oversimplification, but it has been influential.[1] However, if international structures "shape and shove," as Kenneth Waltz has famously argued, then leaders are also capable of pushing back.[2] Believing that leaders possess no agency leaves us poorly positioned to understand why these same leaders respond to the same circumstances with different foreign policies. Indeed, Waltz himself conceded that some leaders "transcend the limits of their instruments and break the constraints of systems that bind lesser performers."[3] To understand the different foreign policies of nuclear powers, one must assume that leaders do have some freedom of choice in foreign policy making. This chapter develops a theoretical framework to explain how leaders of new nuclear powers perceive the opportunities and constraints raised by the possession of nuclear weapons and how these influence their approach to the dilemma of nuclear assertion and foreign policy.

Key insights from decades of psychological research can help in understanding leaders' actions, for three reasons.[4] First, foreign policies are designed by people, not states, and people are vulnerable to the limitations of the human brain. Psychologists focus on how people tend to behave rather than how they should rationally behave. Second, psychologists have documented several tendencies in the way people in high-stakes contests respond to uncertainty and risk. Indeed, international politics is characterized by uncertainty and risk. Leaders of new nuclear powers are usually unaware of the opportunities and limitations that nuclear weapons present. The dilemma of nuclear assertion looms large: it can sustain revisions to an untenable security environment, but it also carries the serious risk of nuclear escalation. Third, despite the ability of psychological research to assist in understanding the major strategic choices of leaders in new nuclear powers, no one has yet taken up the challenge. Scholars have documented many biases and applied several of them to international relations, and the argument put forward here is that two psychological mechanisms through which people perceive and respond to information—availability and fear—profoundly and systematically influence nuclear powers' foreign policies.[5]

Psychological approaches to international relations assume that variation in how people perceive, analyze, and cope with the complex world around them explains the variation in their beliefs, preferences, and behaviors. They rest on the robust empirical finding that human cognition is inherently constrained by innate limitations on one's information-processing capabilities and the capacity of one's working memory. Attention span is finite, a systematic search for information can be costly, and information that is relevant to an issue may be ambiguous, inaccessible, or misinterpreted if it is missed.[6] Earlier research differentiated between unmotivated and motivated biases.[7] Unmotivated biases are the product of the complexity of the environment and the inherent limitations of human cognitive abilities. Motivated biases arise from the emotions that are generated by conflicts in personal needs: they often minimize the discomfort that is created when value trade-offs are fully appreciated.

A psychological approach to international politics assumes that leaders' perceptions, beliefs, and policy preferences are crucial to understanding state foreign policy and the outcomes of geopolitical contexts. The key insight is that while the balance of international military and economic power poses severe constraints on foreign policy making, leaders' engagement with these international systemic pressures determines the final policy outcomes. Most leader engagement with the world is active, not passive. There are usually multiple lessons to be learned from any given geopolitical episode, as well as lessons from history rather than the lesson of history. As Jack Levy has argued, if there was only one lesson from any historical event, events would matter much more than lessons.[8] In psychological models such variation in perceptions, beliefs, and preferences—the content and speed of lessons learned—is both effect and cause. As Levy points out, the "rational choice and neorealist approaches assume that people recognise changing environmental conditions but that there are predictable relationships between informational and structural antecedents and behavioural responses."[9] Variation in individual perceptions and the processing of external stimuli within these frameworks is either not modeled or assumed away. The psychological approach expects that even when given similar information, leaders will have different preferences that are due to variation in prior beliefs, attention spans, information-processing capabilities, and personal feelings. These differences will not cancel each other out over time.

Decades of psychological research demonstrates that people commonly resort to inferential shortcuts in order to proceed in the face of large amounts of data and inherent limitations on information processing.[10] The efficiency gain that these cognitive shortcuts offer is necessary for people to make important decisions in information- and uncertainty-rich environments. Shortcuts are a natural way by which people interpret information quickly and efficiently; they help one assess and respond to his or her surroundings and simplify what are otherwise complex (and more normatively appropriate) inferential procedures.

These heuristics aid the speed and utility of human inference, even if not always the accuracy of that inference, and can cause significant and systematic biases in decision-making. Inattention to crucial data points and incorrect estimations of the value of diagnostic observations lead to preferences that are substantially different from more normatively appropriate expected utility models. These biases are systematic and do not cancel each other out in aggregate. Much early research found these biases in college undergraduates, but more recent studies have shown that foreign policy elites in high-stakes political contests suffer from similar biases when they perceive information, assess risks, and make decisions.

Since Robert Jervis's seminal contribution on the importance of psychological variables to international conflict, scholars have shown how psychological mechanisms bias leaders' explanations of others' behaviors, their own learning from history, and their propensity for risk, even when they have strong incentives to behave rationally.[11] Deborah Welch Larson has shown that the psychology of attribution explains the important change in US foreign policy in 1947. Soviet domination of Eastern Europe did not arouse fears of further expansion, because Stalin's insistence on friendly governments was attributed to his desire to avoid exposure to another German invasion. Soviet pressure on Iran, Greece, and Turkey, however, could not be explained as a legitimate security need, so Moscow's probes in the Mediterranean caused US policy to change.[12]

Yuen Foong Khong argues that the historical episodes cognitively available to President Lyndon Johnson and his advisers explain their response to the deteriorating situation in South Vietnam in 1965: those who had learned from Munich in 1939 and Korea in 1950 favored intervention, but those who had learned from Dien Bien Phu in 1954 favored withdrawal.[13] Dan Reiter has found that states' alliance choices after the First and Second World Wars are better predicted by the lessons that their leaders learned from the wars rather than any variation in balance of power or external threat: leaders who believed that their alliance policies succeeded during a war tended to maintain their policies after war, while those that believed their policies had failed, changed policies.[14] Jonathan Mercer shows that in the years leading to World War I, states' reputations were not influenced by their past behaviors but by how desirable their policies were. Desirable behaviors were attributed to the situation, but undesirable behaviors were attributed to the leader's disposition. Because only dispositional attributions can cause reputations, Mercer shows why allies rarely demonstrate resolve but their adversaries do.[15]

Dominic Johnson and Dominic Tierney have developed a psychological argument about the European crisis in 1914: World War I occurred following the July 1914 crisis but not the preceding crises because by that July leaders believed that war was actually imminent. A belief that war is imminent encourages policies that cause war even when war is in fact not imminent.[16] Availability biases also seem to influence scholars as well as policymakers. In a recent survey of over one thousand international relations scholars, about half of those who had graduated from college during the Cold War believe that Moscow and Washington are headed for a new Cold War today. Only one-third of those who graduated after the Cold War agree.[17]

Levy's definition of learning is "a change of beliefs, degree of confidence in one's beliefs, or the development of new beliefs, skills or procedures as a result of the observation and interpretation of experience."[18] As Levy points out, organizational learning is accomplished through individuals who learn and "encode individually learned inferences from experience into organizational routines and governmental procedures."[19] However, learning is neither necessary nor sufficient for policy change, and it does not necessarily lead to more-accurate, more-efficient, or more-complex beliefs. Leaders of new nuclear powers could learn much about nuclear strategy, posture, proliferation, and foreign policy. But the focus here is on leader learning about foreign policy and, more specifically, on nuclear assertion: how do leaders learn about the opportunities and dangers associated with the use of nuclear weapons to revise unfavorable security environments, and how do these lessons and attitudes influence their foreign policies?

Nuclear weapons present leaders with a fundamental choice. When a country lacks sufficient conventional military power to sustain revisions to undesirable security challenges, after developing nuclear weapons a leader can attempt to revise such parts of his country's status quos through land grabs, coercive threats, insurgency support, and displays and uses of force. Such leaders can threaten to respond to conventional or nuclear retaliation with further challenges that risk nuclear war. This strategy is called *foreign policy assertion*. The problem with assertion is that an adversary can also respond with assertive policies that further increase the probability of nuclear escalation.

As former US secretary of state Dean Rusk pointed out, "One of the quickest ways to have a nuclear war is to have the two sides persuaded that neither will fight."[20] Leaders can avoid this risk and restrict the role of nuclear weapons to deter other attacks, pursuing security imperatives through confidence-building measures, diplomacy, and tacit cooperation; this is called *foreign policy restraint*. While restraint does reduce the risk of nuclear war, it also relies on tools that likely had previously failed to substantially revise serious security threats. Leaders of new nuclear powers must also make many other secondary choices associated with the development, maintenance, and security of an operational nuclear deterrent. But this dilemma is *the* fundamental strategic question; assertive and restrained foreign policies are the only choices. The strategy that a leader selects will exert a strong influence on second-order decisions.

Leaders facing assertive challenges by new nuclear powers face a similar fundamental dilemma. They have two basic options: restraint or assertion. They can pursue inaction, cheap talk, or military mobilizations suited to defending and maintaining the status quo. This foreign policy restraint may prevent a new nuclear power from revising the status quo. But if the leader of a new nuclear power is resolved enough to behave assertively, a restrained foreign policy will unlikely stop him.[21] The alternative foreign policy assertion—military mobilizations suited to destroy troops or capture territory, and credible threats to do so—may stop a new nuclear power's assertion, but it can be very costly and dangerous.

This raises a thorny question: How do we know which foreign policies made by nuclear powers are *nuclear* assertion? Dwight D. Eisenhower's decision to "put all his chips in the pot" in response to Soviet challenges in Western Europe seems to be a nuclear strategy, but Pakistani sponsorship of the Kashmir insurgency in the 1990s appears less so. For the discussion here, we will assume that nuclear assertion can involve both the logic of coercion and military victory.[22]

Nuclear weapons might cause leaders to use force rather than issue threats. Moreover, if an emboldened leader planned to revise a small part of the status quo and then issue a coercive threat, he may not issue the threat if the initial territory grab fails; a strict focus on coercive threats would not code such an event as nuclear assertion. So addressing the logic of compellence threats *and* compellence itself is required. Indeed, most cases of nuclear assertion are better thought of as coercion rather than coercive threats. As Robert Pape notes, "Since war fighting itself can also be an effective coercive strategy . . . insisting on this distinction would exclude many important cases and ignore the most important coercive dynamics in others."[23]

Also, a foreign policy should be considered a case of nuclear assertion only if there is evidence that a leader believed his and only his nuclear weapons enabled a foreign policy that he believed was untenable before the acquisition of nuclear weapons. A differentiation should be made between explicit nuclear assertion, which involves threats to use force if some concession is not made, and implicit nuclear assertion, which involves the use of force absent a threat but where a leader nonetheless believed that nuclear weapons offered assertive advantages. This kind of implicit nuclear assertion is more commonly found than explicit nuclear assertion. Any reference to implicit nuclear assertion will also present evidence either that the leader believed that nuclear weapons offered assertive advantages or that she planned to issue future explicit threats.

For example, Pakistani leaders believed that their nuclear weapons allowed them to sponsor the Kashmir insurgency and pressure Delhi for concessions because the possession of weapons shielded Islamabad from Indian retaliation. Indeed, the intensification of Pakistan's sponsorship of the Kashmir insurgency began precisely when Islamabad developed nuclear weapons. Conversely, there is no evidence that President Kennedy believed that US nuclear weapons were necessary for his decision to sponsor an attack on Cuba in April 1961, so this is not considered "nuclear assertion." The theory developed here does not predict whether a leader will authorize explicit or implicit nuclear assertion.

Finally, the term "nuclear strategy" usually refers to all decisions related to a nuclear doctrine or posture. But any decision to authorize assertive or restrained foreign policies are first and foremost foreign policies, even though they can also be thought of as core elements of nuclear strategy because they address what leaders will ultimately do with their nuclear weapons. A nuclear power's decision to revise or accept the status quo is surely as much a *nuclear* strategy as is a decision about which types of weapon platforms or command-and-control infrastructure will be used.

Psychology and Foreign Policy: Availability

The availability heuristic inclines people to assess the probability of an event or outcome based not on a systematic empirical assessment but on its ease of accessibility or mental construction. Rather than directing sufficient attention to current, past, or plausible data points to estimate probabilities that are close to objective probabilities, psychological research has shown that cognitively accessible and available data—that which is salient, dramatic, personally experienced, recent, or vivid—absorbs too much attention and causes misinterpretation or neglect of other important but less accessible information. As Susan Fiske and Shelley Taylor have pointed out, "Recently and frequently activated data is more cognitively accessible; it comes to mind more easily than unactivated ideas. Such data profoundly influence the encoding of external stimuli into internal cognitive representations, and guides interpretation and mental representation of relevant, moderate and ambiguous stimuli."[24] Daniel Kahneman and Amos Tversky explain that people employ the availability heuristic when they

> assess the frequency of a class or the probability of an event by the ease with which instances or occurrences can be brought to mind. . . . Availability is a useful clue for assessing frequency or probability, because instances of large classes are usually reached better and faster than instances of less frequent classes. However, availability is affected by factors other than frequency and probability. Consequently, the reliance on availability leads to predictable biases.[25]

In one famous study, spouses were asked to estimate their contribution to household maintenance. The self-estimated contributions should have together added up to 100 percent, but they always added up to more. People recall their own efforts much more clearly than the contributions of others and hence they overestimate their own.[26] Similar effects are reported in estimations of responsibility for quarrels and collaborative outcomes: 23 percent of British men and 15 percent of British women who were divorcing or considering a breakup acknowledged that their decision had been strongly influenced by personal friends who experienced temporary happiness after separation.[27] Availability causes egocentric biases in attribution when one person's contributions to a joint product are more readily available and more easily and frequently recalled.[28] Individuals accept more responsibility for the end result rather than attributing the result to other participants. Tellingly, people correct their estimations of responsibility when another participant's contributions are made more cognitively available.[29]

The availability heuristic both intentionally and automatically substitutes the question of objective frequency for that of subjective mental availability.[30] As Kahneman and Tversky show, "Classes [of decisions] whose instances are easy to construct or imagine . . . will be perceived as more frequent than classes of the same size whose instances are less available."[31] Jervis shows that leaders tend to learn from events that are experienced firsthand, early in life, or otherwise important to one's own state or organization.[32] Yuen Foong Khong observes that the senior US advisers who found the events of Munich in 1939 and Korea in 1950 cognitively accessible favored intervention in Vietnam in 1965, but those who found the events of Dien Bien Phu in 1954 cognitively accessible favored withdrawal.[33]

One can argue that Kahneman and Tversky's original formulation of availability rests on something of a grab bag of factors that are difficult to define in a non-tautological way, such as frequency, vividness, and assorted quirks in how we store and recall information. Scholars have addressed the role of ease of recall, factors that influence ease of recall, associated bonds strengthened by repeated examples, and accessibility in memory.[34] The challenge of specifying a priori what sort of observations should be cognitively available to individual persons indeed challenges efforts to systematically test the availability heuristic. But the theory put forward here is based on a simple claim: people are likely to find their own experiences more cognitively accessible and available than either others' experiences or the entire universe of logically possible events. The likelihood that people will be able to learn from any given data point is a direct function of the length of time and quality of their association with that data point.

Kenneth Waltz argues that "the slow spread of nuclear weapons gives states time to learn to live with them, to appreciate their virtues, and to understand the limits they place on their behavior."[35] How does psychological research suggest that such learning will occur? Knowing that leaders of new nuclear powers will be susceptible to the availability heuristic when thinking about the political possibilities of nuclear weapons, there is strong reason to expect that these leaders will be more likely to learn about nuclear weapons and nuclear assertion from their own experiences with nuclear weapons rather than from the historical record or the universe of logically possible but unobservable events related to nuclear weapons. Indeed, research has shown that people are more susceptible to availability biases when they are powerful and "knowledgeable novices" rather than "true experts" on the subject.[36] Two biases related to the availability heuristic are likely to be especially influential on the thinking of leaders of new nuclear powers when they devise foreign policy and confront the dilemma of nuclear assertion.

Cognitive Dissonance

Dissonance theory explains how inconsistent cognitions cause belief and behavior changes.[37] According to the theory, inconsistent beliefs cause a motivational state of mental arousal and discomfort called dissonance, and the drive to reduce dissonance causes one to rearrange one's cognitions.[38] For example, a smoker can believe that smoking is relaxing but also deadly; dissonance is the result.[39] As Fiske and Taylor point out, people tend to respond to dissonance by adding or subtracting cognitions and effectively changing their beliefs to either increase the ratio of consonant to dissonant beliefs (e.g., smoking also causes weight loss) or reduce the importance of the dissonant beliefs (e.g., death is inevitable anyway).[40] Jervis finds that when a policy has high costs, decision-makers are likely to believe that the accomplishment justifies the sacrifice because believing otherwise would be too psychologically painful.[41] Cognitive dissonance causes people to often throw good money after bad and leads to the fallacy of sunk costs.

Jervis has documented several examples. When Germany had invested many resources by 1914 to build a fleet that could deter London, German foreign secretary Gottlieb von Jagow argued that England would not fight because, as he stated, "We have not built our navy for nothing."[42] When Neville Chamberlain learned that his cousin had been killed in the First World War, he claimed that substantial gains were the justification for the war: "Nothing but immeasurable improvements will ever justify all the waste and unfairness of this war."[43] Prior to Pearl Harbor, when Japanese prime minister Hideki Tojo rejected US demands to remove Japanese troops from China, he stated: "We sent a large force of one million men, and it has cost us well over one hundred thousand dead and wounded . . . hardship for four years and a national expenditure of several tens of billions of yen. We must by all means get satisfactory results from this."[44]

Moreover, if the price paid has been so high that it cannot justify the original goal, leaders may not only persist with goal but will expand their objectives.[45] This is apparently one reason why Prussian conspirators' plans to rebel against Napoleon continued after the original goals had been achieved. As Jervis comments, "Once significant energies were invested in the scheme, the leaders felt the need to justify that investment by success—and the more so, the more they put into just keeping their scheme alive."[46]

Nuclear weapons programs require years of financial, technological, bureaucratic, and human investment, and the international pressure, sanctions, and other coercive strategies applied to curb a new proliferator's nuclear ambitions likely make the successful achievement of an operational nuclear weapon more cognitively available. Tests—nuclear and otherwise—that usually follow the development of an operational nuclear weapon are likely to be easily accessible, personally experienced, recent, dramatic, salient, and vivid. In short, a leader's own successful nuclear weapons program is likely to be cognitively available to anyone who has recently developed operational nuclear weapons.[47] When the leader of a new nuclear power confronts the dilemmas of nuclear assertion, it is hard to think of a more cognitively available data point than his or her own successful nuclear weapons program. If leaders are not directly involved in diverting civilian resources to begin a weapons program or otherwise creating an operational nuclear deterrent, they will nevertheless probably have faced the international fallout from their nuclear achievements.

Availability tends to cause people who are favorably disposed toward a technology to focus on its benefits and ignore any risks. Conversely, unfavorable attitudes toward a technology tend to cause people to exaggerate its risks and minimize its benefits.[48] Thus many attitudes toward nuclear power changed after the 2011 Fukushima nuclear disaster. Experiments have shown that providing information designed to influence one's overall evaluation of nuclear power systematically influences its perceived risks and benefits along these lines.[49]

If nuclear weapons are highly accessible to leaders of new nuclear powers, how does this influence their approach to the dilemma of nuclear assertion? The availability heuristic should tend to make leaders in new nuclear powers authorize assertive foreign policies. The cognitively accessible successes associated with their recent development of an operational nuclear capability will likely cause them to form positive estimates of the weapon's assertive potential. When assessing the dilemma of nuclear assertion, leaders usually make two dangerous inferential leaps when formulating foreign policy. First, they will hit on their cognitively available success in development as the key and only evidence to use when assessing the effects of assertive foreign policies. Second, because they tend to view a strategy as positively as the operational nuclear capability itself, they tend to ignore the risk of nuclear escalation. Even if they only consider a nuclear weapon's *defensive* deterrent capability, they will likely reason that a substantial defensive capability implies room for not only a hard-line defensive posture to demonstrate credibility but also *offensive* assertion.[50]

When considering whether to adopt assertive or restrained foreign policies, the key question is how likely assertive strategies will be able to sustain permanent revisions to a security arrangement. Does nuclear assertion "work"? Although assertive foreign policies might serve other purposes, such as sending signals to domestic or international audiences, nuclear assertion will be considered to be working if it tends to allow sustained changes to a state's security environment.

The normatively appropriate procedure to address this question would be to analyze all historical cases of leaders of nuclear powers. Relevant observations would point to other nuclear powers in history that authorized assertive policies, knowing whether those were followed by permanent changes in a security environment or whether other variables may have caused these changes. But these cases will have occurred in distant regions or earlier in time, and likely they had little impact on the leader or state. Because these relevant observations would not be cognitively available, leaders will tend to ignore them.

Even leaders with ample resources to support studies on the effects of nuclear assertion will tend to ignore these distant but relevant historical cases. Robert Jervis finds that "the amount one learns from another's experience is slight even when the incentives for learning are high and the two actors have much in common and face the same situation."[51] If they believe that a specific dyad or rivalry is sufficiently different from others such that only their own pre-nuclear history is probative regarding assertive policies, availability biases should cause them to hit on cases of their adversary's weakness and authorize an assertive foreign policy.

Eliot Cohen and John Gooch point out that German U-boat successes in 1942 were largely attributed to the US failure to learn readily accessible lessons of British experiences in anti-submarine warfare.[52] Before the war, Royal Navy officers repeatedly warned their American counterparts that a convoy system would be necessary to protect Allied merchant ships against U-boat attacks. But only after almost six months of frustratingly high losses following the US entry into the war were coastal convoys established. Cohen and Gooch note the

> absence in many Western armed forces of an institutional locus for applied historical study. . . . It is all too easy to dismiss another decade's or another nation's experience by referring to one or two glaring differences from one's own situation. . . . In the words of one (American) four-star general (in the 1960s regarding Vietnam), "the French haven't won a war since Napoleon. What can we learn from them? . . . *in war there is nothing like the hard school of experience.* (emphasis added)[53]

One might argue that the availability heuristic should cause leaders to learn about nuclear assertion from instances when their own countries were targets of nuclear coercion. Leaders of non-nuclear powers facing more powerful nuclear adversaries may well learn that nuclear weapons would have enabled them to have done better. But many leaders would not find that earlier crisis cognitively available, because it would have occurred several years before they came to power. In 1948 Khrushchev, the Ukrainian Central Committee party leader, was focused on increasing agricultural production, not on the status of Soviet nuclear arms. India and Pakistan developed nuclear weapons at approximately the same time. Mao may well have learned about the power of nuclear assertion from John Foster Dulles's threat and the Taiwan Straits crises in the 1950s, but this would be an exception to the general rule.

Self-Serving Attribution Biases

If nuclear assertion tends to not "work," and if leaders' own failures with an assertive strategy are cognitively accessible, why should they not authorize restrained foreign policies after the first assertive failure? Personal failures with nuclear assertion should be highly cognitively accessible. If availability biases do cause leaders to authorize assertive policies, shouldn't failures cause leaders to authorize restrained foreign policies?

Another bias associated with the availability heuristic is the self-serving attributional bias, which causes people to own success and disown failure. Success is attributed to one's own actions; the role of chance or other factors is neglected; and failure is attributed to the actions of others, to external variables, or to bad luck.[54] Jervis shows that US secretary of state Henry Stimson believed that he was largely responsible for preventing a Russo-Japanese war over Manchuria in 1929, and he attributed Japanese concessions in 1931 to "the stiff tone which I have taken." He apparently didn't realize the complexities of the rivalries in China and Manchuria, nor the Soviets' revolutionary strategy.[55] Stimson's undersecretary was not deeply involved in the earlier crisis and did not believe that Stimson's actions mattered. At the beginning of World War II, the Germans mistakenly attributed the British decision to not bomb German cities not to a shortage of planes but to Germany's restraint against British cities.[56] In the opium war, China misinterpreted every favorable British move as a response to Chinese policy. The United States overestimated the degree to which the French withdrawal from Mexico in the 1860s was caused by US pressure.[57]

In his study of the crises preceding World War I, Jonathan Mercer finds that states tended to attribute desirable events—adversaries backing down, allies standing firm—to their own policies. But they attributed undesirable events—adversaries standing firm, allies backing down—to the actors' disposition.[58] In these situations, the actor is very familiar with his or her own efforts but knows much less about what other variables are relevant. The leader will likely know little about the role played by third parties or the other's domestic processes and internal conflicts. As Jervis states, "In the absence of strong evidence to the contrary, the most obvious and parsimonious explanation is that he was influential."[59]

The self-serving attribution bias suggests that leaders will attribute successes to their own policies.[60] They will tend to ignore other situational variables because these are less cognitively accessible. The bias also suggests that leaders will attribute failures to situational factors or bad luck, and believe that persistence with assertive strategies will pay off. Even after one or more unsuccessful attempts, leaders will not revise their beliefs, because they will tend to underestimate their own responsibility for failure.

In short, there are plausible reasons to expect the availability heuristic to cause leaders in new nuclear powers to authorize and persist with assertive foreign policies. The attribution bias will cause them to believe that nuclear assertion "works," ignoring the risk of nuclear escalation and explaining away any failures associated with the strategy. Leaders that overestimate the success of nuclear assertion will be more likely to authorize it. *Nuclear proliferation is dangerous when leaders learn that nuclear assertion is safe.*

Psychology and Foreign Policy: Availability and Fear

If leaders of new nuclear powers authorize assertive foreign policies and expect a restrained response, an assertive response may be required to cause them to abstain from further nuclear assertion.[61] But while assertive responses are more likely to prevent revisions to the status quo and deter further challenges, they also are costly and may lead to a nuclear crisis that substantially raises the risk of deliberate or inadvertent nuclear escalation. By signaling a higher level of resolve and willingness to accept more risk than the new nuclear power anticipated, an assertive response may cause the new nuclear power to abandon assertive policies in favor of restrained alternatives.

Alexander George concludes that the main variables that increase the probability of "successful" coercive diplomacy are an asymmetry of motivation favoring the coercing state and the target's time urgency and fear of unacceptable escalation.[62] An assertive response by an adversary—usually an experienced nuclear power—signals its motivation to deter challenges to the status quo, but the fear of nuclear escalation that often results creates urgent pressures to de-escalate. An assertive response by an experienced nuclear power is successful nuclear assertion only insofar as it ends the new nuclear power's assertion and restores the status quo. In such cases there is little basis for concluding that nuclear assertion works: the only status quo that it can revise is persistent nuclear assertion.

Leaders of both new and experienced nuclear powers could use nuclear weapons if a conflict directly threatens their territories or if large-scale conventional operations threaten the major elements of their states' nuclear forces.[63] A new nuclear power might worry that an adversary's assertive response to its own nuclear assertion will cause nuclear escalation. The adversary might worry that the new nuclear power will brazenly respond to its efforts to contain it through moves that also cause nuclear escalation. Thoughts of danger that are cognitively accessible and vivid exacerbate fear.[64] However, leaders may fear imminent nuclear war even when nuclear war is not imminent.

Leaders who experience fear of imminent nuclear war—as distinct from a general respect for the dangers associated with nuclear weapons—will tend to avoid any policies associated with causing the fear: they will prefer restrained foreign policies, possibly even against adversaries for whom they had not formerly authorized assertive policies. Leaders who authorize assertive foreign policies against a new nuclear power and experience fear will also likely authorize restrained policies thereafter.

Very little research has addressed the effects of emotion in international politics.[65] And research has not established how fear exacerbates or moderates international conflict. Even the definition of emotions is contested. Rose McDermott defines emotions this way: "One of a large set of differentiated biologically based complex conditions that encompass thoughts, motivations, bodily sensations and an internal sense of experience and are distinct from feelings, mood and affect."[66] Jonathan Mercer defines an emotion as "A subjective experience of some diffuse physiological change and a feeling as a conscious awareness that one is experiencing an emotion."[67] Whether emotional processing requires cognitive processing depends on whether the latter is defined as sensory information processing, or only as abstract and rational thought; this in itself is a hotly contested topic.[68]

There is no strict separation in the human brain between cognitive processes and emotion: emotions typically exert much of their effect through their impact on cognitive processes,[69] and often before cognitive functioning even occurs.[70] Neuroscientists have shown that rational decision-making—the pursuit of what people believe to be in their best interest—depends on both emotional and cognitive processing to provide a foundation for quick and accurate assessments. When the brain identifies an imminent threat, it shuts down the cognitive mechanisms responsible for more-complex procedures and ignites emotional processes to quickly react. This is a learned response to any potentially dangerous cue.[71] Even angry or fearful faces that are presented subliminally can suggest imminent danger and activate the brain's early warning system residing in the amygdala.[72] Fear interrupts ongoing behaviors and directs attention and cognitive effort toward dealing with a threat. It motivates people to remove the danger or remove themselves from the danger. Rational decision-making, therefore, often depends on emotion. As McDermott argues, "If choice is designed to maximize utility, and utilities are influenced by anticipation of regret and rejoicing, then rational models of decision making must take account of emotion as a significant element in assessing and predicting the utility of outcomes."[73]

As Mercer has pointed out, "The separation of thinking from feeling is descriptively inaccurate and provides a shaky foundation for normative or rational-choice theories of decision."[74] Feelings have a "truly privileged status" and retain a "primacy that subtly pervades our mental life."[75] "Feeling *is* believing," according to Mercer, because "people use emotion as evidence."[76] If stable and hierarchical preferences depend on emotion, changes in feelings can lead to changes in preferences.[77] There is extensive psychological research that reveals the systematic tendency for fear to reduce one's acceptance of risk.

Jennifer Lerner and Dacher Keltner developed the "appraisal tendency" framework to show that the experience of fear has systematic impacts on judgment, choice, and risk acceptance. Appraisal themes are processes through which "emotions exert effects on judgement and choice until the emotion-eliciting problem is resolved." Lerner and Keltner systematically link distinct emotions to particular judgment and choice outcomes.[78] Anger produces the optimism about future outcomes and risk acceptance that stem from low levels of uncertainty. Fear is defined by the appraisal themes of uncertainty, unpleasantness, and lack of control in new situations.[79]

From a rational perspective, fear should not affect one's assessment of risk any more than a general sense of danger would, and a risk estimate in one situation should not influence a risk estimate in a logically unrelated situation. But Lerner and Keltner show that these rational assumptions are incorrect. People who experience fear will, as a consequence of an appraisal tendency, perceive greater risk across current *and* new situations: "The same patterns for fear and anger appeared in experimental studies across tasks assessing risk perception, risk preferences, and one's comparative chances of experiencing a variety of positive and negative events."[80]

In one experiment, Lerner and Keltner administered surveys that asked participants the degree of fear they tend to feel in response to known fear-inducing objects, such as snakes and enclosed places. When asked a standard question that assessed orientation to risk when probabilities were known and choice outcomes had little personal relevance, fearful people avoided uncertainty and reduced their risks. A second experiment involved risk assessments with unknown probabilities of relevant outcomes: undergraduate students estimated the probability that particular desired and undesired events would occur in their own and in peers' lives. Again, fearful people avoided uncertainty and perceived greater risks: more-fearful people tended to have more pessimism about logically unrelated future life events. A third experiment used a highly fear-prone group who were required to report risk estimates to an experimenter; the effect of fear on risk persisted. Lerner and Keltner also found that events that are ambiguous in terms of personal control—that is, when subjects believe that they have little to no control over the source of the fear—lead to greater perceived risks. Extremes of very high or very low certainty about one's future control tend to undermine the effect.[81]

A fourth experiment manipulated the fear rather than measuring chronic tendencies to experience fear and anger. Sixty undergraduate participants were asked to answer two open-ended questions in a detailed and truthful manner. Participants were then asked to rank the likelihood that specific events would happen to them. Fearful people perceived greater risk. Lerner and Keltner speculate from these experiments that fearful people "systematically favor risk-free options over potentially more rewarding but uncertain options."[82]

In a subsequent study of 973 nationally representative Americans aged thirteen to eighty-eight shortly after September 11, 2001, both naturally occurring and experimentally induced fear increased the perceived risks and plans for precautionary measures. Respondents used online surveys to express what made them most afraid about the attacks and to describe in detail what made them most afraid, such that others reading their comments might also be afraid. Respondents then were exposed to stimuli about terrorism that evoked fear, they judged the likelihood of future terrorism events in the United States, and they estimated the probability that they and other average Americans might experience eight terrorist or other dangerous events within the next year. Experimentally priming fear exacerbates risk perceptions well beyond the specific terrorism focus of the stimulus.[83]

Other research has reached similar conclusions about the effect of fear on risk perception and choices. Linda Skitka and her colleagues have found in a series of experiments that in response to the September 11 attacks, people who were angry but not fearful supported the relatively risky option of expanding the war beyond Afghanistan, while fearful but not angry individuals supported the less risky option of deporting Arab Americans, Muslims, and first-generation immigrants.[84] Another study of responses to terrorism indicates that anger and fear predict offensive and defensive reactions: willingness to negotiate is reduced with anger but increases with fear.[85] Leonie Huddy and her colleagues have found that those Americans who experienced high levels of anxiety—an emotion related to but distinct from fear—after the September 11 attacks were "less supportive of aggressive military action against terrorists, less approving of President Bush, and favored increased American isolationism. The majority of Americans who perceived a threat of future terrorism in the United States but were not overly anxious supported the Bush administration's international and domestic anti-terrorism policies."[86] George Marcus and his colleagues find that "fear and perceived threat lead people to express higher degrees of ethnocentrism, to respond more punitively toward outgroups, and to become less politically tolerant."[87]

Another body of research has found that events that prime many people's worst fear—fear of their own death—have profound psychological effects. According to J. Greenberg and colleagues, people's need to suppress their own mortality causes cultural worldviews that reinforce perceptions of immortality but which, in the face of terrorism and other reinforcements of mortality, bolster a worldview and higher ethnocentrism and prejudice.[88] Paul Slovic and his colleagues have concluded that the negative effects elicited by thinking about a recent major natural disaster leads to more pessimistic views of the future: participants who were reminded about the recent tsunami believed that the risk of future negative events was high and that of positive events low.[89] Other literature on fear as a disposition rather than an emotional state has reached similar conclusions.[90] In their review of the literature, Ted Brader and George Marcus state that "fear motivates (and prepares the body for) risk-aversive behavior, including actions aimed at prevention and protection, conciliatory acts, hiding, and flight."[91]

An extremely rare congenital genetic disorder called lipoid proteinosis provides the most fascinating and graphic evidence of the effect of fear on risk. Lipoid proteinosis causes extensive damage to the brain's amygdala and prevents a person from feeling and experiencing fear. Fewer than three hundred diagnosed cases have been reported in the medical literature, and almost one-fourth of them are in South Africa, many among people with Dutch or German ancestry.[92] According to Antonio Damasio and his colleagues, these patients understand what an experience of fear involves because they experienced fear as a child, but from the age of about ten on they never experienced the emotion again. "SM," a forty-four-year-old female patient studied by Damasio and his colleagues for over two decades, exhibits no fear from typically high fear–inducing situations, while her experience of other emotions and competence at other activities is unimpaired and her IQ, memory, and perceptual abilities are normal. "Across standard fear-inducing treatments, many self-report questionnaires, three months of real-life experience sampling, and a life history replete with traumatic events, SM repeatedly demonstrated an absence of overt fear manifestations and an overall impoverished experience of fear."[93] She handled dangerous snakes for over thirty minutes and asked to handle even-more-dangerous ones; she returned to a park where an inebriated man had previously threatened to stab her; and she has had her life threatened numerous times. Yet she has great difficulty in detecting imminent threats and learning to avoid risky situations. Like many war veterans with amygdala lesions, she is immune to post-traumatic stress disorder.[94] Her behavior constantly brings her back to the dangerous situations that she should avoid. Damasio and his colleagues conclude that "without the amygdala, the evolutionary value of fear is lost."[95]

Emotions have strong effects on financial decision-making, where actors have strong incentives to behave rationally.[96] Emotions elicit specific cognitive appraisals that become a perceptual anchor for assessing the future. Defensive reactions to stimuli previously associated with physical threat can recover immediately in the face of stressful events.[97]

Thus Damasio concludes that emotions "serve as a basis for future decisions by providing a sense of what is good and bad and causes pleasure or pain on the basis of prior learning and experiences."[98] Research has also shown that sufficiently strong perceptions of threat can cause an amygdala-mediated recalibration that can last a lifetime: post-traumatic stress disorder.[99] Literature on fear conditioning suggests that a sufficient level of fear can cause an emotional recalibration that can last for the remainder of one's life.[100] Thus Jacques Hymans notes that fears, once activated, are "devilishly persistent."[101]

Will experiencing fear of imminent nuclear war influence a leader's orientation to the dilemma of nuclear assertion? The effect of fear should be strongest when those who experience it believe that they have some control over its source. But a genuine expectation of imminent nuclear war cannot be produced in a laboratory among leader subjects who believe that they had some control over a nuclear crisis.[102] Nevertheless, fear of imminent nuclear war will be cognitively accessible, personally experienced, recent, dramatic, salient, and vivid to such leaders. It is hard to think of a more cognitively available data point for a leader who is contemplating nuclear assertion than a nuclear crisis brought about by his or her own assertive foreign policies.

When leaders think of the implications of imminent nuclear war brought about by an adversary's assertive response to their own assertive coercion, they are likely to substitute the question "What do I think about it?" for the easier question "How do I feel about it?"[103] As in other fight-or-flight challenges, the cognitive brain will give precedence to the emotional brain and produce a quick response to escape the situation that caused the fear. This same response will likely cause leaders to quickly select restrained foreign policies.[104]

Restrained foreign policies are hardly risk free—little in international politics is—but restraint reduces the risk of nuclear escalation and is quite distinct from the assertion that causes a nuclear crisis. Fear also influences people's estimates of the risk of events that are unrelated to the source of the fear. Thus leaders may adopt restrained foreign policies toward states with which they have previously not been in nuclear crises. Moreover, because nuclear crises in one's own country are more cognitively accessible to people than crises in other countries, successors to the leader that experienced fear will likely also authorize or support restrained foreign policies.

If nuclear proliferation is dangerous when leaders learn that nuclear assertion is safe, proliferation is safe when they learn that assertion is dangerous. The availability heuristic resolves the puzzles of nuclear proliferation and conflict: experienced nuclear powers are less conflict prone than new nuclear powers because leaders have experienced fear of imminent nuclear war. Their experiences cause them to desist from earlier assertive foreign policies when the balance of incentives and power remain constant. This explains why leaders in states such as India and Pakistan seem to have learned so little from the Cold War: those events are less cognitively available than their own nuclear crises.

The effect of fear suggests that if a leader prevails in a nuclear crisis but also experiences fear of imminent nuclear war, he or she will likely authorize restrained foreign policies. That leader's successors should also have experienced fear and will therefore also likely authorize a restrained foreign policy.[105] From a rational perspective, the experience of fear should not produce different effects than the general danger caused by earlier nuclear coercion.

Examples from international politics and elsewhere illustrate this dynamic. In November 1983, when Ronald Reagan received intelligence that suggested that the Soviet leadership feared an imminent surprise attack during a recent NATO military exercise, he became "visibly shaken" and afterward substantially changed his approach to Moscow.[106] After a massive arms buildup and threatening statements received throughout his first term, Reagan apparently became "anxious to get a top Soviet leader in a room alone and try and convince him we had no designs on the Soviet Union and Russians had nothing to fear from us."[107] He approved the formation of a small group of experts to reach out to the Soviets to moderate their insecurity, develop relationships, and minimize the probability of inadvertent conventional and nuclear escalation.[108] Former CIA senior analyst and division chief in the Office of Soviet Affairs Melvin Goodman claimed that the Able Archer Crisis was the "turning point: it paved the way for Reykjavik, toned down our [military] exercises and made Reagan feel that we needed to talk to the Soviets."[109]

Developing countries often ignore the hazards that bilateral investment treaties pose both to their ability to internally regulate with discretion as well as the costs of expensive compensation claims—until they become subject to an investment treaty claim. Leaders tend to ignore costly but unlikely risks when they have no cognitively accessible comparable cases.[110] Fear can also precede and shape beliefs and cause a reversal of preferences.[111] Thus while William James asked whether people run from bears due to fear or whether people experience fear as a result of running from bears, it is likely that fear both causes and results from behavior.[112] Leon Festinger argues that while experiencing an earthquake can cause people to experience fear of future earthquakes, fear both results from the earthquake and is central to the belief that more earthquakes are to come; the belief leads them to take preparatory measures. The fear of future events that resulted from the Chernobyl nuclear reactor disaster has more seriously influenced people's mental health than the blast itself.[113] One study showed that the level and types of physical illness from radiation in both affected and unaffected areas was similar, but the psychological distress was much greater in affected areas. While the incident had killed no more than five hundred people by 1996, other results were substantial: resettlement costs of two hundred thousand people, an increase in panic-fueled abortions, and a large drop in the birthrate.

The British and American experiences with strategic bombing in the interwar years lends further plausibility to the effects of availability and fear on foreign policy. As Tami Davis Biddle has shown, many British strategic thinkers and much public opinion overemphasized the impact of the Germans' early zeppelin raids, which had managed to inflict damage on an unprepared Britain, but also neglected the less-effective subsequent attacks. Although British defenses increased the cost of later German attacks, "the early raids were an indelible trauma that could not be wholly erased by subsequent events."[114]

British ideas about the superiority of offensive airpower combined with the familiar psychological patterns of availability and fear also trickled into American strategic thinking. US planners hesitated to learn anything about the limitations of airpower from the Chinese and Spanish civil wars, leading Gen. Hap Arnold to surmise that "a few first class planes and heterogeneous legionnaire pilots operating under loose control can never be called an air force and no true lessons can be drawn therefrom."[115] One Italian colonel wrote in 1938 that "aerial warfare in a European struggle would differ greatly from what it is today in Spain."[116]

The Americans also were unable to learn from the British about the perils of undefended daylight bombing until the devastatingly costly second attack on the Schweinfurt ball bearing factory on October 14, 1943. More than two-thirds of the almost three hundred bombers that had been dispatched were shot down or destroyed, and only when the combined bomber offensive itself was called into question was the production schedule for fighter aircraft recalibrated to prioritize long-range escorts and permission granted to attack through cloud.[117]

Table 2.1 illustrates the ALF two-stage nuclear learning model. Two points are worth clarifying. First, availability consistently influences learning throughout the model. In the first stage, availability biases and related cognitive dissonance and attribution biases cause leaders to authorize assertive foreign policies. Unsuccessful assertive attempts do not cause leaders to desist from this dangerous trajectory. The pathology of availability that bedevils leaders of new nuclear powers is overcome only by another cognitively available data point that pushes in the opposite direction: fear of imminent nuclear escalation. While the availability of a leader's own nuclear program will compel him to authorize assertive foreign policies that drag him into a crisis with his nuclear-powered adversary, the similarly strong cognitive availability of the nuclear brink causes him to authorize restrained foreign policies similar to most experienced nuclear powers. The fear of being at the epicenter of one's nation's nuclear crisis trumps the availability of a leader's own nuclear program because it is directly experienced. Such fear also causes risk aversion when the costs and probability of nuclear escalation remain constant.

Second, just as it is difficult to specify the conditions when a new nuclear power's adversary will respond to an assertive policy with its

Table 2.1. The ALF Two-Stage Nuclear Learning Model

	Stage 1	Stage 2
Independent variable	Nuclear proliferation	Assertive foreign policy
Intervening variable	Availability biases (cognitive dissonance, attribution)	Adversary's assertive foreign policy Availability biases (fear)
Dependent variable	Assertive foreign policy	Restrained foreign policy

own assertive policy (and plunge the pair into a nuclear crisis), it is difficult to predict when the adversary's assertion will cause the new nuclear power to experience fear of imminent nuclear escalation. Khrushchev, for example, experienced fear within days of the beginning of Kennedy's blockade to turn back Soviet ships. Musharraf, however, did not experience fear of imminent nuclear war after the Indian mobilization in December 2001 and only reached the nuclear brink in May 2002.

It is worth emphasizing that in the ALF model, availability biases influence foreign policy decision-making only after leaders have developed nuclear weapons. Thus one might ask whether cognitively available experiences from a leader's political career can germinate positive lessons about nuclear assertion. If so, leaders of new nuclear powers would behave assertively long before they develop nuclear weapons. Khrushchev, for example, should have been much more assertive between 1953 and 1956, such as in opposing a peace treaty with Austria rather than pushing for one, or supporting Vyacheslav Molotov's hard-line policies rather than criticizing them. The Soviet leader became much more assertive after his apparently successful Suez experiences and his development of the capability to target the United States with nuclear missiles in 1959. If the availability model explains Pakistani assertiveness in Kashmir, then at least one Pakistan Army general should have learned that assertiveness works; intensified sponsorship of the Kashmir insurgency should have occurred before Pakistan developed nuclear weapons in 1990. Only after Pakistan developed nuclear weapons did Pakistani assertiveness in Kashmir increase, however. In the case of China, the national politics availability model would expect Mao to have thrown his weight around the contested Zhenbao Island and perhaps elsewhere long before he developed nuclear weapons in 1964.

One might ask how the pathologies of availability and fear are distinct from other motivated and unmotivated biases such as attribution, bolstering, wishful thinking, groupthink, and analogical reasoning. Availability itself does not predict policy preferences without further specification. But it does have the distinct and unique pathology of causing leaders to learn from data points that they have either spent much time on or been closely involved with. When the data points used as a basis happen to be a nation's successful nuclear weapons program, the resulting foreign policies will tend to be assertive and very dangerous. Fear has the unique effect of causing risk aversion, which for a leader in the midst of a nuclear crisis should cause restrained foreign policies and have a stabilizing effect.

Without further specification, though, many other psychological biases, while relevant to the challenges associated with new nuclear powers, tell us little about the foreign policies that they will exhibit. In his landmark works, *Perception and Misperception in International Politics* and *Psychology and Deterrence*, Robert Jervis outlines how attribution, bolstering, and wishful thinking can cause deterrence failures and international conflict.[118] His psychological findings have stood the test of time.[119] A number of psychological biases related to attribution—the fundamental attribution error and the actor-observer effect—cause people to believe that their own behavior is constrained by structural pressures but that others have much more freedom to buck the same pressures. The tendency for people to adhere to these beliefs in the face of discrepant evidence can lead to persistent beliefs that adversaries are unconstrained and hostile, that one's own state is weak and pushed into a corner, and that one's allies are ultimately unreliable.[120] These findings might lead us to expect international conflict but in fact say little about how many deterrence failures to expect. Attribution biases suggest much about the sources of threat perceptions but little about what policies leaders of new nuclear powers will use to respond. They also do not address the conditions when leaders might be able to live with menacing security environments.

Jervis has also studied motivated biases. These involve domestic or international pressures that cause policy where beliefs are more a reflection of structural pressures than independent choices.[121] A closely related concept is wishful thinking, by which people believe what they want to believe to avoid painful choices and value trade-offs. But while structural constraints are often severe, leaders rarely have only one policy choice, and the concepts of motivated bias and wishful thinking provide little insight into policy choices. As Jervis points out, "It is hard to draw specific propositions about what decision-makers will think and do from the general concept of wishful thinking."[122]

To be able to explain how leaders navigate their way through such painful value trade-offs as the nuclear assertion dilemma, we need to, as Jack Levy has pointed out, explain the interaction between psychological variables and domestic and political structures by integrating them into a more comprehensive theory of foreign policy and strategic interaction.[123] The ALF two-stage model does precisely this. Individual characteristics are related to national policy implementation through the supreme power that leaders like Khrushchev, Mao, and Musharraf hold over nuclear strategy and foreign policy.

Analogical reasoning involves leaders learning and operationalizing policies learned from past events that resemble the circumstances, alternatives, and potential outcomes of present ones.[124] While analogical reasoning models share an explicit focus on learning with the ALF model, the similarities end there.[125] In the ALF model, leaders in new nuclear powers confronting the dilemma of nuclear assertion and contemplating foreign policy choices do not hit on relevant analogies; they learn only from their own experiences with nuclear weapons. The rational-signaling model expects leaders to learn from certain historical cases and so more closely approximates analogical learning models.

Groupthink occurs when members of a decision-making group prioritize consensus over assessing alternative positions and tend to shun policies that do not conform to the majority position.[126] Such groups exhibit self-censorship and feelings of invulnerability and will not tolerate (and sometimes even punish) contrary viewpoints and dissent in order to consolidate unanimity. Like many of the psychological biases discussed here, it is hard to predict policy outcomes, given the presence of groupthink, without further information, such as knowing the majority policy; groupthink pressures could cause war or peace. Moreover, in the cases addressed here leaders exert substantial influence over strategic decisions regarding nuclear assertion such that while groupthink surely occurs, it is more an *effect* of a leader's policy preferences than a *cause* of it.

Another possible psychological explanation is the Rubicon Theory of War: an implementation mind-set reduces receptivity to incoming information, increases vulnerability to cognitive dissonance and illusions of control, and causes war.[127] While these dynamics are certainly inherent in the ALF model, the transition from deliberation to implementation is central to nuclear emboldenment but exogenous to the Rubicon theory. Nor can the Rubicon model explain nuclear emboldenment, because it does not explain the conditions when actors adopt implementation mind-sets.

One might ask how the mechanisms in the ALF model are different from those outlined in the literature on conventional crisis decision-making, and specifically whether the effects are different from those caused by stress. Nuclear crises certainly involve high levels of stress, but the literature has not specified which psychological mechanisms cause what sort of policy preferences.[128] Escalatory dynamics in crises between two nuclear powers are likely to be distinct from the dynamics experienced between conventionally armed powers in at least two ways: speed and control. "Nuclear crises" are likely to exert different effects on decision-making than crises between adversaries not armed with nuclear weapons. Nuclear crises threaten, at least since the onset of the missile age in the late 1950s, to inflict greater destruction with greater speed, thus depriving decision-makers of control over escalation much more quickly than a conventional crisis might. Nuclear weapons should be expected to both increase the level of fear in a crisis and the rapidity with which leaders are likely to experience it.

While the cognitive and emotional mechanics of the human brain have not changed, the destruction and speed of nuclear weapons present different effects on crisis decision-making. Johnson and Tierney have shown that the belief that war was imminent in July 1914 caused risky war plans by both sides and plunged the major powers into war. But leaders are less likely to authorize first strikes and dangerous mobilizations when war can result in the total destruction of one's state or region within hours rather than months.[129] The mechanisms of crisis decision-making in operation in 1914 are still relevant today, but their impact on policy choices in the nuclear age—where uncontrolled escalation can occur almost instantaneously—are problematic. Crises and armed conflicts between nuclear powers are thus rarer, briefer, and less violent than those between conventionally armed adversaries because of the much greater and quicker destruction that they ultimately promise.

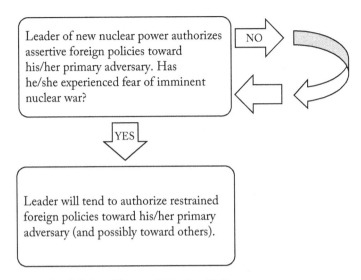

Figure 2.1. Availability, Fear, and Foreign Policy

Rational Choice, Nuclear Weapons, and Foreign Policy

Psychologically biased reasoning about nuclear weapons and foreign policy presupposes unbiased rational calculations. A diverse and influential body of rational-choice scholarship has addressed many issues related to international conflict and the onset and resolution of wars. But no one has developed rational models to explain how leaders approach the dilemma of nuclear assertion, even though several alternatives could be rational. This claim might appear odd in light of the influential work on nuclear weapons and interstate conflict by Robert Powell, Harrison Wagner, and Barry Nalebuff.[130] Their literature, however, has a critical limitation: it explains the implications of a given foreign policy conditional on the distribution of information and resolve rather than explaining the sources of such resolve. Foreign policy and nuclear strategy as a subject in the rational-choice literature is the independent rather than dependent variable. The tendency to take rational approaches and assume rather than puzzle at a given foreign policy has diverted attention from developing an explanation of the fundamental variation in risk propensity and foreign policy decisions made by leaders of nuclear powers. Because rational-choice scholars have neglected this multiplicity of policies, two rational models developed here will help predict how leaders think about foreign policy after developing nuclear weapons, what strategies they buy into, what foreign policies they authorize, and what would cause their policies to change.

Most rational-choice explanations in international relations employ expected utility theory in game theoretic models. Behavior here is conceptualized as choices from a group of alternatives, each of which has a utility value and probability of occurrence. According to expected utility theory, people assess the probability and calculate the utility of each outcome and choose the option that maximizes probability-weighted utility. Learning outcomes in most rational-choice models have two key characteristics: people are assumed to be attentive to enough information to accurately estimate the utility and probability of alternative choices and select the choices that maximize probability-weighted expected utility; and people adjust their preferences to a changed distribution of information (e.g., leaders update their beliefs as new information suggests that probabilities or utilities should be revised). These assumptions imply that in order to explain how leaders learn about the usefulness of nuclear assertion, we only have to model the signals that others send about their resolve rather than include the beliefs and perceptions of the coercer; all leaders are assumed to be attentive to the relevant information and interpret it correctly, or at least behave similarly.

Harrison Wagner's rational-learning model of the Cuban Missile Crisis illustrates these assumptions. According to Wagner's model, in order to understand how President Kennedy's behavior might have caused Nikita Khrushchev to revise his estimate of the probability of an American strike on Cuba, we do not need to address the Soviet leader's beliefs or information-processing abilities; anyone with preferences and information similar to Khrushchev's would be attentive to the same important parts of President Kennedy's behavior and reach the same conclusions and authorize the same policy.[131]

The key assumption here is that all individuals in Khrushchev's position who possess the same preferences would have made the same best or near-best decision. Rational-choice learning models assume that individuals with equal preferences exposed to the same information will exhibit equal or near equal behaviors. In Michael Tomz's model, investors update their beliefs in response to new facts. At each stage in the learning process, investors strike a compromise between their prior views and fresh data. Although Tomz claims that his argument "does not require that all people possess identical cognitive abilities," it does assume that all people will use their different cognitive abilities to reach similar conclusions from the same information.[132]

Rational-choice approaches have not modeled leaders' assessments of foreign policies in the aftermath of developing nuclear weapons.[133] Such explanations might model a two-player game with complete information about a change in the distribution of capabilities but incomplete information about the distribution of resolve. That is, in a scenario when a new nuclear power is deciding foreign policy toward an experienced nuclear power, leaders in both states will be aware of their nuclear weapons but unaware of their resolve to revise a status quo or tolerate assertive foreign policies. Rational-choice approaches would model the optimal foreign policy choice, given the most relevant information about the balance of resolve and historical precedents.

Most rational-choice learning models also assume that bargaining and learning stop once bargaining fails and a crisis, conflict, or war begins.[134] But learning *may* occur and foreign policies *may* change during nuclear crises.[135] Other research has modeled learning after a bargaining failure, but it has assumed that learning ends after one or a few interactions in a crisis or conflict.

These models also have limited application to the question of how a leader learns about nuclear weapons and foreign policy because learning may occur after a few crisis or conflict interactions.[136] Some recent research has, however, modeled bargaining and learning during any time in a crisis or conflict. In Robert Powell's model, one learns about another's type "by watching how that actor behaves and then updating [his or her] beliefs about that actor's type in light of the observed information."[137] In Branislav Slantchev's model, "players use all the information available"; "the uninformed state learns about its opponent by observing both its strategic behaviour at the bargaining table and the nonmanipulable battlefield performance."[138] In Mark Crescenzi's model, states assess the information available from *all* the possible other states in the system to determine what their dyadic partner would do in crisis situations;

"learning is assumed to be experiential in that states learn from the experiences and behavior of other states; diagnostic in that states use the experiences of others to update their beliefs about the intentions of others; and vicarious, or diffuse, in that states learn from experiences in which they are not directly involved."[139]

Rational models also assume that while people are attentive to a lot of information, they learn about an actor's resolve only from that behavior that an irresolute actor could not have sent. Because there are incentives to misrepresenting one's military power or resolve in bargaining, leaders must differentiate between signals that are accurate indicators and those that are not. Rational-choice models assume that only "costly signals" allow actors to credibly reveal these values and therefore warrant the revising of beliefs.[140] As Slantchev claims, "To achieve credibility, an actor must engage in an action that he would not have taken if he were unresolved."[141] Optimal attention and information-processing assumptions ensure that behavior that offers no costly signal (and thus no new information) but that might otherwise be salient will not cause learning. Wagner stipulates that if one player is expected to issue a costless threat and does, his opponent will not change his probability estimate of further undesirable behaviors, because no new information has been received.[142]

Rational-choice approaches usually define costly signals as ones that incur audience costs. James Fearon differentiates between the costs of conceding the issues at stake, which are not influenced by when concessions are made, and the costs that are generated throughout a crisis. The latter are audience costs. As distinct from the physical costs of the crisis and the risk of accidental or preemptive war, "international and domestic audience costs" consist of "signaling costs in the eyes of these audiences when a leader backs down after making a show or use of force or public demand or threat."[143] Tomz defines them as "the domestic price that a leader would pay for making foreign threats and then backing down."[144] According to audience cost theory, domestic publics believe that backing down compromises a leader's or country's reputation for making credible commitments, and that leaders who back down are incompetent in foreign affairs and should be removed from office.[145] Slantchev states that the audience cost mechanism "requires the demanding assumption that leaders incur sufficiently high audience costs; so high, in fact, that peace becomes worse than war."[146]

Rational-learning models might expect leaders to be attentive to historical cases of nuclear assertion. The specification of exactly what probability-weighted expected utility rational-choice learning models would expect leaders to assign to nuclear assertion "working"—with "working" defined as causing sustained revisions to a state's external security environment—is problematic. It is unclear which cases should be assessed in a rational analysis of nuclear assertion. One could argue that, given the small number of nuclear powers, the relevant "universe" of cases should be the entire historical record since 1945. But one could also argue that historical and regional variation renders particular regions or times more relevant to leaders than others.

The coding rules for selecting events to include in the relevant universe of cases could therefore be cases involving the same dyad, cases with at least one state in the dyad, cases with some connection to the region that the state or dyad inhabits, cases with different temporal domains, and cases of all dyads with at least one nuclear power. Powell's and Slantchev's models both include only leaders who learned about an adversary's resolve from direct interactions on the battlefield or at the bargaining table. Crescenzi modeled leaders who learn from the entire historical record.

Other rational-nuclear-learning models that use any subset of the universe of cases could be developed. But further complicating the specification of a rational model is the fact that in all models to date, what knowledge leaders based their assessments of nuclear assertion on is unclear. The expected outcome of rational learning about nuclear assertion is therefore indeterminate: the cases and variables that a leader deems relevant will determine the subjective utility of the choices made.

Empirical studies have reached mixed conclusions regarding whether and how often nuclear coercion works. Few scholars have argued that nuclear assertion often or always works; while many have noted the potential power of nuclear assertion, they usually have carefully qualified those claims. Glenn Snyder and Paul Diesing find "some empirical grounds" to suggest that nuclear weapons offer coercive bargaining advantages.[147] Richard Betts found that nuclear weapons correlated but did not necessarily cause coercive success during several Cold War crises.[148] Several other studies have more boldly pointed to the limits of nuclear assertion. McGeorge Bundy claimed that "When we add up the achievements of atomic diplomacy we find a thin record . . . but the fact that atomic diplomacy has attracted advocates only makes the absence of its effective practice all the more impressive."[149] Morton Halperin has found that "nuclear weapons have never been central" in nineteen US crises.[150]

Recent quantitative research has produced mixed results but also suggests that nuclear assertion tends not to work. Kyle Beardsley and Victor Asal argue that nuclear states tend to "win" their crises: states armed with nuclear weapons win about 75 percent of the time against non-nuclear adversaries in crises over high-salience issues. But what constitutes winning is unclear, and in other cases the probable effect of nuclear weapons is close to a coin flip.[151] Matthew Kroenig argues that states that have more nuclear weapons than their nuclear weapon–equipped adversaries tend to "win" about half the time. But what counts as winning here is unclear, and his conclusion assumes that leaders were aware of the nuclear balance. Even so, the effect of nuclear superiority appears equal to chance.[152] On the other hand, Todd Sechser and Matthew Fuhrmann have modeled the initiation of and outcome from coercive threats in a data set of over two hundred cases between 1918 and 2001. They find that coercive threats by nuclear powers are followed by desired outcomes for the challenger in no more than ten of forty-eight cases involving nuclear-armed challengers.[153] Of these ten, two were Soviet threats to Britain and France in the Suez Crisis, where it could be argued that Soviet nuclear threats likely had no effect. Coercive nuclear threats, then, may have caused desired outcomes in at most 16 percent of Sechser and Fuhrmann's cases, a figure that assumes that nuclear weapons influenced US, British, and French threats to Serbian, Haitian, Iraqi, and Afghani leaders in the 1990s.

The literature suggests two rational-learning models as they relate to nuclear crises. Kenneth Waltz's model argues that nuclear weapons are useful only for deterrence; it expects leaders to learn from all historical cases of nuclear assertion that it hardly ever works and thus leaders will always authorize restrained foreign policies. The second model—rational-signaling—relaxes assumptions about learning from all historical cases.

It expects leaders to learn that nuclear assertion works and expects them to authorize assertive foreign policies to display their resolve to revise or at least defend a status quo. However, it also expects that if a defender displays resolve to maintain the status quo by authorizing a costly signal, the challenger should be expected to authorize a restrained foreign policy.

The Waltzian Learning Model

When leaders must rationally assess the probability that nuclear assertion will work, they can improve their assessments only by analyzing more cases.[154] This procedure is most likely to generate a subjective probability that is close to the objective probability. Leaders may differ in the importance that they attach to particular cases and variables, but the diagnostic value of having more cases of nuclear assertion in other dyads, regions, or time periods will always be greater than zero. Time constraints that operate in nuclear crises should not prevent leaders in peacetime from considering the costs and benefits of assertive foreign policies in the shadow of nuclear weapons. Because most scholarly assessments have concluded that nuclear assertion usually does not work, the Waltzian learning model expects leaders of nuclear powers to always authorize restrained foreign policies.

Nuclear weapons do not allow challengers to credibly threaten to seize disputed goods or territories, usually because using nuclear weapons would be highly costly to the challenger. Rational assumptions about attention and information processing might explain why scholars working with rational-choice assumptions have not addressed nuclear assertion: if it does not work, leaders should know this and never authorize it. One might argue that the Waltzian learning model should not apply to events before 1960 because there were almost no cases of nuclear assertion to assess. But the small number of episodes in this period reduces the number of cases and the amount of effort that leaders like Khrushchev and Eisenhower had to expend in order to rationally estimate the effects of an assertive foreign policy. In the Waltzian learning model, leaders rely on a systematic analysis of all available diagnostic information about all cases involving at least one nuclear power since the beginning of the nuclear age. Leaders are expected to accurately estimate the low effectiveness of assertive foreign policies and authorize restrained foreign policies.

The Rational-Signaling Model

It is possible that leaders will rationally estimate the low effectiveness of nuclear assertion but nevertheless authorize it as a calculated gamble in the face of pressing security threats.[155] Leaders might rationally believe that information from the dyadic relationship at hand is the only relevant information to use in assessing the utility of nuclear assertion. They might rationally learn from other historical cases that nuclear assertion is ineffective but that a different application might be more suitable for current challenges, especially if the adversary made concessions after they themselves developed nuclear weapons.

Leaders might also authorize nuclear assertion to generate domestic audience costs.[156] Under these conditions, nuclear coercion can be considered a rational choice.[157] The rational-signaling model expects leaders in new nuclear powers to authorize assertive foreign policies against a primary, usually nuclear weapon–equipped adversary simply to demonstrate resolve. However, if a leader authorizes nuclear assertion and a defender responds with a costly signal to rationally demonstrate his or her own resolve to defend the status quo, the leader of the new nuclear power should, according to standard rational assumptions, thereafter always authorize a restrained foreign policy toward that adversary.[158]

Leaders can rationally authorize assertive foreign policies toward other states or even toward leaders who have not yet produced a costly signal. Daryl Press shows that when leaders assess military threats, their assessments in one crisis have no rational implication for other crises.[159] The rational-signaling model assumes that a costly signal will be necessary and sufficient for an emboldened and assertive leader to authorize a restrained foreign policy. Costly signals are, however, distinct from assertive foreign policies: restrained foreign policies can also be costly signals.

While the rational-signaling model expects leaders of new nuclear powers to authorize assertive foreign policies, there is no reason to believe that assessments of the utility of nuclear assertion—that is, the probability and cost of nuclear escalation—would be based on the deeply emotional experience of fear rather than on a sense of general danger short of fear. Nor are there rational grounds to expect fear to influence assessments of nuclear assertion—the subjective probabilities and costs of nuclear escalation—any more than fear of general danger would. In the rational-signaling model, leaders learn from some subset of the universe of cases about nuclear assertion, and then they authorize it. The adversary's costly signal is necessary and sufficient for them to authorize a restrained foreign policy. (I assess the particular conditions of each case in the empirical chapters to assess the degree to which leaders confront the dilemma of nuclear assertion along these lines.)

Table 2.2 summarizes the causal process observations and foreign policies that can be expected from each of the three learning models: Waltzian, rational-signaling, and ALF two-stage. Psychological models locate the sources of learning within the perceiver rather than within the sender, so whether a signal is costly is determined by the perceiver. As Mercer argues, "Assessments of credibility depend on one's selection and interpretation of evidence and one's assessment of risk, both of which rely on emotion."[160] Experiences that trigger the emotional brain to act quickly and efficiently to perceived danger will be cognitively available to leaders of new nuclear powers in order for them to authorize restrained foreign policies. Psychological models expect that costly signals by the defender will not cause a leader to adopt restrained foreign policies: the presence of fear of imminent nuclear war, usually caused by assertive foreign policies, is necessary and sufficient to cause leaders of new nuclear powers to authorize restrained foreign policies.

Table 2.2. Three Nuclear Learning Models

Model	Sources of learning about nuclear assertion	Expected foreign policy	Source of change and new foreign policy
Waltzian	Historical record	*Restrained*	No policy change: *Restrained*
Rational-signaling	Any subset of the historical record	*Assertive*	Adversary's costly signal: *Restrained*
ALF Two-Stage	Success(es) with weapons development	*Assertive*	Adversary's assertion and fear of imminent nuclear war: *Restrained*

The Waltzian model expects *new* nuclear powers' leaders to be attentive to the historical record of nuclear assertion, to be able to estimate its limited power, and to always authorize restrained foreign policies. The rational-signaling model expects leaders to learn that nuclear assertion works from any subset of cases and then to authorize it. It expects leaders to always authorize restrained foreign policies toward adversaries that produce costly signals. The ALF two-stage model expects leaders to authorize assertive foreign policies until they experience more than a costly signal; they must also experience fear of imminent nuclear war, which will usually be caused by an adversary's authorization of assertive policies. All three models should apply to leaders of *experienced* nuclear powers as well. If a leader of an experienced nuclear power finds his state's nuclear weapons cognitively accessible, he will authorize assertive foreign policies until he experiences either fear or a costly signal.

One can argue that insofar as the two rational-learning models developed here are not part of the literature, they may be straw men theories only. But rational-choice scholarship has not addressed how leaders learn about nuclear weapons nor how they come to terms with the fundamental trade-off of nuclear assertion. The rational-nuclear-learning models are based on core insights from the most influential rational-choice scholarship in international relations. Different rational assumptions about the sources of learning are transparently incorporated into the two rational-choice alternative models, but those who want a competitive test against extant theory will not be satisfied.[161] Extant rational theories on nuclear power foreign policy do not exist.

Notes

1. Waltz, *Man, the State, and War.*
2. Waltz, "Reflections on Theory," 343. See also Byman and Pollack, "Let Us Now Praise Great Men"; and Jervis, "Do Leaders Matter?"
3. Waltz, "Reflections on Theory," 344.
4. The key variables found in constructivist explanations—actor identities, shared norms, and constitutive structures of normative values—presuppose assumptions about beliefs, perceptions, and information. People must learn their own and others' identities, and what is learned and relearned depends on the

distribution of information and variation in beliefs, perceptions, and interests. Social psychological variables constrain the construction of identities in a way that cultural and institutional variables do not. See Goldgeier, "Psychology and Security," 142.

5. For a review, see Stein, "Rational Deterrence."

6. See, for example, McDermott, *Political Psychology*; Fiske and Taylor, *Social Cognition*; Kahneman, Slovic, and Tversky, *Judgment under Uncertainty*; and Nisbett and Ross, *Human Inference*.

7. Jervis, Lebow, and Stein, *Psychology and Deterrence*, 4.

8. Levy, "Learning and Foreign Policy."

9. Ibid.

10. Simon, "Behavioral Model of Rational Choice"; and Kahneman, *Thinking, Fast and Slow*.

11. Jervis, *Perception and Misperception*; and McDermott, *Risk Taking in International Politics*.

12. Larson, *Origins of Containment*, 326.

13. Khong, *Analogies at War*.

14. Reiter, *Crucible of Beliefs*.

15. Mercer, *Reputation and International Politics*.

16. Johnson and Tierney, "Rubicon Theory of War."

17. Maliniak et al., "Snap Poll."

18. See Levy, "Learning and Foreign Policy," 283.

19. Ibid. For a different definition of learning, see Gross Stein, "Political Learning and Political Psychology," 107–15, 112.

20. *FRUS*, 1961–1963, Vol. 14, Doc. 234.

21. Fearon, "Selection Effects and Deterrence."

22. Sechser, "Militarized Compellent Threats," 381–82; and Sechser and Fuhrmann, "Crisis Bargaining and Nuclear Blackmail." See also McAllister and Labrosse, "What We Talk About."

23. Pape, *Bombing to Win*, 14n3.

24. Fiske and Taylor, *Social Cognition*, 74.

25. Kahneman and Tversky, "Judgment under Uncertainty," 11.

26. Kahneman, *Thinking, Fast and Slow*, 131.

27. McDermott, "Feeling of Rationality," 701; and "Seeing Friends Divorce Inspires Couples to Split," *Daily Telegraph* (UK), October 18, 2013, 11.

28. Ross and Sicoly, "Egocentric Biases."

29. Ibid.

30. Kahneman, *Thinking, Fast and Slow*, 130.

31. Kahneman and Tversky, "Judgment under Uncertainty," 166.

32. Jervis, *Perception and Misperception*, 217–87. See also Khong, *Analogies at War*.

33. Khong, *Analogies at War*.

34. Schwarz et al., "Ease of Retrieval as Information"; Wanke, Schwarz, and Bless, "Availability Heuristic Revisited"; Collins and Loftus, "Spreading-Activation Theory"; MacLeod and Campbell, "Memory Accessibility and Probability Judgment"; Manis et al., "Availability Heuristic in Judgments"; and Rothman and Hardin, "Differential Use."

35. Waltz, "Spread of Nuclear Weapons," 26; and Knopf, "Concept of Nuclear Learning."

36. Kahneman, *Thinking, Fast and Slow*, 135.

37. Festinger, *Theory of Cognitive Dissonance*.

38. Elliott and Devine, "Motivational Nature of Cognitive Dissonance"; and Losch and Cacioppo, "Cognitive Dissonance May Enhance."

39. Fiske and Taylor, *Social Cognition*, 235.

40. Ibid., 235–36. For a good general discussion, see Jervis, *Perception and Misperception*, 382–92.

41. Jervis, *Perception and Misperception*, 394.

42. Cited in ibid., 397.

43. Cited in ibid., 395.

44. Ibid., 398.

45. Ibid.

46. Ibid.

47. Research has shown that the availability heuristic is the optimal mental strategy under some conditions. But these conditions—time pressure, information scarcity, and information redundancy—do not characterize those who face leaders of new nuclear powers that are contemplating the trade-offs of nuclear weapons and foreign policy. See Gigerenzer, Czerlinski, and Martignon, "How Good Are Fast?"

48. Slovic and Alhakami, "Psychological Study of Inverse Relationship."

49. Finucane et al., "Affect Heuristic in Judgments."

50. See Snyder, "Balance of Power," 198–99; and Cohen, "How Nuclear South Asia." One can counter that a more simple explanation for leaders authorizing coercive nuclear strategies is the selection effect: only leaders who expect great benefits from the bomb will attempt to develop it. But this begs the question of why leaders expect great benefits from the bomb, and ignores the fact that leaders who decide to develop nuclear weapons are rarely in power long enough to authorize assertive nuclear policies.

51. Jervis, *Perception and Misperception*, 241–42.

52. Cohen and Gooch, *Military Misfortune*, 63.

53. Ibid., 233–36.

54. See Miller and Ross, "Self-Serving Biases"; Arkin, Cooper, and Kolditz, "Statistical Review"; and Mullen and Riordan, "Self-Serving Attributions."

55. Jervis, *Perception and Misperception*, 345–46.

56. Ibid.

57. Ibid., 344–45.

58. Mercer, *Reputation and International Politics*.

59. Jervis, *Perception and Misperception*, 348.

60. Jervis, "Perceiving and Coping with Threat," 23.

61. Fearon, "Selection Effects and Deterrence."

62. George and Simons, *Limits of Coercive Diplomacy*.

63. Posen, *Inadvertent Escalation*.

64. Kahneman, *Thinking, Fast and Slow*, 139.

65. For exceptions, see McDermott, "Emotions and War"; Mercer, "Emotion and Strategy in the Korean War"; and Rosen, *War and Human Nature*.

66. McDermott, "Feeling of Rationality," 692.

67. Mercer, "Emotional Beliefs."

68. LeDoux, "Emotion," 224. For contrasting positions, see Zajonc, "On the Primacy of Affect"; Lazarus, "On the Primacy of Affect"; McDermott, "Feeling of Rationality"; Elster, *Alchemies of the Mind*, 270; Nussbaum, *Upheavals of Thought*; Damasio, *Descartes' Error*; Frijda, Manstead, and Fischer, "Feelings and Emotions."

69. See Jervis, "Understanding Beliefs," 652–54; Gilovich and Griffin, "Judgment and Decision Making," 561; Damasio, *Descartes' Error*; and LeDoux, "Emotion," 224.

70. McDermott, "Feeling of Rationality."

71. Ibid., 693; and LeDoux, *Emotional Brain*.

72. Morris, Öhman, and Dolan, "Conscious and Unconscious Emotional Learning."

73. McDermott, "Feeling of Rationality," 699; and Clore and Gasper, "Feeling Is Believing," 38.

74. Mercer, "Emotional Beliefs."

75. Damasio, *Descartes' Error*, 159.

76. Mercer, "Emotion and Strategy in the Korean War."

77. Ibid.; and Kahneman, "New Challenges."

78. Lerner and Keltner, "Beyond Valence"; and Lerner and Keltner, "Fear, Anger, and Risk."

79. Certainty is the degree to which future events seem predictable and comprehensible. Control is the tendency to which events seem to be brought about by individual agency or situational variables. See Smith and Ellsworth, "Patterns of Cognitive Appraisal."

80. Lerner and Keltner, "Fear, Anger, and Risk"; Lerner et al., "Effects of Fear and Anger"; and Fischhoff et al., "Evolving Judgments of Terror Risks."

81. Leaders in nuclear crises will, however, be unlikely to believe that they have total or no control over nuclear escalation. On this point, see George and Smoke, *Deterrence in American Foreign Policy*, 527–29. Lerner and Keltner claim that events that are ambiguous in terms of control and predictability "should serve as inkblots that are open to interpretation," hence they magnify the emotions' effect on cognitions ("Fear, Anger and Risk," 151, 156). Other

research has shown that decision-makers are more likely to regret negative outcomes if they were in control when decisions were made. See Markman et al., "The Impact of Perceived Control." See also Sanderson, Rapee, and Barlow, "Panic Induction via Inhalation."

82. Lerner and Keltner, "Fear, Anger, and Risk," 155.

83. Lerner et al., "Effects of Fear and Anger," 147.

84. Skitka, Bauman, and Mullen, "Political Tolerance"; and Skitka et al., "Confrontational and Preventative Policy."

85. Giner-Sorolla and Maitner, "Angry at the Unjust."

86. Huddy et al., "Threat, Anxiety, and Support." See also Huddy, Khatid, and Capelos, "Trends."

87. Marcus et al., *With Malice Toward Some*; Marcus, Neuman, and MacKuen, *Affective Intelligence and Political Judgment*. See also Brader, "Striking a Responsive Chord."

88. Greenberg, Solomon, and Pyszczynski, "Terror Management Theory"; Pyszczynski, Greenberg, and Solomon, "Why Do We Need What We Need?" See also Becker, *Denial of Death*.

89. Vastfjäll, Peters, and Slovic, "Affect, Risk Perception, and Future Optimism," 69–72.

90. See, for example, Hatemi et al., "Fear as a Disposition"; Kendler, Myers, and Prescott, "Etiology of Phobias"; and Neale and Fulker, "Bivariate Path Analysis of Fear Data."

91. Brader and Marcus, "Emotion and Political Psychology," 178.

92. DiGiandomenico et al., "Lipoid Proteinosis."

93. Feinstein et al., "Human Amygdala," 1–5; and Scott et al., "Impaired Auditory Recognition."

94. Koenigs et al., "Focal Brain Damage."

95. Feinstein et al., "Human Amygdala," 38.

96. Lee and Andrade, "Fear, Social Projection." See also Lerner, Small, and Loewenstein, "Heart Strings and Purse Strings."

97. LeDoux and Debiek, "Fear and the Brain," 815.

98. Damasio, *Descartes' Error*.

99. Tooby and Cosmides, "Evolutionary Psychology of the Emotions," 119; and Pitman and Orr, "Psychophysiology."

100. See Öhman and Mineka, "Fears, Phobias, and Preparedness."

101. Hymans, *Psychology of Nuclear Proliferation*, 30.

102. We could prime fear of nuclear war in the laboratory, but the subjects would know that they had no control over its outcome. The effects of fear would be much weaker.

103. Kahneman, *Thinking, Fast and Slow*, 139.

104. The experience of fear of imminent nuclear war may not cause risk aversion in the sense that it need not cause leaders to revise their estimates of

the probability or undesirability of nuclear war. Rather, assuming that leaders believe throughout a crisis that there is a fixed probability of nuclear escalation, fear should cause them to prefer policies that eliminate that risk.

105. For more on the conditions when nuclear restraint is passed on to later leaders, see chap. 6.

106. DiCicco, "Fear, Loathing, and Cracks," 262.

107. Reagan, *An American Life*, 589.

108. DiCicco, "Fear, Loathing, and Cracks," 263.

109. DiCicco, "Fear, Loathing, and Cracks," 262.

110. Skovgaard Poulsen and Aisbett, "When the Claim Hits."

111. Öhman and Wiens, "Concept of an Evolved Fear Module."

112. James, "What Is an Emotion?"

113. Specter, "Ten Years Later," 267.

114. Biddle, *Rhetoric and Reality*, 74.

115. Ibid., 171.

116. Ibid., 172.

117. Ibid., 224–28.

118. Jervis, *Perception and Misperception*; and Jervis, "Perceiving and Coping with Threat," 13–33.

119. See, for example, Fiske and Taylor, *Social Cognition*, 169–73.

120. Jervis, "Perceiving and Coping with Threat," 24; and Mercer, *Reputation and International Politics*.

121. Jervis, "Perceiving and Coping with Threat," 24–27.

122. Jervis, *Perception and Misperception*, 365.

123. Levy, "Political Psychology and Foreign Policy," 275.

124. Mintz and DeRouen, *Understanding Foreign Policy Decision Making*, 103.

125. Khong, *Analogies at War*.

126. Mintz and DeRouen, *Understanding Foreign Policy Decision Making*, 44.

127. Johnson and Tierney, "Rubicon Theory of War," 13–23.

128. Holsti, "Crisis Decision Making," 26–36.

129. Johnson and Tierney, "Rubicon Theory of War."

130. See, for example, Powell, "Crisis Bargaining"; Wagner, "Nuclear Deterrence"; and Nalebuff, "Brinksmanship and Nuclear Deterrence."

131. Wagner, "Uncertainty, Rational Learning," 201.

132. Tomz, *Reputation and International Cooperation*.

133. For a partial exception, see Feaver and Niou, "Managing Nuclear Proliferation."

134. Nalebuff, "Brinkmanship and Nuclear Deterrence"; Morrow, "Capabilities, Uncertainty, and Resolve"; Powell, *Nuclear Deterrence Theory*; Wagner, "Nuclear Deterrence, Counterforce Strategies"; Kilgour, "Domestic Political

Structure"; Bueno de Mesquita and Lalman, *War and Reason*; and Fearon, "Signaling versus the Balance of Power."

135. Wagner, "Bargaining and War."

136. Smith, "Fighting Battles, Winning Wars"; Slantchev, "Power to Hurt"; and Smith and Stam, "Bargaining and the Nature of War."

137. Powell, "Bargaining and Learning While Fighting," 358–59.

138. Slantchev, "Principle of Convergence," 622.

139. Crescenzi, "Reputation and Interstate Conflict," 384.

140. Fearon, "Domestic Political Audiences"; Schultz, "Domestic Opposition and Signaling"; Smith, "International Crises and Domestic Politics"; and Tomz, "Domestic Audience Costs." Recent game theory approaches have explored the conditions when "costless" signaling can cause belief change. See Trager, "Diplomatic Calculus in Anarchy."

141. Slantchev, "Feigning Weakness," 359.

142. Wagner, "Uncertainty, Rational Learning," 186.

143. Fearon, "Domestic Political Audiences," 579–81.

144. Tomz, "Domestic Audience Costs," 821.

145. Smith, "International Crises and Domestic Politics"; and Guisinger and Smith, "Honest Threats."

146. Slantchev, "Military Coercion in Interstate Crises," 544. See also Trager and Vavreck, "Political Costs of Crisis Bargaining," 526–27.

147. Snyder and Diesing, *Conflict among Nations*, 460–62.

148. Betts, *Nuclear Blackmail and Nuclear Balance*.

149. Bundy, *Danger and Survival*, 597.

150. Halperin, *Nuclear Fallacy*.

151. See Beardsley and Asal, "Winning with the Bomb," 290.

152. It is not clear that the United States won the 1956 Suez Crisis or the 1967 Six-Day War, nor that the Soviet Union won the 1961 second Berlin Crisis, the 1975 Angolan Crisis, or the 1979 Afghanistan invasion. These five events account for 25 percent of Kroenig's cases. See Kroenig, "Nuclear Superiority."

153. Sechser and Fuhrmann, "Crisis Bargaining and Nuclear Blackmail."

154. Crescenzi, "Reputation and Interstate Conflict."

155. Goemans and Fey, "Risky but Rational."

156. One can, however, argue that leaders should rationally know that audience costs would be unlikely to enable them to prevail. See Snyder and Borghard, "Cost of Empty Threats"; and Trachtenberg, "Audience Costs."

157. One might argue that leaders rationally learn that nuclear coercion does not work but authorize it anyway, due to random error. The tendency for new nuclear powers to be systematically more conflict prone than they were before and long after developing nuclear weapons, however, suggests that the errors are not random.

158. One might also argue that a defender's reputation could rationally deter a nuclear power from challenging the status quo. But because rational

approaches tend to model reputations as remaining constant, a constant reputation cannot explain variation in nuclear strategy. See Guisinger and Smith, "Honest Threats."

159. Press, *Calculating Credibility*.

160. Mercer, "Emotion and Strategy in the Korean War," 3.

161. For other research that develops rational alternative explanations because no alternative rational models exist, see Yarhi-Milo, *Knowing the Adversary*.

3

Blind Moles and Mutual Extermination: The Soviet Union, 1956-1962

AT THE 1955 SUPERPOWER SUMMIT in Geneva, Switzerland, US president Dwight D. Eisenhower informed the Soviet minister of defense, Georgi Zhukov, that "it would take some time until the present psychological state of distrust and fear were overcome . . . what was necessary were some events or series of events which might change the psychological climate."[1] By the end of the Cold War Thomas Schelling had suggested that the Cuban Missile Crisis had had the effect Eisenhower called for: "The Cuban Missile crisis was the best thing to happen to us since the Second World War" because "it helped us avoid further confrontation with the Soviets, it resolved the Berlin issue, and it established new basic understandings about U.S.-Soviet interaction."[2]

The most dangerous years of the Cold War and two lingering puzzles related to it are best explained through the lens of the ALF model's availability heuristic and fear. Soviet foreign policy became explicitly assertive—and the Cold War became much more dangerous—beginning in 1959 because Nikita Khrushchev developed the capability to target the United States with nuclear missiles, after learning in 1956 that nuclear weapons allow assertive foreign policies to have substantial effects. Then, despite having pushed hard to revise the superpower competition, Khrushchev authorized restrained foreign policies in Berlin and Cuba in 1963—and made the competition much safer—because he personally experienced fear of imminent nuclear war during the Cuban Missile Crisis.

Although Stalin first tested a nuclear bomb in 1949, it wasn't until 1959 that the Soviets developed a nuclear missile capable of reliably targeting the United States. Even by the time of the Berlin Crisis, Soviet conventional power did not allow Khrushchev to realize his ambitious security objectives because US retaliation elsewhere would have challenged any Soviet effort to sustain changes to the status quo.[3] The Waltzian model would expect Khrushchev to have authorized a restrained foreign policy and accepted the status quo in 1959 rather than in 1963. The rational-signaling model would expect Khrushchev to have authorized an assertive foreign policy in 1959 but authorized restraint in 1961 after Kennedy authorized a costly signal.[4] The ALF model would expect Khrushchev to have learned of the power of nuclear assertion from his own successes with Soviet nuclear weapons in 1959 and then have authorized assertive foreign policies. But the experience of fear of imminent nuclear war in 1962—caused by Soviet designs on both Cuba and Berlin—was necessary to cause him to authorize restraint.

Khrushchev likely learned of the power of nuclear assertion on the basis of a superficial assessment of only one case. His apparently successful Soviet policies in the 1956 Suez Crisis were cognitively accessible, personally experienced, and dramatic. The lessons he learned from Suez likely caused him to authorize assertive foreign policies in the Middle East and Western Europe immediately after. By the time of the Cuban Missile Crisis, however, the experience of fear of imminent nuclear war had caused him to give up on nuclear assertion—even though assertion had been the basis of Soviet foreign policy for the previous five years and the status quo remained undesirable. The Waltzian learning model cannot explain why Khrushchev authorized assertive policies from 1959 through 1962, and the rational-signaling model cannot explain why Kennedy's 1961 costly signal did not deter Khrushchev's third attempt to compel Kennedy out of West Berlin in 1962. The events in West Berlin played a central role in Soviet grand strategy, and the three "nuclear learning" models will be tested in light of those events.

Soviet Strategy in West Berlin

The central issue of the early Cold War was the division of occupied Germany.[5] At the end of World War II, Washington, London, Paris, and Moscow had agreed that Germany would be divided between them. Western troops had reached Berlin, so that city was also divided. This gave the United States and its allies occupation rights to part of the former German capital located deep within an East German state that Washington refused to recognize diplomatically. Most acknowledged that the occupation of Germany was not a viable long-term solution because much of the German population was sympathetic to unification and it was widely believed that they would eventually demand unification, or at least more autonomy. Though some feared that the occupation might cause the German militarism that the division was designed to avoid, memories of Hitler's 1941 invasion remained vivid. Stalin worried that a rearmed West Germany, or perhaps a unified Germany, would threaten the Soviet Union once again; his major goal was to prevent occupied Germany from joining the Western bloc.[6] Partly as a result of the first Berlin blockade, the Western powers unified their territories into West Germany in 1949 and then granted it NATO membership in 1955.

Thus Khrushchev inherited a German status quo that was much more threatening than the one Stalin experienced. The integration of the allied German territories into West Germany, the admission of West Germany into NATO, and the increasing economic aid the new state received from the United States through the Marshall Plan together substantially increased the threat. East Germany had become both the centerpiece of Moscow's influence in Eastern Europe and the litmus test of the viability of Soviet communism. Before 1949 the future of the allied Germanys was unclear. By 1955 they were integrated into West Germany, and the relative economic power of that state over communist East Germany was large and growing larger. West German chancellor Konrad Adenauer could interfere in East German affairs knowing that any Soviet reaction would encounter a US response. To make matters worse, by 1958 Eisenhower openly spoke of sharing US nuclear weapons with West Germany through the multilateral nuclear force agreement.

While Khrushchev had little control over these serious external threats to East Germany, the internal threat of West Berlin to East Germany was also severe. West Berlin was able to undermine the economic self-sufficiency of East Germany, and every month following the June 1953 East German uprising an average of fifteen thousand people fled East Germany through West Berlin.[7] By 1955 almost three hundred thousand of the state's most skilled people, including doctors, engineers, and scientists, had escaped; by 1959 one-sixth of the country's population had fled.[8] During the first five months of 1961 more than one hundred thousand had fled and another twenty thousand fled in June 1961 alone; this was followed by thirty thousand in July and fifty thousand in August.[9]

Countless East Berliners took advantage of the East's low cost of living but worked in the more lucrative West Berlin market, further drying up sources of East German economic dynamism. Many West Berliners came to East Berlin to take advantage of cheaper state-subsidized goods and services. Both of these further increased the incentive for East Berliners to move west. By July 1961, shortly after Kennedy offered Khrushchev a settlement committing to keep the bomb out of West Germany but with no concessions regarding West Berlin itself, the Western presence in that city was critically undermining East German sovereignty. Khrushchev worried that East Germany's demise might throw doubt on his commitment to other communist satellite states and undermine the Soviets' influence in the East European buffer zone, perhaps even within the Soviet Union itself. The open border between the two halves of Berlin also allowed the United States and Britain to communicate with their agents fairly easily.[10]

Marc Trachtenberg argues that West Germany's nuclear ambitions drove Soviet policy during this period. But Trachtenberg admits that additional factors must have been at work after 1960 because in late 1961 Khrushchev rejected Kennedy's offer that guaranteed a non-nuclear West Germany.[11] If West German nuclear plans truly were the main driver of Soviet policy, Khrushchev would have accepted Kennedy's terms. Trachtenberg himself admits, "I had no really adequate evidence from Soviet sources to work with, so it seemed best to just let it be."[12] The evidence seems to show that the status of West Berlin mattered more to Khrushchev than the prospect of a West German bomb and that the nuclear brink was necessary to temper his assertive moves.

Hope Harrison has found that Bonn's nuclear ambitions were mentioned much less frequently in Khrushchev's interactions with both the East Germans and the Western powers than his concern about the threat that West Berlin posed to East Germany.[13] In a typical exchange with Americans, Khrushchev told visiting US senator Hubert Humphrey in 1958 that Berlin was a "bone in my throat" and that he intended to "cut this knot."[14] Foreign Minister Andrei Gromyko justified his policy proposal in November 1958 on the grounds that it "would draw attention to the problem of the preparation of a peace treaty [with East Germany]."[15] Khrushchev even stated to his Presidium colleagues in May 1961 that "we are not afraid of German aggression."[16]

While the August 1961 building of the Berlin Wall stemmed the flow of refugees out of East Germany, it did not address all the challenges that Western occupation posed.[17] Allied access routes in and out of the city remained intact and daily violated East German sovereignty. Since Adenauer, Kennedy, and others refused to diplomatically recognize East German sovereignty because there was no formal peace treaty that ended World War II, the legitimacy of the East German government was weakened.[18]

Another challenge that West Berlin posed was intelligence: East German leader Walter Ulbricht often complained that West Berlin allowed West German and American intelligence agencies to undermine him.[19] Khrushchev's ideological commitment to the viability of communist East Germany, as well as Ulbricht's strong desire to shore up East German sovereignty by ending Allied access routes to West Berlin, help explain why Soviet pressure on West Berlin persisted after the Berlin Wall had stemmed the massive exodus of refugees.[20] In short, Khrushchev's desire to revise the status quo in West Berlin was the Soviets' central grand strategy during Khrushchev's reign.[21]

Many have argued that Soviet local military superiority in West Berlin hardly rendered Khrushchev unable to realize his goals.[22] The problem with this claim is that it assumes that only the local balance of power influenced Khrushchev's calculations about the West Berlin status quo. Khrushchev would have correctly considered whether the regional and global balance of military power permitted him to sustain revisions that his local superiority may have allowed. At the time it was clear to everyone that the Soviets could take West Berlin if they wanted, but it was far from clear that they could prevail in another all-out conventional war in Europe.

Several scholars have argued that the "Soviet superiority" thesis is incorrect and that Khrushchev would not have been able to sustain revisions to the Berlin status quo. One influential study of the military balance in the 1960s concludes that "NATO and the Warsaw Pact were roughly equal in terms of soldiers, guns, vehicles, infantrymen, and the like. In many respects, we were 'superior'; in some respects, they were."[23] Neither equality nor inferiority of force allows a revised status quo to be sustained; superiority is usually required.

Other scholars have addressed the status quos of earlier and later periods and reached similar conclusions. Matthew Evangelista focuses his assessment on the 1947–48 period and finds that "Soviet troops were not capable of executing the kind of invasion feared in the West during the late 1940s."[24] Barry Posen and John Mearsheimer addressed the 1980s and reached similar conclusions. Mearsheimer argues that "the common image of overwhelming Pact materiel superiority, created by misleading 'bean counts' of unrepresentative classes of equipment, is simply incorrect." Posen concludes that "NATO forces are fully competitive with the Warsaw Pact in Central Europe" and "would probably thwart a conventional attack."[25] Moreover, at the time, Khrushchev lacked any allies that could have offered military or economic assistance to achieve any goals in Berlin. Mao Zedong had long received more benefits from the Soviet Union than he had offered in return, and by 1960 Mao's growing radicalism had substantially undermined the Sino-Soviet alliance.[26] Khrushchev himself confessed to his Presidium colleagues on January 8, 1962, that "the enemy is strong and not weaker than we are."[27]

The Soviet Union obviously became a nuclear power in 1949. But in a more important sense it became a nuclear power in 1959 when Khrushchev acquired the ability to target the United States with nuclear weapons. As late as 1955 Khrushchev had no means of reliably delivering a nuclear bomb to a target on the US mainland. The most current Soviet bomber at the time, the M-4, had a combat radius of only five thousand miles and thus could not reach either US coast; a Soviet sea-launched nuclear capability was years away.[28] Thus Khrushchev admitted to Polish leader Wladyslaw Gomulka in 1958 that "five years ago . . . we could not reach the USA."[29] Later aircraft, which entered service in 1957 and remained until 1959, were the only means the Soviets had for reaching US territory with nuclear weapons, but those were through suicidal one-way bombing runs, and vulnerability to American air defenses limited their deployment.[30] The Tu-16 gave Khrushchev credibility in Europe by the late 1950s, but these planes were also vulnerable to NATO's anti-aircraft defenses.[31] Khrushchev's decision to limit production of long-range bombers, coupled with his lack of long-range missiles, meant that in any war as late as 1958 the Soviet Union would be overwhelmed by US nuclear forces and have no comparable response.[32]

Since the Soviet Union could not deploy bombers close to US borders, the need to deliver nuclear weapons to US territory required intercontinental ballistic missiles. Khrushchev thus revealed in his autobiography that "the most difficult task was the problem of delivering nuclear bombs to targets located at great distances from our territory"; the 3M bomber "could fly as far as the United States but couldn't get back."[33] The Kremlin had approved a plan in March 1955 to deploy to East Germany some R-5M medium-range nuclear missiles—the first ones capable of targeting London and Paris—so that NATO members could be targeted. The accepted history dates the deployment to 1956.[34] But recent archival evidence shows that the deployment did not take place until 1958 and that the nuclear warheads were not transferred to East Germany until April 1959.[35]

The first Soviet ICBM capable of targeting the United States, the R-7, was initially used to put Sputnik 1 into space in October 1957. But the satellite was not ready to be mated with a nuclear warhead at the time. The first successful nuclear launch occurred almost two years later, when the Soviets acquired the ability to launch a three-megaton warhead and aimed it at the United States in the summer of 1959.[36]

Khrushchev's Soviet Union in 1959 was thus in many ways a new nuclear power. Having finally developed the capability to target Washington with nuclear missiles, Khrushchev wanted to shore up East Germany in order to provide a stronger buffer against rising West German power, to undermine Western intelligence against the Soviet bloc, to consolidate the Soviet regime, and to facilitate the ideological victory that he was convinced Moscow would win.[37] But he found himself lacking options.

US resolve to defend West Berlin from a Soviet challenge was widely viewed as a litmus test of its resolve to defend Western Europe as a whole, and Eisenhower and Kennedy rejected Khrushchev's many proposals to change the status of the city. Khrushchev and his colleagues agreed with Defense Minister Rodion Malinovsky, who said that "our inferior position was impossible to us."[38] Yet, as Sergei Khrushchev notes, with "things still going poorly," all Kruschchev could do was "grasp at straws."[39]

Thus in April 1956 Khrushchev bluffed to Prime Minister Anthony Eden's wife that "our rockets can go even farther [than Britain's]," while admitting in his memoirs that "at that time we didn't have any intercontinental missiles at all . . . we were [only] able to threaten England."[40] He knew that "the United States was beyond our reach at the time" and "mainly stressed our military might."[41] Khrushchev, however, did admit in his memoirs that as late as 1959 "we didn't have the necessary number of missiles to deliver those weapons. We couldn't reach the United States with our planes either . . . the United States itself was beyond the range of our [nuclear] weapons."[42] By the summer of 1961 Marshal Sergei Varentsov explained to American secret agent Col. Oleg Penkovsky that "with respect to ICBMs, we still don't have a damn thing."[43]

It is now clear that Khrushchev largely consolidated his power within the Presidium by 1960 and was the man most responsible for developing and authorizing Soviet assertive foreign policy throughout the following decade. Khrushchev had assumed leadership in the Soviet Presidium (formerly Politburo) in 1955 after coordinating the marginalization or death of the three colleagues who found themselves in charge of Soviet decision-making following Stalin's death in 1953. While a dozen senior Presidium members influenced decision-making in the mid-1950s, over time Khrushchev replaced the older Stalin-era conservatives with younger loyalists, which consolidated his influence over Soviet policy.[44]

An unsuccessful coup in 1957, partly caused by competition over whether the underlying Stalinist principles of Soviet foreign policy were

Table 3.1. Soviet-Deployed ICBMs, 1955–1964

1955	1956	1957	1958	1959	1960	1961	1962	1963	1964
0	0	0	0	4	4	14–24	14–24	109	191

Source: Podvig, *Russian Strategic Nuclear Forces*; Zaloga, *Kremlin's Nuclear Sword*; and Volkogonov, *Autopsy for an Empire*.

to be retained or discarded, resulted in the political isolation of the remaining Stalinists. Thus William Taubman states that by October 1957, about one year before the first Soviet Berlin ultimatum, the rout of Molotov, Georgy Malenkov, Lazar Kaganovich, and Georgi Zhukov left Khrushchev as the USSR's undisputed leader.[45] By the time of Khrushchev's first coercive threat in 1959, he held immense power in the Presidium and faced little competition over his foreign policy decisions. His more outlandish hawkish policies were often moderated, primarily by the cautious Anastas Mikoyan, but Khrushchev usually got his way with minimal pushback.[46] Signs of his authority had appeared the previous year: the British ambassador observed in 1956 that Khrushchev drank liberally at an open air party and "insulted literally every country in the world."[47]

In 1958 Khrushchev proposed the sudden signing of a peace treaty with East Germany but was forced to concede to a six-month ultimatum. In the 1961 Berlin Crisis, Khrushchev fathered all the offensive policies directed at the United States; there was no pressure by military officials for more-aggressive policies. By early 1962 Khrushchev's two unsuccessful Berlin bluffs had caused no outward revolt among Presidium members. At the May 1962 Presidium meeting Khrushchev first announced his Cuban missile strategy for Berlin, which quickly caused intense disagreement and led to a three-day recess and subsequent unanimous vote.[48] Khrushchev was able to secure all the available intermediate and tactical missiles for the Cuban deployment and with this one vote radically transformed Soviet Berlin policy.

The Middle East Crises, 1956–1958

The Kremlin's relationship with Egyptian president Abdel Gamal Nasser had become the centerpiece of Khrushchev's strategy of building alliances in the Third World and consolidating Soviet influence in the resource-rich Middle East. Khrushchev told the Egyptian leader that "we needed a new active diplomacy because the impossibility of nuclear war [means] that the struggle between us and the capitalists was taking on new forms."[49] In late July 1956 Nasser announced the nationalization of the Suez Canal, through which two-thirds of all the oil imported by

Europe passed. It was not good timing for Khrushchev since Soviet R-5M medium-range ballistic missiles were not yet operational and he thus lacked the power to defend his Egyptian client from Anglo-Israeli aggression.[50] Israeli forces invaded Egypt on October 29 of that year, followed by British and French troops on November 5. Nasser's military position quickly deteriorated, and Khrushchev faced the sudden prospect of losing an important ally and source of regional influence.

As William Taubman has shown, Khrushchev bluffed his way through the problem. Though the R-7 ICBM was far from operational in 1956, the Soviet leader was already "using" it in encounters with Western statesmen.[51] Within hours of the British and French intervention he suggested sending a threatening letter to the British, French, and Israelis that repeated an implicit reference to the use of nuclear weapons that had been broadcast on Moscow radio: "In what position would Britain have found herself had it been attacked by more powerful states possessing all types of modern weapons of destruction? We are full of determination to crush the aggressor and re-establish peace in the East by using force."[52]

Anthony Eden called for a cease-fire on November 7, despite having neither removed Nasser nor reestablished control of the canal; French support for withdrawal was quickly forthcoming.[53] But Khrushchev's coercive bluff did not cause an Anglo-Israeli retreat. Instead, the Allies' supreme allied commander in Europe, US general Alfred Gruenther, proclaimed that if Moscow attacked London or Paris, it would in turn be destroyed "as surely as night follows day."[54] A day before the cease-fire, British and French intelligence chiefs apparently had only one question to ask the CIA station chief in London at their tense meeting. And when they learned that Khrushchev did not possess the capability to target London with nuclear missiles, "everyone in the room visibly relaxed."[55]

Even in light of the emptiness of the Soviet nuclear threat, Eden's finance minister told him that without American assistance Britain could not afford a war. Anglo-Israeli aggression in Egypt had raised concerns over Britain and France's oil supply, which forced Eden and French prime minister Guy Mollet to abruptly call "time" on a military gambit. In the eight days following the initial Israeli attack, extensive sales of the pound sterling had lowered its value, and Eden was struggling to soak up enough of the outflow to stop the fall. The British believed that their World War II association with Eisenhower would cause him to join the fight, happily provide oil, and perhaps even "tide them over" through the purchase of excess British pounds. They did not grasp that Eisenhower, in light of his desire to make the United States more appealing to the Arab world, would actively oppose what he viewed as European imperialism. Britain and France's severe lack of oil forced Eden and Mollet to seek an immediate cease-fire. Eden faced a stock of oil that would have lasted less than fifty days and an almost-collapsed British pound. Khrushchev's coercive threat did not compel Eden and Mollet to withdraw from Suez; they understood that Khrushchev's threat was a bluff and would likely have retreated if Khrushchev had not issued it.[56]

The Waltzian model would expect Khrushchev to have systematically assessed the effectiveness of nuclear assertion in the first ten years of the Cold War. But while absence of evidence is not evidence of absence, still, there is no evidence in the extensive primary and secondary literature that Khrushchev made such assessments.[57] The Waltzian model also would have expected him to learn that assertive foreign policies, backed by nuclear weapons, would not have saved Nasser from foreign aggression and therefore not have issued the November 5 threat. Insofar as Khrushchev hinted that he was threatening to use *nuclear* weapons to salvage Nasser's position—and the British certainly worried that he was—the Waltzian learning model cannot explain his foreign policy decisions. The failure of the Waltzian model to explain this episode is further supported by the fact that Soviet R-5M missiles were not yet operational in November 1956: Khrushchev, by Waltzian accounts, should not have issued coercive nuclear threats if he could not fulfill them.

The rational-signaling model can be used to explain Khrushchev's nuclear assertion because it would expect him to have learned—from some subset of historical cases—that nuclear assertion works. He would be predicted to issue a threat in order to display his resolve to shore up his influence in Egypt and the wider Arab world. Moreover, Khrushchev received no costly signal from the United States, Britain, France, or Israel during the Suez Crisis—Eisenhower did not follow Gruenther's vague threat with any further statements or deployments—so the rational-signaling model would expect him to have persisted with nuclear assertion. In the face of Britain and France's retreat from Egypt within forty-eight hours of the Soviet nuclear threat, coupled with apparent US inactivity when Khrushchev believed that Eisenhower supported the move against Nasser, further nuclear assertion to display Soviet resolve was hardly an irrational choice.

The ALF model would expect Khrushchev to have relied on his cognitively available Suez experience as the only evidence to use in assessing the effectiveness of nuclear assertion. He would be expected to ignore the possibility that Washington, London, and Paris knew his threat was a bluff, and not have considered the central but less cognitively accessible fact that British and French oil needs and the currency crash were the causes of their retreat from Egypt. The ALF model expects Khrushchev to have persisted with nuclear assertion until he experienced fear of imminent nuclear war.

Some evidence supports this hypothesis. Months before Suez, Khrushchev proclaimed to a British audience that because of missiles, "which can be fired at targets great distances away . . . a new situation has taken shape."[58] Khrushchev's son, who intimately experienced his father's foreign policy decision-making, claimed that the lessons his father learned from Suez were based only on the temporal association between Khrushchev's coercive threat and immediate British and French compliance; Khrushchev did not recognize the role that oil and currency problems played in allowing Nasser to survive. Rather, he attributed that specific outcome to his own threat and learned that coercive nuclear threats can have powerful effects. As Sergei Khrushchev claims:

> The cease-fire resulting from our message made an enormous impression on Father. He was extraordinarily proud of his victory. He had a way to influence the course of international affairs and would return to it more than once. He resorted to similar arguments when tensions arose around Syria, Iran, Jordan and Iraq. Father became convinced that the mere mention of nuclear-armed missiles had a powerful effect. . . . The consequences of Suez were felt throughout the years to come. Its echo could even be heard in the . . . Cuban Missile Crisis. Over and over again he recalled the previous year's events in Suez, the phenomenal effect produced by the mere mention of the R-5.[59]

Other evidence supports this assertion. Khrushchev declared to Mao Zedong in July 1958 that "when we wrote letters to Eden and Mollet during the Suez events they immediately stopped their aggression."[60] He asserted to the Yugoslav ambassador that the cease-fire was the direct result of the Soviet threat.[61] And in his memoirs, written years after 1956, Khrushchev still maintained his belief: "The main point is that within twenty-two hours after the receipt of our warning the aggression was ended . . . this was a big victory for the Soviet Union, a victory for its authority and its military might. Our voice proved to be so powerful that it forced the aggression to cease."[62]

A Soviet Foreign Ministry analysis in late 1956 made no reference to Anglo-US alliance dynamics; it concluded that Washington was "the most active supporter of a peaceful settlement of the situation in Egypt."[63] Khrushchev, however, believed that the British and French would not have acted as they did unless America had given them "a green light to go ahead."[64] In his memoirs he stated that London and Paris knew that Eisenhower's behavior was a "ruse" that "would have no consequences."[65] But Eisenhower's aloofness was the principal reason why the British and French strategy floundered. One of Khrushchev's colleagues, Anastas Mikoyan, pointed out in June 1957 that "the Americans were conducting a different policy from the English." He nonetheless concurred that "everyone recognizes" that the threat to "the use of missile weapons by us . . . decided the fate of Egypt."[66] A further test of the ALF model could assess the lessons learned by Khrushchev's colleagues—that is, whether they found different events cognitively accessible—but insufficient data exists to test this hypothesis.

The Soviet leader learned from Suez that "nuclear weapons were all-powerful and that he didn't need many of them."[67] As Taubman points out, Khrushchev believed nuclear weapons were so destructive that they would never be employed, so he understood that he could threaten nuclear war without actually risking it.[68] Because no one wanted nuclear war, he believed that he could gain significant political concessions from nuclear bluff and bluster. Apparently when the Soviet leader first learned about nuclear power, he "couldn't sleep for several days. Then I became convinced we could never possibly use these weapons and . . . I was able to sleep again."[69] As he noted in his memoirs, "I believed what he [Eisenhower] said—that he feared war, that is, a real full-scale war."[70]

Khrushchev "simply beamed" after the launch of Soviet satellites and disingenuously announced in August 1957 that the Soviet Union had intercontinental rockets capable of reaching "any part of the globe."[71] He believed that ICBMs were so powerful that between 1955 and 1958 he unilaterally reduced Soviet Army strength by 2.3 million troops. Long-range bombers, fighter aircraft, artillery, and navy materiel—which Khrushchev referred to as "fodder for sharks"—all faced substantial cuts.[72] After a successful series of rocket launches in September 1958, Khrushchev was "smiling broadly" and "simply in raptures over what he had seen."[73] In 1959 he justified further substantial cuts to the Soviet armed forces on the grounds that "we have an assortment of rockets to serve any military purpose . . . that can virtually shatter the world."[74] He maintained in his autobiography that in 1971 he would have authorized further Soviet arms cuts because "we have the main thing—ICBMs and other strategic long-range missiles . . . the correct choice for us today is missiles, nuclear weapons and a submarine fleet."[75]

One might ask whether high-level political competition in the aftermath of Stalin's death was a more important cause of Soviet grand strategy and foreign policy than Khrushchev's personal beliefs. As Aleksandr Fursenko, Timothy Naftali, James Richter, and others have noted, Khrushchev faced a "double bind": he had to compete militarily with the United States but also steward resources toward the precarious Soviet command economy that he was convinced would eventually prevail over US global capitalism. Even so, these political constraints left room for many combinations of weapons platforms, geopolitical strategies, and five-year economic plans; the availability heuristic explains why the Soviet leader zeroed in on the lessons of Suez in the face of these pressing constraints. By effectively basing Soviet grand strategy on the highly dubious claim that nuclear assertion works, Khrushchev could waste little time in subjecting the Soviet armed forces to substantial cuts. The argument that nuclear missiles could compensate for massive ground forces and allow a focus on economic competition "addressed the same internal and external pressures recognized by Malenkov in 1953."[76]

Regional and domestic political structures undoubtedly shaped and shoved the Soviet leader, but the pathologies of availability powerfully influenced how he pushed back. Moreover, it is now fairly clear that after he ousted the instigators of the 1957 coup and forced the retirement of Georgi Zhukov, who advocated massive ground forces, from 1958 through late 1964 Khrushchev was "alone at the top" and usually got his way with minimal concessions.[77] As Richter points out, "if one coalition enjoys a preponderance of power in the decision-making process, international events are unlikely to force it to lose influence or alter its policies."[78]

In October 1957 Khrushchev had mobilized Soviet forces along the country's southern border to prevent Turkey, a US ally, from attacking Syria in retaliation for Damascus's decision to sign a trade pact with Moscow. According to Fursenko and Naftali, when Turkey did not invade, Khrushchev learned that Soviet military threats were able to deter the US from challenging his allies.[79] Khrushchev also expressed to Mao Zedong his belief that nuclear assertion would be key to saving the new regime in Iraq.[80] A day after the July 14, 1958, coup in Iraq and related unrest in Lebanon, Eisenhower deployed a battalion of troops to Beirut. British paratroopers were flown into Amman to defend against Syrian aggression. By July 16 US troops in Lebanon numbered eight thousand and the British contingent in Jordan exceeded three thousand.[81] Moscow declared that day that "the Soviet Union cannot remain indifferent to events creating a grave menace in an area adjacent to its frontiers, and reserves the right to take the necessary measures dictated by the interests of peace and security."[82]

Khrushchev also ordered military maneuvers by Soviet forces and the Bulgarian Army near Turkey and Iran. He then sent a back-channel message to Eisenhower through Soviet military intelligence officer Yuri Gvozdev and Frank Holeman, president of the National Press Club, which declared that "any United States or British move toward Iraq will mean war."[83] According to Mohamed Heikal, Khrushchev stated that "we had learned a lesson from Suez, so we didn't wait for the Turks to start aggression but sent them an ultimatum straightaway."[84] Gvozdev warned that Khrushchev would respond to challenges against the new regime in Iraq by airlifting Russian volunteers into the Middle East and threatened that "if there is war, the Russians will ignore European bases and attack the United States directly."[85]

Eisenhower and Harold Macmillan decided to recognize the Iraqi regime and not march to Baghdad. But they did this for reasons unrelated to Khrushchev's threat. The leader of the Iraqi coup, General Qasim, had consolidated his control of the country, and the former prime minister, a key to any hope for a counterrevolution, had been captured and executed. On July 17 the British foreign secretary wrote to John

Foster Dulles that "if the new Government of Iraq obtained effective control of the country it would be out of the question to consider reconquering the country from the military stand-point."[86] When Iraq signed an alliance with the United Arab Republic (UAR), effectively consolidating General Qasim's authority in Iraq and ensuring that any US incursion would drag Egypt, Syria, and possibly others into a regional war, Dulles agreed with his British and French counterparts "not to back a military effort to retake Iraq."[87] Qasim further reduced the incentives for Washington and London to attack Baghdad by reaffirming Iraq's previous oil commitments to Britain and its allies.

Khrushchev would not have known of the content of the Washington-London diplomatic cables at the time, but it seems that he neglected the impact of the widely publicized assassination of the Iraqi prime minister and Iraq's alliance with UAR. He assumed, from his cognitively accessible coercive demands and his apparently successful Suez threats, that he had deterred Eisenhower from ordering US troops in Beirut to march on Baghdad. He informed his Presidium colleagues that for the second time in eighteen months a Soviet threat had prevented the militarily and economically stronger United States from destroying one of the Soviet Union's allies in the Third World.[88] Sergei Khrushchev claimed that his father "celebrated a victory."[89] And following a meeting with Khrushchev, Bulgarian leader Todor Zhivkov reported on the "collapse of the American plans to invade Syria."[90]

The Waltzian model cannot explain Khrushchev's apparent inattention to the historical record. Given Khrushchev's inability to reliably target the United States with nuclear weapons, the model does not explain the causes and occurrence of the dangerous turn in Soviet foreign policy toward nuclear assertion. The rational-signaling model can explain Soviet assertion: Khrushchev had not yet received a costly signal, and Eisenhower's low-profile deployment of a mere battalion of troops likely only reinforced Khrushchev's suspicions that the American leader was not highly resolved to address Soviet nuclear ultimatums. The ALF model also can explain Khrushchev's nuclear assertion because he had not yet experienced fear of imminent nuclear war.

Throughout this period, Eisenhower had ignored Soviet bluff and bluster and effectively authorized restraint toward the Soviet Union. Khrushchev was never going to experience fear of imminent nuclear war under such conditions, and he was more likely to find in Eisenhower's limited responses confirmation of his belief in the long shadow that nuclear threats provide. Further confirmation of his belief in the power of nuclear assertion imminently took Soviet foreign policy in a very dangerous direction.

The First Berlin Crisis, 1958–59

Four months after the coup in Baghdad, Khrushchev channeled to West Berlin his newfound nuclear assertiveness. He declared on November 10, 1958, that if the Allied powers did not sign a peace treaty with the Soviet Union that formally recognized East Germany, he would sign a separate treaty with that state and upend all earlier postwar superpower agreements, forcing the US and its allies to seek admission to West Berlin through East Germany. Eisenhower would have been forced to overturn long-standing US policy and diplomatically recognize the East German regime, which may have ended Western access rights to and eventually presence in West Berlin.[91]

By November 1958 over ten thousand NATO soldiers were stationed in the city and the air and rail transport corridors that Khrushchev threatened to eliminate were used multiple times daily. Two days after Khrushchev's speech, Soviet guards stopped three US Army trucks that were leaving West Berlin by the Babelsburg checkpoint. The commanding US officer refused to permit inspection, and the standoff ended hours later only when a platoon of American tanks reinforced the transport.[92] At the next Presidium meeting on November 20, Anastas Mikoyan rallied the group to derail Khrushchev's Berlin policy. The role the Babelsburg incident played is unclear, but Khrushchev's plan to force a treaty was canceled.[93] The subsequent Soviet policy, represented in a note delivered to Eisenhower on November 27, reflected a middle ground between Khrushchev and Mikoyan. Moscow promised to wait six months before unilaterally signing its peace treaty with East Germany. Khrushchev wrote that since "only madmen" could want war, he would have to "provide straitjackets."[94]

Given that the East German strategic nuclear missile deployment was expected to be operational within six months, Khrushchev abandoned bluff in favor of a threat that he could actually carry out. The new proposal, which called for negotiations regarding the occupation regime in West Berlin for it to become a free city, was linked neither to NATO nor to the Warsaw Pact. According to Sergei Khrushchev, his father hoped to "give them a good scare, and thereby extract their agreement to negotiate."[95] He lied to visiting senator Hubert Humphrey that the Soviets had a rocket capable of traveling nine thousand miles and asked where the senator lived, "so I don't forget to order them to spare the city when the rockets fly."[96]

Eisenhower, however, probably suspected that Khrushchev was bluffing and that doing nothing would leave the Soviet leader with the uncomfortable choice of either taking military action that might cause nuclear escalation or backing down.[97] During Khrushchev's time in Washington in September—four months after the ultimatum expired—he informed the outgoing president that he would refrain from further demands regarding Berlin. But Khrushchev, according to his aide Oleg Troyanovsky, nevertheless believed that Eisenhower's invitation was "a tangible result of the pressure that had been exerted on the Western powers since the November 27 note about West Berlin."[98]

The Waltzian learning model cannot explain Khrushchev's attempt to coerce Eisenhower out of Berlin: it expects leaders to always use nuclear weapons to maintain the status quo. The president had signaled publically and privately that he was not prepared to be negotiated or coerced out of West Berlin. He believed that the United States had made an error in trying to control territory that far behind Russian lines and felt a need to negotiate, but he never went further than insisting that "we do not seek a perpetuation of the status quo in Berlin." As French president Charles de Gaulle later told John Kennedy, there would not be "any retreat from Berlin, any change of status, any withdrawal of troops [and] any new obstacles to transportation and communication."[99]

While Khrushchev possessed undisputed local military superiority and could have taken over West Berlin if he had wished to do so, carrying out his threat would have further undermined the Soviet position. Increasingly severe threats to East Berlin and Moscow and a worsening economic plight for East Germany would have resulted. Khrushchev was aware of the brutal reality that a Soviet takeover of West Berlin would have put all of Europe up for grabs at a time when the US could have preemptively destroyed the small Soviet nuclear missile force and then selectively wiped out Soviet military power and cities at will. Eisenhower could also have responded to any Soviet move on West Berlin by imposing an economic blockade on East Germany that would have surely brought it to the brink of collapse and thereby posed deeper problems for Moscow. Nuclear assertion was never going to work in 1959, because Khrushchev had to make the first move on Berlin—a core US interest—in the face of long odds.

While several scholars at the time partly explained Khrushchev's behavior as a desire to shore up the shaky Soviet nuclear deterrent, it is unclear how coercive threats could have consolidated the Soviet nuclear deterrent when they also risked a preemptive American attack.[100] Insofar as the assertion was designed to remove the Western presence in Berlin rather than just signal a resolve to eliminate it, the Waltzian model cannot explain the Soviets' foreign policy. It would expect Khrushchev to have accepted the intolerable threat that West Berlin posed to East Germany and to have authorized a restrained foreign policy toward West Berlin.

The rational-signaling model can explain Khrushchev's nuclear assertion. Khrushchev had incentives to display his resolve to revise the status quo in Berlin, but Eisenhower had not authorized a costly signal. The platoon of US tanks at the Babelsburg checkpoint did not differentiate between resolved defenders and bluffers, so Khrushchev was unlikely to have learned of Eisenhower's resolve to stem Soviet nuclear assertion. He informed his colleagues in February 1959 that if the Western powers "wish to force [their] way through, using all appropriate means . . . we will answer with all appropriate means."[101] Evidence shows that Khrushchev believed his 1958–59 Berlin ultimatum would be dangerous. He told Polish leader Wladyslaw Gomulka that "there will be tensions of course . . . there will be a blockade. They will test to see our reaction . . . we will have to show a great deal of cold blood in this matter."[102] The ALF learning model can also explain Khrushchev's nuclear assertion because he had not yet experienced fear of imminent nuclear war.

The Second Berlin Crisis, 1961

Khrushchev issued his second coercive nuclear threat in early June 1961, perhaps holding back throughout 1960 to help his preferred candidate,

John Kennedy, defeat Richard Nixon in a tight US election. The Soviet embassy had informed him that while Kennedy was likely to stand firm on Berlin, the president was "not a mediocrity" but was "unlikely to possess the qualities of an outstanding person."[103] The Soviet leader informed visiting US columnist Walter Lippmann in mid-April that "there are no such stupid statesmen in the West who would unleash a war in which hundreds of millions would perish just because we sign a peace treaty with the GDR."[104]

According to his son, Khrushchev "couldn't stop thinking about Germany."[105] He first offered an interim agreement on West Berlin with a fixed time limit, after which West Berlin would become a "free city" without any occupying forces. When Kennedy proved unwilling to accept the agreement, he resorted to an ultimatum: if Kennedy did not concede to Soviet terms by December 31, he would sign a peace treaty with East Germany that would turn over to the East German government the control of all air, rail, and road access routes into and through Berlin.

As Khrushchev stated in his memoirs, he "kept the pressure on" to "force [Kennedy] to recognise the necessity of meeting us halfway."[106] Khrushchev's desperation at East Germany's economic plight and Ulbricht's persistence caused the construction of the Berlin Wall. While it stopped the flow of East German refugees into the West, it did not resolve the underlying geopolitical and economic pressures that motivated Soviet policy. A weak East Germany—which Kennedy refused to recognize diplomatically—exacerbated US and West German influence in Eastern Europe and threatened the legitimacy of communism in the Soviet Union.

Kennedy remarked to Deputy National Security Adviser Walt Rostow that "Khrushchev is losing East Germany. He cannot let that happen. If East Germany goes so will Poland and all of Eastern Europe."[107] Daily violations of East German sovereignty weakened the legitimacy of the East German government. Sergei Khrushchev wrote that his father "had nightmares about it: the German problem gave him no peace."[108] A further cause of Khrushchev's desire to achieve East German sovereignty through a peace treaty was the strong desire of East Germany's Ulbricht to receive what Khrushchev had in 1959 and 1961 threatened to give him.[109]

During his election campaign and first months in office, President Kennedy had made repeated promises to defend West Berlin's security and Western access routes to the city. Like his predecessors, he viewed access in Berlin as the key indicator for his reputation to defend Western Europe; as he told Khrushchev, "when we are talking about West Berlin, we are talking about Western Europe."[110] Unlike Eisenhower's cool non-response to Khrushchev's November 1958 threat, Kennedy produced a costly signal and announced substantial military preparations for a potential Berlin conflict. He announced in a televised presidential address on July 25 that he would request from Congress a massive defense budget increase of $3.25 billion, he would issue a call-up of some reserve troops and the National Guard, and he would initiate a new program of civil defense. "We cannot and will not permit the communists to drive us out of Berlin, either gradually or by force."[111] By mid-October the first of forty thousand reinforcement troops landed in France to begin the buildup. Another three thousand soldiers and one hundred tanks arrived at Bremerhaven in mid-November and quickly became operational.[112] Half of the US long-range bombers were also put on fifteen-minute ground alert.

On September 24, before US troops arrived in Europe, Khrushchev informed Kennedy through his press secretary that "the storm in Berlin is over."[113] Khrushchev wrote to Ulbricht four days later that "since the measures for the safeguarding and control of the GDR borders with Berlin have been implemented successfully . . . steps that could exacerbate the situation, especially in Berlin, should be avoided."[114] However, he also told the commander of Soviet forces in East Germany, Ivan Konev, to "scare them."[115]

Ulbricht was emboldened by Khrushchev's threats to himself deter Allied entry into West Berlin. On October 22 East German police prevented a senior American diplomat in West Berlin from crossing into East Berlin until Soviet officers arrived at Checkpoint Charlie three hours later and permitted entry. The next morning Ulbricht further complicated US access when he announced that civilians crossing the Berlin sector border required identification cards. On October 25 Kennedy authorized a series of daily probes by civilians accompanied by an armed escort. The civilian vehicle was allowed access only when it was joined by an M48 tank.[116] Two days later ten Soviet tanks positioned themselves in front of Checkpoint Charlie in anticipation of the now daily US armed probe. After US tanks approached the front of the Western side, the Soviet tanks were reinforced to thirty to match the total number of US tanks in Berlin. After this famous standoff that lasted almost twenty-four hours and which was shown all over the world, Khrushchev withdrew his tanks.

The Waltzian model cannot explain Khrushchev's 1961 nuclear assertion. Little had changed since 1959: the status quo in Berlin had arguably deteriorated some, but the few extant Soviet nuclear missiles remained highly vulnerable to more numerous and reliable US ICBMs; Kennedy was inexperienced but had said many times that he would not concede in Berlin. Given that he had the remainder of his first term to face any domestic and international repercussions of an ignominious retreat from West Berlin, Khrushchev might have expected Kennedy to have been much more resolved than the almost-retired Eisenhower was in 1959. The Waltzian model would expect the Soviet leader to have authorized a restrained foreign policy and accept the continuing deterioration of East Germany: Khrushchev simply did not have the military or economic resources to resolve the problem.

The rational-signaling model can explain Soviet nuclear assertion because neither Eisenhower nor Kennedy had authorized a costly signal. In the face of more severe threats to the crucial Soviet position in West Berlin, the rational-signaling model would expect Khrushchev to have persisted with nuclear assertion in order to display his resolve to revise the untenable status quo. It cannot, however, explain why Khrushchev continued to authorize nuclear assertion after Kennedy's 1961 military buildup.

Kennedy's response to Khrushchev's 1961 ultimatum was a costly signal. He told the American public several times that he would not concede on US access to or occupation rights of West Berlin, and he publically announced then carried out a major military mobilization and deployment in response. The standoff at Checkpoint Charlie was shown all over the world. Kennedy did not attempt to destroy the Berlin Wall; he accepted it in the hope that it would moderate Khrushchev's appetite for coercive aggression.[117] The rational-signaling model would expect Khrushchev to have authorized restrained foreign policies in response.

However, by October 1961, weeks after he canceled his second Berlin ultimatum, Khrushchev told Polish president Wladyslaw Gomulka: "If we do not apply pressure, then we will have to give up on signing a peace treaty with the GDR."[118] Khrushchev also told Ulbricht in early 1962 that "we must put pressure to get a peace treaty."[119] He elaborated his belief that nuclear assertion would help realize his Berlin objectives at a January 8, 1962, Presidium meeting: "It is now too early to say that we will not win. We should still press on. I take the worst case: They won't agree. But it means agreeing right now that it will bring nothing. It's too early. So it's worthwhile playing this game."[120] Khrushchev continued to harass US ground and air access to Berlin by restricting flights in the northern and southern corridors, and he ordered Soviet fighters to fly in or near US flights, buzzing them and dropping metal chaff to confuse radars.[121] Kennedy authorized the flight of civilian and military planes through the corridors at Soviet reserved attitudes. More damning for the rational-signaling model, Khrushchev deployed nuclear missiles to Cuba in what now appears to have at least partly been a third assertive Berlin grab.

Khrushchev believed that his 1961 assertive strategy had a risk of nuclear escalation. As he told his Presidium colleagues, "The risk that we are taking is justified; if we look at it in terms of a percentage, there is more than a 95% probability that there will be no war."[122] In August 1961 he expressed to the Italian prime minister that "I think there will not be any war."[123] Khrushchev told Ulbricht that if he signed a peace treaty he would "have to put our rockets on military alert," and expressed to members of the Warsaw Pact that after the construction of the Berlin Wall, "no one can guarantee that there will be no war."[124]

When it became clear that there would be no Western efforts to remove the wall nor otherwise penalize the Eastern Bloc, Khrushchev remarked that "war might have broken out."[125] However, Khrushchev did not experience fear of imminent nuclear war in the 1961 Berlin Crisis. The ALF model explains his nuclear assertion and his persistence with it even after Kennedy authorized a costly signal. Kennedy's signal was mostly designed to defend Western interests in Berlin from Soviet encroachment. Khrushchev, therefore, was unlikely to experience fear of imminent nuclear war. The Cuban Missile Crisis was required to temper Soviet revisionism.

The Cuban Missile Crisis, 1962

President Kennedy left the Vienna summit believing his performance had only served to embolden Khrushchev. As he said to *New York Times* journalist James Reston, "If he thinks I'm inexperienced and have no guts, until we remove those ideas we won't get anywhere with him. So we have to act."[126] But Kennedy did not know that the Suez Crisis six years prior had already emboldened Khrushchev to assertively throw his weight around the Middle East and Western Europe. Khrushchev came to Vienna already poised to cause trouble in West Berlin. After Kennedy revealed to Khrushchev that he was well aware that the United States was miles ahead in the nuclear arms race, Khrushchev likely felt great pressure to somehow compensate for the Soviets' weakness if he was to successfully wrestle the US out of West Berlin.

Much scholarship has argued that Soviet motivations during the Cuban Missile Crisis were different from the ones at work during the two Berlin crises.[127] The 1989 declassification of files related to Operation Mongoose, which detail US covert operations against Cuba after 1961, reinforce claims that the threat from Washington was the prime catalyst for the Soviet missile deployment.[128] While the two Berlin crises were understood to have been motivated by revisionist Berlin concerns or West German nuclear ambitions, the deployment of strategic nuclear missiles to Cuba was understood to have been motivated by a desire to defend Castro's Cuba from a US invasion.[129] During the crisis President Kennedy, his chief Sovietologist Llewellyn Thompson, and many other advisers believed that the primary purpose of the deployment was to enable Khrushchev to eliminate the West's position in West Berlin.[130] It is now clear that the deployment was motivated by offensive Berlin-related and defensive Cuba-related objectives: it was an assertive foreign policy, and much of the assertion was aimed squarely at West Berlin.

The error in the claim that the defense of Cuba was the *only* cause of Soviet policy there in 1962 is that after authorizing a smaller deployment, Khrushchev then authorized a much larger one that we now know he himself claimed had *offensive* purposes. In September 1961 Fidel Castro had asked Khrushchev to position anti-aircraft shore-based missiles and ten thousand troops in his country. In April 1962 Khrushchev and his colleagues approved the missiles as well as a training program for the Cuban military and three thousand Soviet troops. This deployment seems to have been designed to defend Cuba from a US invasion. Khrushchev, however, told his Presidium colleagues on May 21 that the deployment "will be an offensive policy."[131] "He persuaded them to agree to fifty thousand troops plus tactical, intermediate, and strategic nuclear missiles."[132] Khrushchev made many belligerent statements about Berlin during the summer of 1962.[133] He linked the situations in Cuba and Berlin in a September 28 letter to Kennedy, even though Kennedy and Secretary of State Dean Rusk repeatedly reassured Soviet Foreign Minister Gromyko as late as October 20 that they did not plan to invade Cuba.[134]

The Soviet deployment seems odd if the only goal was to defend Cuba from a US invasion.[135] Fidel Castro remarked in 1992 that "if it was a matter of defending Cuba without creating an international problem the presence of tactical weapons would not have created the same problem that the strategic weapons did."[136] It is unclear when Khrushchev began to associate Berlin objectives with the deployment of Soviet forces in Cuba. The defense of Cuba was likely the original motivation for the deployment, and Khrushchev may have believed that Kennedy was planning a second invasion.[137] Khrushchev stated in an October 22–23, 1962, meeting that "we wanted to intimidate and restrain the USA vis-à-vis Cuba."[138] Much evidence shows, however, that during the summer of 1962, as the Cuban deployment grew, Khrushchev devised a Berlin assertive strategy centered around his Cuban missile base.

It appears that Khrushchev planned to coerce Kennedy out of West Berlin after privately stipulating his demands and then publically announcing the establishment of the base in Cuba and bringing a complaint to the United Nations.[139] Khrushchev revealed his new offensive Berlin policies at a July 1 Presidium meeting: within two years all Western troops would be replaced by UN troops, and within six years the UN troops would be removed.[140] This proposal denied the international access for Western planes and trains in East Germany that Kennedy had intimated he might be able to accept.[141]

Khrushchev wrote a letter to Kennedy on July 5 in which he demanded an immediate 50 percent reduction in the Western troop contingent stationed in Berlin, to be replaced by troops supplied by countries of the Warsaw Pact and other neutral and smaller NATO countries that would serve under the auspices of the United Nations. His goal was that this UN contingent would be phased out over four years.[142] Kennedy responded to Ambassador Anatoly Dobrynin that he could not accept such terms. But Khrushchev encouraged Ulbricht to tighten border controls around West Berlin anyway.[143]

On July 25 Khrushchev asked the US ambassador if he wanted to deal with another Berlin crisis before or after the November 6 congressional elections.[144] Kennedy learned in August that Khrushchev was likely to raise the Berlin issue at the United Nations.[145] Khrushchev then told the West German ambassador on September 11 that after the November congressional election he would push for the establishment of a free city of West Berlin and that "we have already prepared everything for this."[146] Fursenko and Naftali have found that as part of this November initiative, in July the Soviet foreign ministry wrote to Soviet embassies in the Middle East demanding information about the liquidation of Western military bases and the status of UN forces in their countries.[147] After learning of the Soviet nuclear missile base in Cuba, Kennedy had drafted a letter to Castro stating that "the Soviets have quietly suggested to others that the threat these weapons represent may make it worthwhile to the US to trade concessions on Berlin for Soviet abandonment of Cuba."[148]

As Soviet nuclear missiles were sailing to Cuba, Khrushchev had formulated and was operationalizing a third assertive Berlin push. It is unlikely that Khrushchev's Cuban missile deployment, at least from mid-May on, was not also designed to achieve offensive Berlin objectives. Khrushchev's aide Troyanovsky claimed that after receiving Kennedy's initial letter about the blockade and the demand for the removal of the missiles, Khrushchev proudly exclaimed that "we've saved Cuba."[149] But his initial reply was not to exchange the missiles for Cuba's security: he upped the ante and demanded the removal of the Jupiter missiles without waiting for Kennedy's response. When he did settle for the pledge there was little elation that the main goal of the Cuban missiles had been achieved. Thus Arnold Horelick claims that "to regard the outcome of the Cuban missile crisis as coinciding in any substantial way with Soviet intentions or interests is to mistake the skillful salvage of a shipwreck for brilliant navigation."[150]

The events of the crisis are well known. Kennedy learned of the Soviet nuclear missiles in Cuba about a month before Khrushchev planned to announce them, and in turn announced a US blockade of the island and the immediate authority to call up 150,000 reserve troops. By the time the blockade went into effect two days later, Soviet ships still in the Mediterranean and submarines more than two days away from Cuba had turned back to their Black Sea ports. But some Soviet submarines and a few ships were still headed for Cuba. Khrushchev wrote to Kennedy, offering to remove the missiles from Cuba if Kennedy promised not to invade the island, and then he quickly wrote another letter asking for the further removal of the Jupiter missiles in Turkey as well. Kennedy accepted these terms on the condition that the Jupiter concession remain secret, and he threatened to attack Cuba if Khrushchev did not accept these terms within twenty-four hours. But he promised to accept Castro's regime if they were. Khrushchev removed the missiles and eventually the other Soviet weapons, and the crisis was resolved.[151]

The Waltzian model can explain Khrushchev's decision to defend Cuba from a US invasion: no number of US assurances could have removed all doubts about US designs on Havana. But the Waltzian model cannot explain Khrushchev's nuclear assertion over West Berlin in 1962. The deployment of an extensive tactical and medium-range missile force to a locale across the Atlantic Ocean and within a state that was geographically close but deeply hostile to the United States would inevitably be located before all missiles became operational. Such missiles would inevitably have been attacked or forced to return. The commander of the Soviet military mission in Cuba thus warned Khrushchev that U-2 spy planes would make it difficult if not impossible to keep the operation secret once the missiles reached Cuba.[152] But Khrushchev ignored this advice: his successful and cognitively available Suez experiences led him to cling to his belief that nuclear assertion worked. The main military planner of the operation later wrote: "Considering all its risks, it is surprising that the plan came so close to success."[153]

Troyanovsky wrote that Khrushchev's Cuban missile scheme "stretch(ed) even a sound idea to the point of absurdity;" his initial proposal to the Soviet ambassador to Cuba "nearly turned me to ice."[154] Consistent with the pathologies of availability, Khrushchev ignored the resolve Kennedy displayed in his costly signal the previous year and sincerely believed that his Cuban missile base would turn the tide in West

Berlin. Khrushchev thus proclaimed on June 10, "I think we'll win this operation."[155]

The rational-signaling model cannot explain Khrushchev's nuclear assertion in 1962: considering the circumstances, he would have been expected to authorize a restrained foreign policy toward Berlin after Kennedy's costly signal in 1961. Moreover, Kennedy had proclaimed throughout 1962 that grave circumstances would arise if Khrushchev had placed offensive weapons in Cuba.

The ALF model assumes that credibility is determined by the perceiver rather than the sender. It is sensitive to the reality that while the pathologies of availability can reduce the deterrent effects of otherwise clear costly signals, the experience of fear of imminent nuclear war can make a signal credible. While it does not appear that Khrushchev experienced fear of imminent nuclear war before the Cuban Missile Crisis, much evidence suggests that he did so between Tuesday, October 23, when Soviet ships began to turn away from Cuba, and Thursday, October 25. Kennedy's reaction to Khrushchev's Cuban strategy was not only an embargo and acceptance of Khrushchev's terms but a threat that he would attack Cuba within twenty-four hours if Khrushchev rejected them. Kennedy finally deployed an assertive foreign policy in response to Khrushchev's six years of strategic assertion.

Khrushchev should have known that Kennedy was highly resolved to remove the missiles: the president had announced publically that he would never allow them. The Soviet leader knew that tactical as well as strategic nuclear weapons were already based in Cuba and that a US attack would kill many Soviet troops and cause a tactical if not strategic nuclear retaliatory act that likely would have escalated to nuclear war. He knew that this scenario could all occur within twenty-four hours. Under these conditions, Khrushchev was highly likely to experience fear of imminent nuclear war.

After learning of Kennedy's blockade of Cuba, Khrushchev sent Kennedy a letter on October 24 that informed him that "we will not simply be bystanders with regard to piratical acts by American ships on the high seas."[156] However, by the end of the next day he seems to have become primarily concerned with de-escalating the crisis. As Sergei Khrushchev has written, "During the night father had already begun to doubt the advisability of the evening's decision to continue straight ahead [and challenge the blockade]; that Thursday was when a change took place in his thinking."[157] Furthermore, when Rudolf Anderson's U-2 was shot down on October 27, "It was at that very moment—not before or after—that Father felt the situation slipping out of control . . . that the missiles had to be removed, that disaster loomed."[158]

When the Presidium received a briefing on the effects of nuclear war, according to his son, Khrushchev "listened with half an ear."[159] During the summer of 1962 he had claimed that "every idiot can start a war, but it is impossible to win this war . . . the missiles have one purpose—to scare, to restrain them so that they have appreciated this business to give them back some of their own medicine."[160] He had repeatedly mocked the idea of accidental nuclear war at the Vienna summit. His first letter to Kennedy was rich in his standard bluff and bluster. But by the time of the second letter, at the height of the crisis, his tone was much more emotional. He haphazardly expressed the dangers of inadvertent escalation with reference to a rope and the knot of war. He described the situation as "blind moles" facing "mutual extermination," and noted that if "war should break out, then it would not be in our power to stop it, for such is the logic of war":

The more the two of us pull, the tighter the knot will be tied. And a moment may come when that knot will be tied so tight that even he who tied it will not have the strength to untie it. And then it will be necessary to cut that knot, and what that would mean is not for me to explain to you, because you yourself understand perfectly well of what terrible forces our countries dispose.[161]

When a colleague suggested a new challenge in Berlin at the height of the crisis, Khrushchev scolded him to "Keep that kind of advice to yourself. We don't know how to get out of one predicament and you drag us into another."[162] At the October 25 Presidium meeting he announced that it was time to seek an urgent way out of the crisis.[163] He claimed to his colleagues that "we started out and then got afraid" and that "we didn't want to unleash a war." He noted that "the tragedy is that they can attack, and we shall respond. This may end in a big war."[164] Khrushchev admitted in his memoirs that on the night of Friday, October 26, he was "actually very concerned" and "at one particularly worrisome time, I spent the whole night in the Kremlin."[165] One Soviet deputy foreign minister told his colleagues that Khrushchev "shit his pants" when he heard that the US Strategic Air Command was moving to the nuclear alert level DEFCON-2.[166] As he stated to the president of Czechoslovakia on October 30, 1962, he believed the two countries "were truly on the verge of war."[167]

At the height of the crisis the Soviet ambassador to the United Nations, Valery Zorin, explained to UN Secretary General U. Thant that "it is necessary to act quickly . . . since the situation cannot be allowed to get out of control."[168] Barely one month after the crisis ended in early December, Khrushchev informed peace activist Norman Cousins of his fear of imminent nuclear war during the crisis: "Of course I was scared. It would have been insane not to have been scared. I was frightened about what could happen to my country—or your country or all the other countries that would be devastated by a nuclear war. If being frightened meant that I helped avert such insanity then I'm glad I was frightened."[169] One of the 1964 coup plotters claimed that the missile crisis had "frightened terribly the organizer of this very danger."[170]

In his memoirs, Khrushchev stated that the crisis "reached a boiling point of the highest intensity. We were close to war, standing on the brink of war. . . . Fortunately we were able to come to an agreement. Why? We feared a nuclear exchange."[171] Khrushchev told the American ambassador in November that "we may not love each other, but we have to live together and may even have to embrace each other if the world is to survive."[172]

Khrushchev misunderstood the US political system and seems to have believed Robert Kennedy's messages—one of which was delivered on October 27 through Georgi Bolshakov—that the president could not control the powerful and independent joint chiefs of staff.[173] He grew alarmed about Castro's increasingly panicky and reckless behavior, which culminated in the shooting down of a U-2 spy plane and a letter from Castro encouraging him to authorize a preemptive nuclear strike against the United States.[174] Khrushchev stated in his memoirs that after hearing of the contents of the letter, "we sat there in silence, looking at one another for a long time."[175]

Khrushchev also knew that Soviet forces on Cuba had tactical missiles armed with nuclear warheads and that a US invasion would lead to a major clash between US and Soviet forces; at one point in the crisis he authorized tactical nuclear weapons to be used against invading US forces, only to quickly retract this order.[176] Thus by late October Khrushchev vigilantly looked for any and all signs of a US invasion. His fear caused an otherwise inexplicable reaction: he took seriously a spurious tip from a Washington Press Club bartender that an invasion of Cuba was imminent.[177]

Given Roswell Gilpatric's speech that dispelled the nuclear and missile gap and that recent revealing of Oleg Penkovsky's spying, Khrushchev may have reasonably believed that Kennedy believed he could get through a nuclear war with little damage. Robert McNamara had told columnist Stewart Alsop in February 1962 that "in some circumstances we might have to take the initiative."[178]

It is not surprising that Khrushchev experienced fear of imminent nuclear war at the climax of the crisis. He had deployed a massive Soviet nuclear missile force, accompanied by a huge deployment of conventional troops and naval flotilla, across the Atlantic on the territory of a US adversary. Khrushchev never believed that he was near the nuclear brink in the earlier two Berlin crises. But by late October the blockade and exchange of coercive notes left little doubt that the current crisis could escalate out of control.

It is not clear why, from a rational perspective, Khrushchev rejected the risks of nuclear assertion from the experience of fear rather than from the general danger he had provoked beginning in 1959. Why, for example, did Khrushchev not concoct a fourth Berlin grab against the inexperienced Lyndon Johnson in 1964? Given how far Khrushchev went with a plan that most would agree was crazy, his lack of even contemplating a fourth Berlin push in 1964 is astounding. The effect of fear, captured in the ALF model but neglected in the rational-signaling model, explains this drastic Soviet policy change.

Realism would lead one to expect that the greater military power that was gained through rough parity would lead to a more- rather than less-aggressive foreign policy.[179] So Khrushchev's authorization of a restrained foreign policy and acceptance of the status quo in Berlin after the Cuban Missile Crisis of 1962 is deeply puzzling. Why, given three costly attempts over the four previous years to get his way in Berlin, did he finally accept the unbearable status quo now?

By November Castro refused to go along with plans to remove the tactical nuclear weapons from Cuba, Kennedy demanded that the Il-28 bomber fleet that Khrushchev had deployed there also had to be removed, and the Chinese were challenging the Soviets' communist bloc leadership. Even if Khrushchev did not believe Kennedy would invade Cuba, he might have worried that Kennedy's successor would. The embattled Soviet leader could have attempted to salvage his position either through another Berlin threat or possibly a secret force of troops and weapons stationed in Cuba. However, he accepted the status quo in Berlin, hightailed Soviet forces out of Cuba, and abandoned nuclear assertion. It is difficult to think of a more dramatic foreign policy change.

In early December Khrushchev wrote letters to Kennedy that explicitly promised no further Berlin ultimatums.[180] He still wanted a revision to the status quo in Berlin but was no longer willing to authorize assertive nuclear strategies to get it. A month later he repeated his desire for US troops in Berlin to operate under a UN mission force, but he did not demand it.[181] As he told the US and British ambassadors to Moscow on April 23, 1963, "You don't want to decide the German issue, but it's the most important one."[182] Earlier in the month he had written to Kennedy that Soviet surface-to-air missiles would remain in Cuba and that further U-2 flights would be shot down.[183] By June he admitted to members of the Presidium that "We will not get an agreement [on Berlin] from the Americans: let's change the tactic."[184] This comment represents a fundamental change in Soviet foreign policy: while nuclear assertion—or nuclear bluff—had been the basis for Soviet foreign policy in Berlin and elsewhere for the previous eight years, following the Cuban Missile Crisis Soviet grand strategy turned to restraint. Only the ALF model can explain the shift.

If Kennedy's blockade of Cuba displayed new information about US resolve, why didn't Khrushchev challenge it and persist with nuclear assertion? Because his previous experience of fear reduced his willingness to run risks. From a rational-signaling perspective, the fear experienced in the crisis should have had no additional influence over Khrushchev's feelings of general danger. Nor should the emotion he experienced have had any impact on Soviet foreign policy toward states other than East Germany or Cuba (i.e., the Middle East or Southeast Asia). But an experience of fear triggers the emotional brain to supersede the mechanisms responsible for cognitive mental processing and makes a prompt fight-or-flight decision.

When the brain perceives situations that are similar to experiences that caused fear in the past, the emotional brain will be given priority and cause a response similar to the earlier situation.[185] Thus when a leader who has experienced fear of imminent nuclear war subsequently experiences a situation that resembles the original fear-inducing one (whether in terms of the adversary or the potential for nuclear escalation), that leader will authorize restrained rather than assertive foreign policies.

The ALF model also helps explain other aspects of Soviet foreign policy in the aftermath of the Cuban Missile Crisis that are puzzling if viewed only from a rational-signaling perspective. A comparison of Khrushchev's responses to challenges in Iraq and Laos before and after the Cuban Missile Crisis displays the effects of experiencing the nuclear brink. When the Iraqi monarchy was deposed in 1958, Khrushchev threatened war if Eisenhower were to move against Baghdad. Though the stakes in Iraq in 1963 were not great enough to warrant Soviet nuclear assertion, had Khrushchev not experienced fear of imminent nuclear war a year earlier he likely would have at least towed a harder line. After General Qasim was overthrown and murdered by elements of the anti-communist Ba-ath party in 1963, Khrushchev might have been expected to issue threats to the new Iraqi government or to President Kennedy to restore the earlier regime. However, by then he viewed the new status quo in Iraq through a different lens. He immediately recognized the new government and did nothing to prevent the subsequent Ba-athist massacre of the Iraqi communist party.[186] Rather than challenging Kennedy he authorized a restrained foreign policy because it offered the least risk of nuclear escalation.

While arguably the stakes in Laos were never great enough to warrant risking nuclear escalation, it is likely that Khrushchev would have been willing to accept greater escalation of the conflict had he not earlier reached the nuclear brink. In May 1962 Khrushchev had ignored the Chinese and North Vietnamese sponsorship of an invasion of the Nam Tha region in Laos by the communist organization Pathet Lao, which led to the deployment of additional US troops in Thailand. By November Khrushchev believed that further communist gains would lead to the deployment of US troops in Laos as well. Whether or not this would have escalated to nuclear war, the workings of the emotional brain likely caused Khrushchev to view this as a potential source of escalation with the United States that was best avoided. Unlike his earlier violations of the neutrality agreement, he declined Pathet Lao's request for more secret assistance and told his colleagues that "if we continue pursuing the same policy [of allowing sponsorship of the Pathet Lao] then it will not be in the interests of the leftists."[187] These policies may have left Khrushchev vulnerable to other risks, but they also reduced the probability of further conflict with Washington.

Khrushchev's time at the nuclear brink taught him that negotiations and mutual restraint were more effective than assertive demands. In September 1962 he had offered a partial nuclear test ban were Kennedy to commit to a five-year moratorium on underground testing followed by a permanent ban. But then negotiations stalled through early 1963. Washington and London demanded at least three on-site inspections of Soviet facilities; Khrushchev rejected the terms, worrying that agreeing would reveal Soviet weakness. However, by July 1963 he offered an unconditional cessation of Soviet underwater and atmospheric tests. The superpowers, which had earlier fought so hard over the status of Berlin, put that issue aside to stem the spread of nuclear weapons. Such an agreement would not have been possible following the failed 1958–59 and 1961 Berlin ultimatums. Indeed, in October 1961 Khrushchev tested a fifty megaton Soviet warhead that exhibited the largest-ever blast yield. As Fursenko and Naftali aptly note, by 1963 Kennedy "would get a partial test ban without paying the Berlin price."[188]

A further review of the experiences and beliefs of Khrushchev's successors—Leonid Brezhnev (general party secretary), Alexei Kosygin (premier), and Nicolai Podgorny (Presidium chairman)—would test the relevance of the ALF model. It is likely that Brezhnev, Kosygin, and Podgorny experienced fear of imminent nuclear war during the Cuban Missile Crisis alongside Khrushchev, so the model should expect them to have adopted restrained foreign policies. It took Khrushchev three to five years after Stalin's death to consolidate his power, and Brezhnev took at least that long.[189] It is nonetheless telling that by March 1965, although Moscow had grown alarmed by Lyndon Johnson's escalation of the Vietnam War, and despite again raising the problem of European security and a German peace settlement, Brezhnev did not take advantage of Johnson's preoccupation with Southeast Asia to take another crack at West Berlin. Consistent with the ALF model, McGeorge Bundy had noted in November that Anatoly Dobrynin, two years after the Cuban Missile Crisis, "referred nostalgically to the period in which there was intimate communication with President Kennedy."[190]

The expansionistic, risk-taking Soviet policies in the 1970s following nuclear parity and the Vietnam War pose a challenge for the ALF model.[191] If Brezhnev and Kosygin experienced fear of imminent nuclear war during the Cuban Missile Crisis, doesn't the model expect them to have adopted restrained foreign policies? Following Khrushchev's exit from power, Soviet assertive policies were, however, mostly seen in peripheral areas, such as Afghanistan and Africa. The issues at stake were sufficiently low to never make US-Soviet armed conflict a likely prospect, and in some cases (the Middle East) it is not clear that Soviet policy was expansionistic or risk-acceptant. It may have been supporting clients in contests with US-sponsored adversaries. Soviet policies during this period therefore do not falsify the ALF model: there is no evidence to suggest that Brezhnev and his associates' policies were caused by nuclear emboldenment. Moreover, Soviet foreign policy in Western Europe during the latter half of the 1960s was mostly restrained: Brezhnev publically demonstrated his acceptance of parity (rather than striving for superiority) by agreeing to the SALT I and ABM treaties.

More problematic for the ALF model is the Soviet nuclear threat to China in 1969, which was made only seven years after the Cuban Missile Crisis in response to a lethal Chinese ambush on aggressive Soviet patrols on the disputed Zhenbao Island. Like Kennedy's policy in the Cuban Missile Crisis, Soviet nuclear assertion was directed at what may have been perceived as Chinese nuclear assertion on a peripheral contested island (see chapter 5). Nuclear threats to the United States in 1962 were much more assertive and accepting of risk than nuclear threats to quell further Chinese surprise attacks on a marginal locale. Nonetheless, any evidence that Brezhnev and his associates experienced fear in the Cuban Missile Crisis but also believed that nuclear assertion in 1969 would have effects beyond stopping Chinese assertion at Zhenbao would undermine the ALF model.

One might argue that the changed nuclear balance and elite Soviet politics by 1969 would lead Brezhnev and his associates to have little basis to draw on lessons from Cuba. Perhaps they would authorize a more assertive policy. But since the Soviet leaders experienced fear of imminent nuclear escalation in 1962, that experience may well have influenced their foreign policy decisions regarding China seven years later. The fear of imminent nuclear war has a long impact on foreign policy decision-making. More research on the Brezhnev era is required to further test the ALF model.

Summary

The historical record shows that in the Soviet Union's case, nuclear proliferation was dangerous when Nikita Khrushchev believed that nuclear assertion is safe, but it became safe only when he came to learn that it is dangerous. Khrushchev "overlearned" about nuclear coercion from his cognitively accessible Suez experiences and "underlearned" from less cognitively accessible variables (the experiences of others, the historical record, etc.). He accepted the subjective risk of nuclear escalation and authorized an assertive foreign policy. He continued to authorize it in the Middle East, Berlin, and Cuba despite its repeated failure and the costly signal from President Kennedy in 1961.

The fear of imminent nuclear war, caused by Kennedy's assertive reply at Cuba, was necessary for Khrushchev to authorize a restrained foreign policy. The evidence clearly shows that the Soviet leader experienced fear of imminent nuclear war and that this fear led to a fundamental change in Soviet foreign policy. Multiple sources suggest that Khrushchev learned dangerous lessons about nuclear assertion just as the pathologies of availability expressed in the ALF model predict. Kennedy's costly signal in 1961 was insufficient to temper Soviet assertion; the experience of fear of imminent nuclear war explains why he decided to accept an unbearable status quo that he had earlier pushed so hard and risked so much to revise.

It is not clear whether Brezhnev experienced fear of imminent nuclear war in 1962, but his foreign policy is broadly consistent with the ALF model. The next superpower nuclear crisis—Able Archer, in 1983—didn't occur until twenty years later, and it exhibited a greatly reduced risk of nuclear escalation. One might argue that Kennedy's policies in

Table 3.2. Nuclear Learning Models: Soviet Union, 1956–1963

	Waltzian	Rational-Signaling	ALF Two-Stage
Assertion in 1956 Suez Crisis	✗	✓	✓
Assertion in 1958–59 Berlin Crisis	✗	✓	✓
Assertion in 1961 Berlin Crisis	✗	✓	✓
Assertion in 1962 Cuban Missile Crisis	✗	✗	✓
Restraint, 1963–	✓	✓	✓

the Cuban Missile Crisis suggest that nuclear assertion might work under some conditions. But this was one of the very few cases among the many assertive episodes in the Cold War that "worked," and it worked only because the status quo that was revised was nuclear assertion.

Table 3.2 summarizes the explanatory power of the three nuclear-learning models in light of the Soviet case. The Waltzian model cannot explain Khrushchev's nuclear assertion. It expects him to have accepted the status quo in Berlin and not caused the most dangerous years of the Cold War. Waltz accurately argues that nuclear weapons are good for deterrence only, but this perspective neglects the crucial question of how leaders come to learn this lesson. Inattention to this learning mechanism robs the theory of an ability to explain the origins of the most dangerous years of the Cold War. The rational-signaling model explains Soviet nuclear assertiveness but does not explain the most dangerous episode of the Cold War, since it assumes that leaders rationally learn from costly signals in a manner that psychological approaches have long shown is incorrect. The ALF model explains why an experience of fear of imminent nuclear war was necessary for Khrushchev to authorize a restrained foreign policy in Berlin and Cuba. It further predicts that had Khrushchev not experienced fear of imminent nuclear war in October 1962 he may have persisted with nuclear assertion into 1963 and 1964. Without the radical scheme to deploy strategic nuclear missiles to Cuba, Khrushchev may have issued another Berlin ultimatum, backed down, yet again not experienced fear of imminent nuclear war, and authorized another assertive Berlin threat in 1963.

The three learning models can explain Khrushchev's restrained foreign policy in 1963—nuclear assertion cannot continue forever—but the

Waltzian and rational-signaling models fail to explain why this did not occur five years and three nuclear crises earlier. The ALF nuclear learning model explains how nuclear weapons influenced Soviet foreign policy during the Khrushekev years. The evidence shows that Khrushchev's response to the dilemma of nuclear assertion influenced the dangers and opportunities that nuclear weapons presented throughout the Cold War. His policies were strongly influenced by the psychological biases of availability and fear. At the height of the Cold War, nuclear proliferation became dangerous when the Soviet leader learned that nuclear assertion is safe but became safe when he learned that it is dangerous.

Notes

1. *FRUS*, 1955–1957, Vol. 5, Doc. 203.
2. Blight and Welch, *On the Brink*, 104.
3. Nevertheless, President Kennedy was probably willing to concede more, and he may have been willing to grant Khrushchev the important concession of a *public* trade of the Jupiter missiles in Turkey.
4. One can argue that while calling up the reserves would have been costly, it was cheap compared to what was at stake in Berlin; the model might not discriminate between a tough actor and a bluffer. However, costly signaling models do not specify how costly costly signals must be, so it is not unreasonable to assume that Khrushchev should rationally have learned about Kennedy's resolve from this signal alone.
5. See, for example, Trachtenberg, *A Constructed Peace*; and Gaddis, *Strategies of Containment*.
6. See, for example, Zubok, *A Failed Empire*; and Gaddis, *Strategies of Containment*.
7. "Telephonogram from Miroshnichenko and Lun'kov to Soviet High Commissioner V. Semyonov Regarding Inter-zone Travel," July 4, 1953, Cold War International History Project, http://digitalarchive.wilsoncenter.org /document/110400.
8. Harrison, *Driving the Soviets Up the Wall*, 114–15.
9. Smyser, *Kennedy and the Berlin Wall*, 12, 83.
10. "East German Ministry of State Security, 'Brief Assessment of the Investigation Results Achieved in 1961 in Work on Crimes of Espionage,'" January 9, 1962, Cold War International History Project, http://digitalarchive .wilsoncenter.org/document/118657.
11. Trachtenberg, *A Constructed Peace*, 251–56.
12. Ibid., x.

13. Harrison, *Driving the Soviets Up the Wall*. Harrison elaborates that Ulbricht tried to push Khrushchev to raise the West German nuclear issue in public more frequently because he believed the German public would be much more supportive of a campaign against West Germany possessing nuclear weapons than a campaign for a peace treaty with the Soviet Union.

14. *FRUS*, 1958–1960, Vol. 8: Doc. 84.

15. Fursenko and Naftali, *Khrushchev's Cold War*, 192.

16. Ibid., 356.

17. "Notes on the Conversation of Comrade N. S. Khrushchev with Comrade W. Ulbricht on August 1, 1961," August 1, 1961, Cold War International History Project, http://digitalarchive.wilsoncenter.org/document/110206.

18. Thus Khrushchev's Berlin ultimatums indirectly threatened to increase the responsibilities and sovereignty of East Germany by undermining the access rights of the Allies.

19. Smyser, *Kennedy and the Berlin Wall*, 9, 52. See also Paul Maddrell, "Exploiting and Securing the Open Border in Berlin: The Western Secret Services, the Stasi and the Second Berlin Crisis, 1958–1961," Working Paper 58, Cold War International History Project (February 2009), http://www.wilsoncenter.org/sites/default/files/CWIHPWP58_maddrell.pdf.

20. Kennedy remarked to Deputy National Security Adviser Walt Rostow that "Khrushchev is losing East Germany. He cannot let that happen. If East Germany goes so will Poland and all of Eastern Europe." Quoted in Kempe, *Berlin*, 293. Regarding the argument that Ulbricht pressured Khrushchev into policies that he would have otherwise avoided, see Harrison, *Driving the Soviets Up the Wall*, 212. For an example of Ulbricht's persistence, see "Letter from Ulbricht to Khrushchev," January 18, 1961, Cold War International History Project, http://digitalarchive.wilsoncenter.org/document/117140.

21. For similar claims about the importance of West Berlin to Soviet strategy, see Harrison, *Driving the Soviets Up the Wall*, 5; and Zubok, *Failed Empire*, 109.

22. Influential examples of the Soviet superiority thesis include Flanagan, *NATO's Conventional Defenses*; Smoke, *National Security and the Nuclear Dilemma*; Gaddis, *Strategies of Containment*; and Powaski, *The Cold War*.

23. Enthoven and Smith, *How Much Is Enough?*, 142.

24. Evangelista, "Stalin's Postwar Army Reappraised," 111. He elaborates: "Soviet divisional manpower has historically numbered 50 to 60 percent of Western divisional manpower, and [considering] that Soviet divisions have far fewer support troops, the picture looks different . . . an image of rough parity emerges" (119).

25. Posen, "Is NATO Decisively Outnumbered?," 189, 200; Posen, "Measuring the European Conventional Balance"; and Mearsheimer, "Numbers, Strategy, and the European Balance," 184.

26. Luthi, *Sino-Soviet Split*.

27. Fursenko and Naftali, *Khrushchev's Cold War,* 412.

28. Ibid., 39.

29. Douglas Selvage, "Khrushchev's November 1958 Berlin Ultimatum: New Evidence from the Polish Archives," *Cold War International History Project Bulletin* 11 (1998): 200–203, 202.

30. See Zaloga, *Kremlin's Nuclear Sword,* 26–31; Podvig, *Russian Strategic Nuclear Forces,* 1–6; and Fursenko and Naftali, *Khrushchev's Cold War.*

31. Fursenko and Naftali, *Khrushchev's Cold War,* 39–40.

32. Ibid., 166, 177.

33. Khrushchev, *Memoirs,* 2:455.

34. Podvig, *Russian Strategic Nuclear Forces,* 3; and Zaloga, *Kremlin's Nuclear Sword,* 238.

35. Uhl and Ivkin, "Operation Atom."

36. Podvig, *Russian Strategic Nuclear Forces,* 181; Zaloga, *Kremlin's Nuclear Sword,* 232; S. Khrushchev, *Nikita Khrushchev and the Creation of a Superpower;* and Fursenko and Naftali, *Khrushchev's Cold War.*

37. Pleshakov, "Studying Soviet Strategies," 233.

38. May and Zelikow, *The Kennedy Tapes,* 422.

39. S. Khrushchev, *Khrushchev on Khrushchev,* 21.

40. Khrushchev, *Memoirs,* 3:69.

41. Ibid., 69, 75, 77.

42. Ibid., 172.

43. Schecter and Deriabin, *The Spy Who Saved the World,* 80, 113.

44. Fursenko and Naftali, *Khrushchev's Cold War.*

45. Taubman, *Khrushchev,* 364.

46. Thompson, *Khrushchev,* 179–84; Taubman, *Khrushchev,* 310–24; and Fursenko and Naftali, *Khrushchev's Cold War,* 15–32, 145–49.

47. Taubman, *Khrushchev,* 348.

48. Miller Center, "Kremlin Decision Making Project, May 21, 1962." These online notes are mostly Vladimir Malin's stenographic accounts of high-level Presidium meetings, as quoted in Fursenko and Naftali, *Khrushchev's Cold War.* The authors refer to them as "Archives of the Kremlin," or AOK.

49. Taubman, *Khrushchev,* 354; and Heikal, *Sphinx and Commissar,* 92.

50. Karabell, *Parting the Desert,* 269.

51. Taubman, *Khrushchev,* 347.

52. Fursenko and Naftali, *Khrushchev's Cold War,* 134n50; and Miller Center, "Kremlin Decision Making Project," November 5, 1956.

53. *FRUS,* 1955–1957, Vol. 16, Docs. 531, 532.

54. Cited in Betts, *Nuclear Blackmail,* 64.

55. Fursenko and Naftali, *Khrushchev's Cold War,* 136n55.

56. Kunz, *Economic Diplomacy of the Suez Crisis,* 116–52.

57. The sources used to make this and other absence-of-evidence claims are Khrushchev, *Memoirs,* vol. 3; S. Khrushchev, *Nikita Khrushchev and the*

Creation of a Superpower; S. Khrushchev, *Khrushchev on Khrushchev*; Schecter, *Khrushchev Remembers*; Talbott, *Khrushchev Remembers*; Taubman, *Khrushchev*; Thompson, *Khrushchev*; and Fursenko and Naftali, *Khrushchev's Cold War*. Translated archival sources include "The Mao-Khrushchev Conversations, 31 July–3 August 1958 and 2 October 1959," *Cold War International History Project Bulletin* 12–13 (2001): 244–72; Douglas Selvage, "The End of the Berlin Crisis: New Evidence from the Polish and East German Archives," *Cold War International History Project Bulletin* 11 (1998): 218–29; Selvage, "Khrushchev's November 1958 Berlin Ultimatum"; Uhl and Ivkin, "'Operation Atom.'" Studies of Soviet foreign policy before the Cuban Missile Crisis are Zubok, *Failed Empire*; Volkogonov, *Autopsy for an Empire*; Zubok and Pleshakov, *Inside the Kremlin's Cold War*; Harrison, *Driving the Soviets Up the Wall*; Smyser, *Kennedy and the Berlin Wall*; Kempe, *Berlin 1961*; F. Taylor, *The Berlin Wall*; Gearson and Schake, *Berlin Wall Crisis*; Beschloss, *The Crisis Years*; and Pleshakov, "Studying Soviet Strategies." Sources for the Cuban Missile Crisis are Fursenko and Naftali, *One Hell of a Gamble*; Dobbs, *One Minute to Midnight*; Gribkov, "The View from Moscow and Havana"; Blight, Allyn, and Welch, *Cuba on the Brink*; Blight and Welch, *On the Brink*; Nathan, *Cuban Missile Crisis Revisited*; May and Zelikow, *Kennedy Tapes*; and Kennedy, *Thirteen Days*. In addition to sources mentioned elsewhere in the chapter, other sources are Richter, *Khrushchev's Double Bind*; Mikoyan, *Tak Bylo*; Bloomfield, Clemens, and Griffiths, *Khrushchev and the Arms Race*; Bundy, *Danger and Survival*; Cousins, *The Improbable Triumvirate*; Nash, *The Other Missiles of October*; and Seaborg, *Kennedy, Khrushchev, and the Test Ban*.

58. Khrushchev, *Memoirs*, 3:75.

59. S. Khrushchev, *Nikita Khrushchev and the Creation of a Superpower*, 211–12, 264.

60. Zubok, "Mao-Khrushchev Conversations," 14.

61. Taubman, *Khrushchev*, 359–60.

62. Khrushchev, *Memoirs*, 3:815, 666.

63. I. Tugarinov, "Third World Reaction to Hungary and Suez, 1956: A Soviet Foreign Ministry Analysis," December 28, 1956, Cold War International History Project, 7–8, http://digitalarchive.wilsoncenter.org/document/111097. See also Richter, *Khrushchev's Double Bind*, 93.

64. Heikal, *Sphinx and Commissar*, 82.

65. Khrushchev, *Memoirs*, 3:816.

66. "Minutes of the Meeting of the CPSU CC Plenum on the State of Soviet Foreign Policy," June 24, 1957, Cold War International History Project, 9–10, http://digitalarchive.wilsoncenter.org/document/110459.pdf?v=93c19 bd6d01a9efe4d7ba12 729ac5402.

67. Fursenko and Naftali, *Khrushchev's Cold War*, 243–44; and Taubman, *Khrushchev*, 359.

68. Taubman, *Khrushchev*, 347.

69. Heikal, *Sphinx and Commissar,* 129; and Taubman, *Khrushchev,* 347.

70. Khrushchev, *Memoirs,* 2:517.

71. Taubman, *Khrushchev,* 378.

72. Ibid., 379.

73. Ibid., 381.

74. "Nikita Khrushchev Memorandum to CC CPSU Presidium," December 8, 1959, Cold War International History Project, http://digitalarchive .wilsoncenter.org/document/117083.

75. Khrushchev, *Memoirs,* 2:514, 516; see also 523.

76. Richter, *Khrushchev's Double Bind,* 106–7, 193; Taubman, *Khrushchev,* 381; and Fursenko and Naftali, *Khrushchev's Cold War,* 243–48.

77. Taubman, *Khrushchev,* 365, 413.

78. Richter, *Khrushchev's Double Bind,* 3.

79. Fursenko and Naftali, *Khrushchev's Cold War,* 160.

80. Zubok, "Mao-Khrushchev Conversations," 14. Mao Zedong also believed this. At the end of 1961 the East German ambassador in Beijing remarked that the Chinese had believed that "in the case of the Suez aggression, the Soviet ultimatum, which was taken seriously, scared the imperialists and forced them to stop their aggression." See Harrison, *Driving the Soviets Up the Wall,* 240.

81. Fursenko and Naftali, *Khrushchev's Cold War,* 173.

82. "Text of Soviet Statement on Mideast," *Washington Post,* July 17, 1958.

83. Fursenko and Naftali, *Khrushchev's Cold War,* 167–68.

84. Heikal, *Sphinx and Commissar,* 83. Mohammed Heikal was the editor in chief of the influential Cairo newspaper *Al-Ahram* from 1957 through 1974; he also worked as a ghostwriter for Egyptian president Nasser, was a member of the Central Committee of the Arab Socialist Union, and was the Egyptian minister of information from 1970 through 1974.

85. Fursenko and Naftali, *Khrushchev's Cold War,* 168.

86. *FRUS,* 1958–1960, Vol. 12 Doc. 122.

87. *FRUS,* 1958–1960, Vol. 12 Doc. 26.

88. Miller Center, "Kremlin Decision Making Project, August 4, 1958."

89. S. Khrushchev, *Nikita Khrushchev and the Creation of a Superpower,* 292.

90. "T. Zhivkov's Report at the Bulgarian Plenary Session on the Middle East Crisis," October 2, 1958, Cold War International History Project, http:// digitalarchive.wilsoncenter.org/document/113222.

91. *FRUS,* 1958–1960, Vol. 8, Docs. 24–118.

92. Ibid.

93. Fursenko and Naftali, *Khrushchev's Cold War,* 203–204.

94. "Soviet Government Note Sent to U.S. Government of November 27, 1958," *Department of State Bulletin* 40, no. 1020 (January 12, 1959): 81–89.

95. Cited in Taubman, *Khrushchev,* 399.

96. Ibid., 407.

97. *FRUS*, 1958–1960, Vol. 8, Doc. 80.

98. Troyanovsky, "Making of Soviet Foreign Policy," 220. See also Harrison, *Driving the Soviets Up the Wall*, 117.

99. *FRUS*, 1958–1960, Vol. 9, Docs. 14–16; and Kempe, *Berlin*, 217.

100. See, for example, Horelick and Rush, *Strategic Power and Soviet Foreign Policy*; Linden, *Khrushchev and the Soviet Leadership*; and Parrott, *Politics and Technology in the Soviet Union*.

101. Miller Center, "Kremlin Decision Making Project, February 21, 1959."

102. Selvage, "Khrushchev's November 1958 Berlin Ultimatum."

103. Note from USSR Embassy to USA relayed by Gromyko to Khrushchev, August 3, 1960, "John Fitzgerald Kennedy: Political Character Sketch," 6, Cold War International History *Project*, http://digitalarchive.wilsoncenter.org /document/115978.pdf?v=3fea81d3b02cfc029b0f3cf66e9a7236.

104. Taubman, *Khrushchev*, 490.

105. Ibid., 505.

106. Khrushchev, *Memoirs*, 3:307.

107. Cited in Kempe, *Berlin 1961*, 293. For the argument that Ulbricht pressured Khrushchev into policies that he would have otherwise avoided, see Harrison, *Driving the Soviets Up the Wall*, 212.

108. Taubman, *Khrushchev*, 482.

109. Harrison, *Driving the Soviets Up the Wall*; and Fursenko and Naftali, *Khrushchev's Cold War*.

110. Fursenko and Naftali, *Khrushchev's Cold War*, 363.

111. J. F. Kennedy, "Report to the Nation: The Berlin Crisis."

112. Donald A. Carter, *The U.S. Military Response to the 1960–1962 Berlin Crisis*, The U.S. Army Center of Military History, http://www.foia.cia.gov/sites /default/files/document_conversions/16/USMilitaryResponse.pdf.

113. Salinger, *With Kennedy*, 191.

114. See http://legacy.wilsoncenter.org/coldwarfiles/files/Documents/1961 0928_Khrushchev_Ulbricht.pdf.

115. Smyser, *Kennedy and the Berlin Wall*, 159n21.

116. Ibid., 137.

117. "Memorandum of Conversation, Secretary's Meeting with European Ambassadors," Paris, August 9, 1961, *National Security Archive*, http://www2 .gwu.edu/~nsarchiv/NSAEBB/NSAEBB354/8–9–61%20Secy%20meeting .pdf; and "State Department Cable 340 to Embassy Bonn, August 13, 1961," *National Security Archive*, http://www2.gwu.edu/~nsarchiv/NSAEBB/NSAE BB354/8–1361%20cable%20Rusk%20statement.pdf.

118. Selvage, "End of the Berlin Crisis," 224.

119. Fursenko and Naftali, *Khrushchev's Cold War*, 422n30.

120. Ibid., 412n10, 414.

121. Smyser, *Kennedy and the Berlin Wall*, 151.

122. Fursenko and Naftali, *Khrushchev's Cold War*, 356.

123. "Italian Prime Minister Fanfani's Visit to Moscow, August 1961," Cold War International History Project, http://digitalarchive.wilsoncenter.org /document/113361.

124. Fursenko and Naftali, *Khrushchev's Cold War*, 341, 381.

125. Schecter, *Khrushchev Remembers*, 170.

126. Beschloss, *Crisis Years*, 224–25.

127. For a summary of the historiography of the Cuban Missile Crisis, see Leffler and Westad, *Cambridge History of the Cold War*, 2:531–32.

128. One of the most important contributions was Blight, Allyn, and Welch, *Cuba on the Brink*, 8.

129. Bernstein, "Understanding Decisionmaking," 150–51.

130. May and Zelikow, *Kennedy Tapes*, 37–41, 62, 67–68, 87, 115, 159–60. Kennedy accurately predicted on October 9 that "As a result of the Soviet actions on Cuba, there was much less prospect of reaching agreement on Berlin" because "Khrushchev might try to force something." *FRUS, 1961–1963*, Vol. 15, Doc. 130.

131. Miller Center, "Kremlin Decision Making Project, May 21, 1962"; and Fursenko and Naftali, *Khrushchev's Cold War*, 435n80. See also Lebow and Stein, *We All Lost the Cold War*, 48.

132. "List of Troops and Commanders to take part in Operation 'Anadyr,'" June 20, 1962, Cold War International History Project, http://digitalarchive .wilsoncenter.org/document/113050.pdf?v=62f13a343e90f0099f8961ae 1c0dc751; and Fursenko and Naftali, *One Hell of a Gamble*.

133. Taubman, *Khrushchev*, 539–40; Fursenko and Naftali, *Khrushchev's Cold War*, 446–47, 458; and May and Zelikow, *Kennedy Tapes*, 426–27.

134. *FRUS, 1961–1963*, Vol. 6, Doc. 56; *Cold War International History Project Bulletin* 8–9 (Winter 1996/1997): 280–81.

135. Allison and Zelikow, *Essence of Decision*, 82–109.

136. Blight, Allyn, and Welch, *Cuba on the Brink*, 250–51.

137. "A Trigger for Khrushchev's Deployment? Alexei Adzhubei's Report on His Conversation with John F. Kennedy, 30 January 1962," *Cold War International History Project Bulletin* 17/18 (Fall 2012): 316–23.

138. Timothy Naftali, "The Malin Notes: Glimpses inside the Kremlin during the Cuban Missile Crisis," *Cold War International History Project Bulletin* 17/18: 299–315, 306.

139. Mikoyan, *Soviet Cuban Missile Crisis*, 101. For similar arguments about Soviet strategy in Cuba in 1962, see Burlatsky, *Khrushchev and the First Russian Spring*, 173–74; Dobrynin, *In Confidence*, 73; and Gribkov, "View from Moscow."

140. The group had not discussed Berlin for several months. "Central Committee of the Communist Party of the Soviet Union Presidium Protocol

No. 39," July 1, 1962, Cold War International History Project, http://digitalarchive.wilsoncenter.org/document/115067.

141. Fursenko and Naftali, *Khrushchev's Cold War*, 441nn7–8.

142. Ibid., 445.

143. Ibid., 445n22.

144. Ibid., 447nn27–28.

145. Ibid., 449n38.

146. Ibid., 457n56, 458; and Smyser, *Kennedy and the Berlin Wall*, 189.

147. Fursenko and Naftali, *Khrushchev's Cold War*, 450nn42–43.

148. National Security Archive, The George Washington University, http://www.gwu.edu/~nsarchiv/NSAEBB/NSAEBB395/docs/mrFC.pdf.

149. Taubman, *Khrushchev*, 562.

150. Horelick, "Cuban Missile Crisis," 365.

151. May and Zelikow, *Kennedy Tapes*, 390.

152. Mikoyan, *Soviet Cuban Missile Crisis*, 101; and Fursenko and Naftali, *Khrushchev's Cold War*, 444n16.

153. Mikoyan, *Soviet Cuban Missile Crisis*, 118n53.

154. Cited in Taubman, *Khrushchev*, 541, 543.

155. "Central Committee of the Communist Party of the Soviet Union Presidium Protocol 35," June 10, 1962, Cold War International History Project, http://digitalarchive.wilsoncenter.org/document/115066; and Fursenko and Naftali, *Khrushchev's Cold War*, 440.

156. *FRUS*, 1961–1963, Vol. 6, Doc. 63.

157. Khrushchev, *Nikita Khrushchev and the Creation of a Superpower*, 572, 576.

158. Ibid., 608; and Schecter, *Khrushchev Remembers*, 178.

159. Khrushchev, *Nikita Khrushchev and the Creation of a Superpower*, 597–98.

160. Fursenko and Naftali, *One Hell of a Gamble*, 182; and Schecter, *Khrushchev Remembers*, 493, 495–96.

161. *FRUS*, 1961–1963, Vol. 6, Doc. 65.

162. S. Khrushchev, *Nikita Khrushchev and the Creation of a Superpower*, 560.

163. Fursenko and Naftali, *One Hell of a Gamble*, 259.

164. Miller Center, "Kremlin Decision Making Project, October 22, 1962."

165. Khrushchev, *Memoirs*, 3:33.

166. Dobbs, *One Minute to Midnight*, 112.

167. "Minutes of Conversation between the CPCz and the CPSU, October 30, 1962," cited in "The Global Cuban Missile Crisis at 50," *Cold War International History Project*.

168. Valerian Zorin, "October 26 Memo," *Cold War International History Project Bulletin* 8–9 (Winter, 1996–1997): 290.

169. Cousins, *Improbable Triumvirate*, 46.

170. Cited in Fursenko and Naftali, *One Hell of a Gamble*, 352.

171. Khrushchev, *Memoirs*, 2:520, 3:350.

172. Fursenko and Naftali, *Khrushchev's Cold War*, 498n27.

173. Anatoly Dobrynin, "October 27 Memo," *Cold War International History Project Bulletin* 5 (Spring 1995): 80; "Letter from Khrushchev to Fidel Castro," October 28, 1962, Cold War International History Project, http://digitalarchive.wilsoncenter.org/document/114504; "Telegram from Soviet Ambassador to the USA Dobrynin to USSR Foreign Ministry, Forwarding Telegram from Georgi Zhukov," November 1, 1962, Cold War International History Project, http://digitalarchive.wilsoncenter.org/document/112648; Schecter, *Khrushchev Remembers*, 497–98; Fursenko and Naftali, *One Hell of a Gamble*, 185; Blight and Welch, *On the Brink*, 264–65.

174. "Telegram from Fidel Castro to Nikita Khrushchev," October 26, 1962, Cold War International History Project, http://digitalarchive.wilsoncenter.org/document/114501; "Letter from Fidel Castro to Khrushchev," October 28, 1962, Cold War International History Project, http://digitalarchive.wilsoncenter.org/document/114503. By October 30 reports of a possible US invasion continued to flow in. See "Telegram from Soviet Deputy Foreign Minister Kuznetsov and Ambassador to the UN Zorin to USSR Foreign Ministry," October 30, 1962, Cold War International History Project, http://digitalarchive.wilsoncenter.org/document/112634.

175. Khrushchev, *Memoirs*, 3:341; Mikoyan, *Soviet Cuban Missile Crisis*; and Alekseev, "Telegram from Soviet Ambassador to Cuba A.I. Alekseev to USSR Foreign Ministry," October 27, 1962, Cold War International History Project, http://digitalarchive.wilsoncenter.org/document/110999.

176. Fursenko and Naftali, *Khrushchev's Cold War*, 471; and Fursenko and Naftali, *One Hell of a Gamble*, 242–43.

177. "Cable from Soviet Ambassador to U.S. Dobrynin to USSR Foreign Ministry," October 25, 1962, Cold War International History Project, http://digitalarchive.wilsoncenter.org/document/111918; and "Telegram from Soviet Ambassador to the USA Dobrynin to the USSR MFA," October 27, 1962, Cold War International History Project, http://digitalarchive.wilsoncenter.org/document/111835.

178. Taubman, *Khrushchev*, 536.

179. See, for example, Waltz, *Theory of International Politics*; and Mearsheimer, *Tragedy of Great Power Politics*. For a possible exception, see Glaser, *Rational Theory of International Politics*.

180. Fursenko and Naftali, *Khrushchev's Cold War*, 508.

181. Ibid., 510n59.

182. Ibid., 520n103.

183. Ibid., 516–17; *FRUS*, 1961–1963, Vol. 11, Doc. 308.

184. Fursenko and Naftali, *Khrushchev's Cold War*, 525n120.

185. Bechara and Damasio, "Somatic Marker Hypothesis"; and Rosen, *War and Human Nature*, 27–70.

186. Fursenko and Naftali, *Khrushchev's Cold War*, 511–13.

187. Ibid., 505n43.

188. Ibid., 521.

189. For a recent assessment of Brezhnev's policies, see Zubok, *Failed Empire*, 192–226; and Bacon and Sandle, *Brezhnev Reconsidered*. One can argue that Brezhnev did not accept the status quo in Cuba, because he attempted to establish a submarine base at Cienfuegos in 1970. See Siniver, "Nixon Administration and the Cienfuegos Crisis."

190. *FRUS*, 1964–1968, Vol. 14, Doc. 141.

191. See, for example, Hopf, *Peripheral Visions*; and Garthoff, *Détente and Confrontation*.

4

The Most Dangerous Place in the World: Pakistan, 1998-2002

US PRESIDENT BILL CLINTON believed that the end of the Cold War left the Kashmir region of South Asia as the most dangerous place in the world. He also believed that "nuclear arsenals made both India and Pakistan less secure."[1] Following Clinton, George W. Bush's senior advisers, if not the president himself, believed that the rapid escalation of conventional conflicts would cause nuclear war in South Asia.[2] One senior Bush administration official described the general American sentiment during the 2001–2002 crisis this way: "We know how mad you are, but this is not the time to let MAD take over."[3] In 2010 Barack Obama issued a secret directive to focus diplomatic efforts in the region on reducing tensions between India and Pakistan.[4] His former coordinator for arms control and weapons of mass destruction (WMD) terrorism claimed: "The risk of a conflict escalating to a nuclear war is probably higher in South Asia than in anywhere else in the world."[5]

Scholars have debated whether nuclear weapons have increased or decreased the probability of conventional war and conflict between India and Pakistan.[6] As usual, it depends on where one looks for evidence. The number of attacks and fatalities in the insurgency in Kashmir increased after 1990 when Pakistan developed nuclear weapons. (India also gained a nuclear capability between 1988 and 1990.) After both adversaries tested nuclear weapons and missiles in 1998, the two countries fought a war in 1999 in the Kargil sector of Kashmir and engaged in a more dangerous ten-month mobilized standoff in 2001–2. But Indo-Pakistani relations since 2003 have been far less prone to conflict: Kashmir saw as many fatalities in 2012 as it had in 1989. Vipin Narang echoes conventional wisdom when he claims: "The superpower model of nuclear strategy and deterrence does not seem to be applicable to India and Pakistan because they have small arsenals and where an active and enduring territorial rivalry is punctuated by repeated crises that openly risk nuclear war."[7]

These arguments are either incorrect or incomplete because they cannot explain variation in Pakistani foreign policy nor, more specifically, the impact of fear of imminent nuclear war on former president Pervez Musharraf's foreign policy choices. Pakistan exhibited an assertive foreign policy after achieving an operational nuclear deterrent in 1990, and Musharraf persisted with that assertion, authorizing the dangerous Kargil intrusion in 1999 and maintaining assertion toward India after that. However, after reaching the nuclear brink in May 2002, fatalities in the Kashmir conflict declined and Musharraf began authorizing a more restrained foreign policy.

Policymakers and scholars who assert that nuclear weapons have made conventional and nuclear conflict between India and Pakistan more or less likely must confront and explain this variation in Pakistani foreign policy. Moreover, while important differences exist between the experiences during the Cold War and more-recent events in South Asia, the effect of fear of imminent nuclear war on Khrushchev and on Musharraf show that the similarities between these two cases outweigh their differences.[8]

Limited data on the beliefs and attention span of army general and (later) president Pervez Musharraf does not allow a systematic test of the Waltzian, rational-signaling, or ALF models. However, there is sufficient documented evidence to rigorously probe them, and the ALF model can explain the available evidence better than the rational-signaling or Waltzian alternatives. Nuclear proliferation was dangerous when Musharraf learned that nuclear assertion is safe, and it became safer when he learned that it is dangerous.

The central puzzle to answer regarding Indo-Pakistani conflict dynamics and nuclear weapons in South Asia is why a weak and becoming relatively weaker Pakistan has not reached a settlement with India. Pakistan has, in Christine Fair's words, "doggedly attempted to revise the geographical status quo and roll back India's ascendancy, and the very instruments it has used to attain these policies have undermined Pakistan's standing within the international community and even its own long-term viability."[9] Fair explains this through her observance of the Pakistani Army's strategic culture. But Fair and others do not come to terms with or explain the substantial variations in the level of violence seen in Kashmir long after the US commitment to Afghanistan ended. Fatalities in the disputed region substantially rose throughout the 1990s, peaking in 2001 at a total of 4,500. The number has substantially declined since then, and 2011 was nearly as safe as the late 1980s (before Pakistan acquired nuclear weapons). Why was Pakistani foreign policy from 1990 through 2002 so much more assertive and dangerous than it was in the subsequent decade? Why did Pakistan push so hard to revise the status quo in Kashmir and then essentially accept it in 2002 even though nothing had changed? Why did Pakistan experience the same dangerous cycles of instability and stability as the Soviet Union had, once it had acquired nuclear weapons?

Pakistan's sponsorship of the Kashmiri insurgency in the 1990s can be viewed as nuclear assertion motivated by the belief that nuclear weapons would prevent overwhelming retaliation by India, which the Pakistani Army would be unable to long resist. Pervez Musharraf's authorization of the intrusion into Indian Kashmir at the Kargil sector in 1999 was fueled by his belief that India's isolation after Delhi's May 1998 nuclear test would lead Washington to tacitly accept Pakistan's gains from nuclear assertion and let India and Pakistan resolve their dispute bilaterally. While Musharraf likely hoped that Clinton would allow Pakistan to hold onto the territorial gains it had made in Kashmir and encourage a new agreement on the region, the president, eager to stem the flow of nuclear weapons, ensured that Pakistan would never appear to have gained anything from nuclear assertion in Kargil.

The Waltzian learning model cannot explain Musharraf's authorization of nuclear assertion in Kashmir. Rather, it would expect Musharraf to have authorized a restrained foreign policy and accept the intolerable Kashmir status quo. But Musharraf did continue to authorize nuclear assertion in Kashmir after Kargil: though he did not authorize further

Kargil-like intrusions, he did continue to sponsor the Kashmir insurgency in an effort to compel Indian prime minister Atal Bihari Vajpayee to negotiate and ultimately revise the Kashmir status quo.

Neither can the rational-signaling model explain Musharraf's actions. Vajpayee's mobilization and military efforts to eject Pakistani troops from Kargil in 1999 was a costly signal, so Musharraf should have refrained from sponsoring the insurgency after the Kargil War. While it is unclear if Musharraf authorized or was aware of the planning for the December 2001 attacks on the Indian Parliament and May 2002 attacks on civilians at an army base in Jammu, he experienced fear of imminent nuclear war on May 30 or 31, 2002, after India deployed its three offensive strike corps in Rajasthan in preparation for an invasion of Pakistan. A restrained Pakistani foreign policy in Kashmir caused the substantial decline in violence in that disputed territory since 2003.

Pakistani Grand Strategy and Kashmir

The partition of British India into India and Pakistan in 1947 left a weak and vulnerable Pakistan. As Paul Kapur and Sumit Ganguly have pointed out, East and West Pakistan, separated by a thousand miles of Indian territory, lacked the financial means, military assets, industrial capacity, natural resources, strategic depth, and central government needed to effectively coordinate national and provincial affairs.[10] Moreover, the need for Pakistani statehood was not accepted by all of British India's Muslims nor the autonomous tribes of the northwest frontier and the province of Balochistan.[11]

The potential acquisition of Muslim-majority Kashmir offered a solution to many of Pakistan's problems: the new country could gain both sovereign legitimacy and strategic depth by increasing the distance between Indian troops and Islamabad.[12] Pakistani leaders decided long ago that to differentiate their polity from and justify its existence against India it had to be nothing less than an Islamic homeland. Pakistan's potential cessation to India of Kashmir—where the states of Jammu and Kashmir are about two-thirds Muslim and the Kashmir valley is about 95 percent Muslim—would be the thin end of the wedge and open the door to the possibility that South Asian Muslims could live in a secular multiethnic Indian state.

On the other hand, India's offering of Kashmir to Pakistan would also "give the game away" by dangerously implying that a religious minority could not live within India's democracy. Doing so would undermine fundamental Indian conceptions of multiethnicity and eat away at the democratic foundations of the Indian state.[13] Pakistan and India therefore have both long viewed possession of Kashmir as a primary political and security objective. Kashmir has dominated Indo-Pakistani relations for much of the time since independence and has been at the center of three of the four wars between the two nations.[14]

Just as Josef Stalin's effort to eject the United States from West Berlin in 1948 made Germany more dependent on Washington, Pakistan's sponsorship of an insurgency against the Maharajah of Kashmir pushed him into Delhi's arms. After several Pakistan-sponsored uprisings began to undermine the Maharajah's power in October 1947, he signed an instrument of accession to India that Pakistani leaders have since refused to accept.[15]

After the first 1947–48 Kashmir war, India controlled two-thirds of the territory, which helped Delhi gain de facto control of the disputed areas. In sympathy to the insurgency's efforts against Indian rule, Pakistan responded by more extensively sponsoring the indigenous uprising in the late 1980s, just when it developed nuclear weapons. General Musharraf echoed many when he claimed that the ultimate goal of "liberating Indian held Kashmir" was the "core issue" in Indo-Pakistani relations.[16]

Musharraf's desire to engage in talks over Kashmir resemble Khrushchev's goals for West Berlin. Just as Khrushchev wanted an audience with Eisenhower and Kennedy to renegotiate the Berlin status quo, US deputy secretary of state Richard Armitage noted in June 2002 that Musharraf was "quite keen on entering into a dialogue on the whole question of Kashmir."[17] Much of Pakistan-sponsored violence has been designed to increase the costs of India's position and encourage the United States to broker regional bargains that Pakistan would be unable to achieve on its own. Even so, the literature has neglected one central question: after having pushed so hard to revise the status of Kashmir through nuclear-backed territory grabs and assertive threats, why did Musharraf change his approach to Kashmir to be one of diplomacy and confidence-building measures beginning in 2003? Vipin Narang argues that the shift in Pakistan's nuclear posture in the late 1990s exerted a systematic effect on its ability to deter Indian challenges.[18] But posture is not policy, and it is unclear why this posture gave rise to sustained revisionism in Kashmir until 2002 and then a tacit acceptance of the status quo thereafter.

The 1990s Kashmir Insurgency

Pakistan had enriched enough uranium in 1987 to produce a nuclear device, but it was not until 1990 that it was able to manufacture all of the components necessary for an operational nuclear weapon.[19] India first readied two dozen nuclear weapons for quick assembly and aerial delivery between 1988 and 1990.[20] The Waltzian learning model would expect Pakistan's leaders to have not been emboldened by nuclear weapons and to not have authorized an assertive foreign policy. The Kashmir insurgency that grew in the early 1990s and peaked in the early 2000s appears to undermine this expectation. As table 4.1 shows, the number of attacks on Indian forces in Kashmir increased dramatically after Pakistan acquired nuclear weapons. Security force, civilian, and terrorist fatalities increased from about thirty in 1988 to over twenty-five hundred in 1993.

The installation of a new chief minister in Jammu and Kashmir amid widespread allegations of electoral fraud in 1987, followed by the dismissal of the government and reinstatement of presidential rule in 1990, complicates any causal inference that could be made here. Pakistan's new nuclear capability could have emboldened Pakistani prime ministers Benazir Bhutto and Nawaz Sharif to intensify sponsorship of the Kashmir insurgency, which may have undermined the government and led to presidential rule. But the allegations of electoral fraud also could have encouraged the conditions that Pakistan's leaders simply took advantage of.

While the weakness of the Kashmir government during the 1990s may have made an assertive foreign policy more attractive to Pakistan,

Table 4.1. Fatalities from the Kashmir Insurgency, 1988–2012

	Civilians	Security force personnel	Terrorists	Total
1988	29	1	1	31
1989	79	13	0	92
1990	862	132	183	1,177
1991	594	185	614	1,393
1992	859	177	873	1,909
1993	1,023	216	1,328	2,567
1994	1,012	236	1,651	2,899
1995	1,161	297	1,338	2,796
1996	1,333	376	1,194	2,903
1997	840	355	1,177	2,372
1998	877	339	1,045	2,261
1999	799	555	1,184	2,538
2000	842	638	1,808	3,288
2001	1,067	590	2,850	4,507
2002	839	469	1,714	3,022
2003	658	338	1,546	2,542
2004	534	325	951	1,810
2005	521	218	1,000	1,739
2006	349	168	599	1,116
2007	164	121	492	777
2008	69	90	382	541
2009	55	78	242	375
2010	36	69	270	375
2011	34	30	119	183
2012	16	17	84	117

Source: Institute for Conflict Management, South Asia Terrorism portal; and Elias, "Pakistan: The Taliban's Godfather?"

evidence suggests that Pakistan's nuclear capabilities loomed large in the intensification of the Kashmir insurgency. Indeed, Pakistan's nuclear weapon development did coincide with an increase in the intensity of the insurgency, but it may be a correlation only. The evidence gathered by Paul Kapur strongly suggests that Sharif and Bhutto were emboldened by their own nuclear capabilities and authorized an assertive foreign policy on these grounds. Bhutto stated that Pakistan's leaders believed that having nuclear weapons allowed them to undermine Indian rule in Kashmir through sponsorship of the insurgency: "Having nuclear capabilities would ensure that India could not launch a conventional war."[21]

Former Foreign Ministry director general for South Asian Affairs Jalil Jilani stated that "since Pakistan's acquisition of nuclear capacity, Pakistan has felt much less threatened" and nuclear weapons allowed policies that could "put a check on Indian ambition."[22] India's Joint Intelligence Committee noted the Pakistani perception in 1991 that "low-intensity conflict was feasible against India because Pakistan's nuclear capability would deter Indian escalation."[23] The Indian government's report of the Kargil War found that without Pakistani nuclear weapons, "It is inconceivable that it could sustain its proxy war against India, inflicting thousands of casualties, without being unduly concerned about India's conventional superiority."[24] Were Pakistani nuclear weapons not a factor that emboldened Islamabad to authorize an assertive foreign policy, the increase in violence in the Kashmir insurgency should have occurred well before 1990.

The Waltzian model cannot explain why Pakistani leaders authorized an assertive foreign policy in the 1990s in order to realize their Kashmir ambitions. Superior Indian military power and a more dynamic economy had allowed Delhi to prevail in the 1948 and 1965 wars over the region. Nuclear weapons, as ever, did not allow Pakistani leaders to credibly threaten a territory grab or demand concessions, because the cost of using them is so high. The rational-signaling model can explain Pakistani assertiveness because Pakistani leaders had strong incentives to display their resolve to revise an unbearable status quo. Only the ALF model would expect newly nuclear Pakistan to have authorized an assertive foreign policy until a crisis caused it to experience fear of imminent nuclear war.

The 1999 Kargil War

The Pakistani intrusion at the Kargil sector of Kashmir in 1999 was qualitatively and quantitatively different from earlier Pakistani assertion in the disputed territory. Pakistani troops were not engaged in combat in the 1990s, and Pakistan limited its support to financial and logistical assistance only. Incursions into Indian territory during this period did not penetrate far beyond the Line of Control (LoC). However, within a year of the 1998 nuclear tests, members of the Pakistani Northern Light Infantry Unit, disguised as tribal mujahedeen, penetrated twelve kilometers into India-held Kashmir at the Kargil-Dras sector of the LoC. A consolidated Pakistani position there would have allowed Pakistan to prevent India from supplying its troops in the Siachen glacier sector and presumably to demand further Kashmir concessions.

Though General Musharraf and Prime Minister Sharif later blamed each other on the aggression once the identity of the Pakistani troops was revealed, it is likely that Musharraf had vaguely informed Sharif of the nature of the operation and that Sharif approved it without realizing its implications.[25] In his autobiography, Musharraf denied that Pakistani troops were involved and claimed that Pakistani maneuvers at Kargil were a response to imminent Indian aggression.[26] However, the former army general has recently come close to admitting Pakistani government complicity in the Kargil intrusion. He stated in 2013: "If we are the rogues in Kargil, then you [India] were the rogues in East Pakistan and Siachen." He also did not deny that he had spent a night with Pakistani troops eleven kilometers within Indian Kashmir.[27]

The former head of analysis of Pakistan's Inter-Services Intelligence (ISI)—the army's intelligence arm—recently stated that Pakistani behavior at Kargil "certainly wasn't a defensive manoeuvre: there were no indications of an Indian attack. Our clearly expressed intent was to cut the supply line to Siachen and force the Indians to pull out."[28] Musharraf restricted knowledge of the operation to the army's chief of the general staff and the director general of military operations—the GOC 10 Corps, Rawalpindi—and did not inform the military's general headquarters of the operation's details until the identity of the intruders became known.[29] Prime Minister Vajpayee and his advisers were deeply surprised at the aggression and took several weeks to redeploy troops and dislodge the Pakistani intruders using intense peak-to-peak combat. It took nearly two months for Indian forces to dislodge most of the Pakistani isolated outposts.

After a meeting with President Clinton in which Sharif unsuccessfully begged and pleaded for anything that he could proclaim was a victory or concession from the operation, Sharif ordered his remaining troops to withdraw to Pakistan-held Kashmir. Clinton was concerned about nuclear escalation and wanted to ensure that Pakistan did not appear to have made any territorial gains. Despite later claims by military officials that the operation itself was highly successful, the political gambit was a depressing failure and Sharif was overthrown in a military coup months later.

One can argue that an Indo-Pakistani conflict similar to the Kargil War would have inevitably occurred by the late 1990s had Pakistan not developed nuclear weapons. But India and Pakistan had not engaged in military combat during the twenty-eight years leading up to 1999, and Pakistan's sponsorship of the insurgency in Kashmir came only after its development of nuclear weapons. Once India won the race in 1984 to establish military control of the Saltoro Mountains, Pakistan launched several attacks with the goal of establishing a position on the range's ridgeline. Since that mountaineering race, India and Pakistan have together sustained over thirty five hundred casualties, with many arising from the harsh requirements of glacier living.[30]

The Kargil plan had been floating in senior Pakistani military circles since 1987. After a successful Indian attack in June 1987, which dislodged Pakistani troops from a forward outpost overlooking Indian deployments, and an unsuccessful Pakistani attempt to recover that position three months later, alternative Pakistani plans were formulated to gain control of the area. Former army general Mirza Alam Beg claimed at a 1989 press conference that Benazir Bhutto refused to authorize a plan to occupy the Kargil heights in order to disrupt the Srinagar-Leh Road.[31] Although the army was optimistic about its ability to make territorial gains by occupying Srinagar, Bhutto apparently and wisely believed that this would undermine Pakistan's position in Kashmir in the long run.[32]

Partly due to the constraints of the winter climate on military operations, border security in the Kargil sector during the winter of 1989 was particularly sparse.[33] The former head of the ISI noted at the time that "the Indian army is incapable of undertaking any conventional operations at present."[34] It is thus not implausible that a Pakistani leader would have eventually authorized the Kargil operation or something resembling it had Pakistan never developed nuclear weapons. Peter Lavoy, Feroz Hassan Khan, and Christopher Clary argue that Pakistani leaders were not emboldened by their new nuclear capability in 1999: "It was this lack of understanding of the meaning of the nuclear revolution that made Kargil planners act as if nothing had changed. Kargil planners at the time still acted as if they lived in a pre-nuclear, conventional world. They were mainly concerned with operational imperatives, restoring honor, and retribution for Siachen."[35]

This assessment is consistent with the Waltzian model because it expects Pakistani leaders to have authorized a restrained foreign policy: if Lavoy and his coauthors are correct, the Kargil War did not result from Pakistani nuclear emboldenment. There are, however, strong reasons to doubt this claim. Much evidence suggests that Pakistani nuclear weapons were central to the Kargil plans and that the intrusion was part of a nuclear weapons–emboldened assertive foreign policy. Indian Army general V. P. Malik at the time noted that "there was a strong belief that Pakistan's demonstrated nuclear weapons capability in May 1998 was sufficient to prevent the escalation of the situation in Kargil to a full-scale conventional war."[36] Benazir Bhutto rejected Kargil-like plans in 1989 and then in 1996 as well, probably because she believed that the United States would force Pakistan to retreat.[37] The strategy, as presented to her, left a large role for Pakistani nuclear weapons. According to Kapur, Bhutto claimed that "the logic was that if we scrambled up high enough . . . we could force India to withdraw. To dislodge us [the Indians] would have to resort to conventional war." She claimed that "our nuclear capability [gave] the military confidence that India cannot wage a conventional war against Pakistan."[38]

Jalil Jilani claimed to Kapur that nuclear weapons "deterred India" and ensured that there would be "no major war" between India and Pakistan.[39] The Waltzian model cannot explain evidence that nuclear weapons emboldened Musharraf to authorize an assertive foreign policy at Kargil. Rather, Pakistani sponsorship of the Kashmir insurgency was nuclear assertion. If Pakistani nuclear weapons did not cause the 1999 Kargil intrusion, it is not clear why the Kashmir insurgency did not intensify before 1990 and Sharif and Bhutto did not authorize the Kargil plan much earlier.

Escalation patterns in the 1965 and 1971 wars also suggest that nuclear weapons exerted a strong influence on the Kargil War. If Pakistani nuclear weapons did not cause the Pakistani intrusion at Kargil, perhaps the Kargil War should have exhibited escalation similar to other wars fought between India and Pakistan prior to their development of nuclear weapons. Variation in escalation in the 1965, 1971, and 1999 wars, however, suggests that Indian and Pakistani nuclear weapons strongly influenced the latter. In 1965 and 1971 India and Pakistan quickly escalated the fighting and opened second fronts. In the 1965 Kashmir War the Indian Air Force (IAF) attacked targets well inside Pakistani territory, and Indian strike corps employed all available weapons systems to attack and seize Pakistani territory over a wide front.[40] The Indian Navy also attacked Pakistani ports and forced a partial blockade from the sea. Pakistanis shelled Indian positions and captured a village fourteen miles within India-controlled Kashmir. After Indian forces reached Lahore, Pakistan introduced seventy tanks and two infantry divisions. For the remainder of the war both sides made extensive use of air operations in support of their ground forces over enemy territory.[41] The Kargil war did not exhibit such escalation.

In the 1971 war Pakistan, unable to deal with the growing strength of the insurgents within East Pakistan and frustrated with their continuing Indian support, launched an air strike at India's northern military bases. The IAF retaliated with its own air strike and quickly established air superiority. The Indian Navy bombarded Pakistan's key port at Karachi, and an Indian air-and-ground offensive made a small intrusion into Pakistan.[42]

The United States did little to influence the outcome of the 1965 war. President Johnson, consumed with US actions in Vietnam, expressed little interest. The United States deployed two ships from the Middle East to Karachi while the US Air Force evacuated all Westerners from West Pakistan. The war was resolved when Leonid Brezhnev brokered the Tashkent cease-fire agreement in January 1966.

During the 1971 war the United States sent the USS *Enterprise* carrier battle group and an amphibious-ready group to the Indian Ocean on behalf of Pakistan. But India had declared a cease-fire and the war ended by the time the deployment arrived. Washington intervened much more quickly in the 1986 and 1990 crises in order to maintain the status quo and prevent escalation.[43]

President Clinton was greatly concerned with nuclear escalation at Kargil. According to aide Bruce Riedel, the president and his colleagues were alarmed from the outset because of its potential for nuclear escalation: "We could all too easily imagine the two parties beginning to mobilize for war, seeking third party support (Pakistan from China and the Arabs, India from Russia and Israel) and a deadly descent into full scale conflict all along the border with a danger of nuclear cataclysm."[44] To this end Clinton hosted Sharif and the Indian foreign minister in an effort to de-escalate and resolve the conflict. Some US and Indian officials have claimed that the Pakistani military took steps to alert its nuclear forces during the Kargil conflict, although this remains unclear.[45] The evidence that Pakistani leaders were emboldened by their new nuclear capability to authorize an assertive foreign policy at Kargil and to sponsor the Kashmir insurgency and penetrate deeply inside the LoC at Kargil in 1999 falsifies the Waltzian learning model. Lavoy and his coauthors are surely correct that operational incentives, honor, and retribution all influenced Pakistani policy at Kargil. But if Pakistani nuclear weapons did not, they need to explain why Bhutto and Sharif did not authorize assertion sooner, once India had successfully dislodged Pakistani troops from the Siachen Glacier in 1984.

The rational-signaling model would expect Pakistan to have authorized an assertive foreign policy to display its resolve to revise Kashmir and also that a costly signal by India would have caused a restrained Pakistani policy in response. It can therefore explain Pakistani policy at Kargil but cannot explain Pakistani persistence with nuclear assertion after India's costly signal during the Kargil War.

After discovering the Kargil incursion, Vajpayee unequivocally displayed his resolve to not make concessions on Kashmir through an intensive and costly ground and aerial military offensive. The operation led to the deaths of over five hundred Indian troops because Indian forces, unlike in earlier conflicts, refrained from occupying Pakistani territory. The intense peak-to-peak effort was much more time consuming and costly than an offensive into Pakistani territory would have been. In a typical public address delivered during the conflict, Indian foreign minister Jaswant Singh proclaimed to the public that India would not consider negotiations over Kashmir before Pakistan restored the status quo: "No solution is possible until Pakistan first agrees to restore the status quo ante."[46] Vajpayee stood firm on his demand to Sharif, transmitted through President Clinton, that Pakistan unconditionally withdraw from Kargil. According to Riedel, "There was no give in."[47] Moreover, the Indian leader intimated that Pakistan's possession of nuclear weapons would not prevent Delhi from defending itself from future Pakistani revisionism. Defense Minister George Fernandes proclaimed in January 2000 that nuclear weapons "can deter only the use of nuclear weapons, but not all and in any war. Indian forces can fight and win a limited war at a time and place chosen by the aggressor."[48]

The rational-signaling model would expect Musharraf to have authorized a restrained foreign policy after the Kargil War. India had decisively prevented Pakistan from revising Kashmir in 1948, 1965, and 1999; in the latter, its formal position was that negotiations could begin only after Pakistan had restored the status quo. Delhi's resolve to defend the status quo from a Pakistani challenge was clearly demonstrated in the Kargil War, when Indian forces took heavy casualties and did not open second fronts. Although India's greater military power was spread between the eastern (China) and western (Pakistan) fronts, Pakistan was able to retain revisions to the status quo for at most a few weeks. Nuclear weapons would not allow any Pakistani leader to overcome these challenges, and Musharraf should have rationally learned that any plan involving nuclear weapons and an assertive foreign policy would not yield his desired Kashmir objectives.

The signal of Delhi's resolve to stay the course in Kashmir, however, seems to have had little effect on the Pakistani leader. The years 2000, 2001, and 2002 witnessed the greatest number of fatalities in the Kashmir insurgency. While the number of incidents was a slight decrease from mid-1990s levels, the number of resulting fatalities increased significantly. The yearly number of fatalities, already almost 2,000 by 1992 and 2,500 by 1999, exceeded 3,000 in 2000 and peaked at 4,500 in 2001. It is unclear how much of this was sponsored by Musharraf, but evidence suggests that a good deal was. While Musharraf stated in his autobiography that by January 2001 he believed the time had come to "turn over a new leaf with India and find a non-military solution to their remaining problems," the solution still rested on his conviction that sponsoring Islamic insurgents in Kashmir had only increased the probability of realizing his Kashmir ambitions by compelling Vajpayee to negotiate at the Agra summit.[49]

When Musharraf was asked in June 2001 if he would reduce Pakistani support for militancy in Kashmir, he replied that "the time has not yet come."[50] Musharraf admitted that once India had agreed to negotiate, sponsoring the Kashmiri insurgency temporarily became less imperative.[51] Shortly after the Kargil War, however, Ashley Tellis and his colleagues concluded that while Musharraf probably learned that intrusions like Kargil would not sustain revisions to the status quo, Musharraf also likely continued to believe that sponsoring the insurgency might still help him realize his Kashmir objectives.[52] The rational-signaling model cannot explain why Musharraf persisted with an assertive foreign policy after Vajpayee's costly signal of India's resolve to defend the Kashmir status quo.

The ALF model would expect Musharraf to have authorized an assertive policy in Kashmir in the 1990s and then persisted with nuclear assertion after the Kargil War because the costly signal by India did not cause him to experience fear of imminent nuclear war. Musharraf and his associates were emboldened to challenge the status quo at Kargil but not earlier, at least partly because they believed that India's cognitively accessible isolation after its nuclear test would lead Washington to allow Pakistan to maintain their gains from the intrusion.

The 1998 nuclear tests isolated India and brought renewed international attention to the Kashmir dispute. As Clinton offered Sharif many incentives to not reciprocate, the Pakistani tests were widely viewed as a defensive response to Indian belligerence. Washington's long Cold War estrangement with Delhi and intense US pressure on and condemnation of it in relation to its nuclear tests probably caused Pakistan to believe that gains at Kargil could be used as a bargaining chip to resolve the dispute bilaterally. Tellis and colleagues conclude that Musharraf seems to have learned that the United States might allow him to maintain any gains in the Siachen Range and that the Kargil intrusion would pressure India to engage in a Kashmir dialogue.[53] Christine Fair reports that to most of her Pakistani interviewees, India's isolation after the 1998 nuclear test loomed large in Pakistani strategy at Kargil.[54]

The desire of Pakistan to enlist international sympathy in order to sustain revisions to Kashmir (which it was unable to generate independently) was a main theme of the Indian government's formal review of the war.[55] According to Feroz Hassan Khan, Kargil planners believed that because Indian forces were overstretched following a decade of dealing with the Kashmir insurgency, the international community would benignly view the episode as standard LoC activity rather than as an act to force India to withdraw.[56] The overestimation of the effectiveness of the Kargil plan in revising the undesirable status quo—based on an exclusive but errant focus on India's behavior in the insurgency and on Delhi's isolation after the nuclear tests, as well as the overall neglect of other episodes of nuclear assertion—is precisely the sort of pathology of availability that the ALF model expects.

Indian military operations during the Kargil War were confined to a defense of the status quo; Vajpayee would not authorize Indian forces to enter Pakistani territory. Despite pressure from the army, and despite the high escalation incentives that would have saved many Indian soldiers' lives, the prime minister did not allow the conflict to escalate.[57] Air force jets, for example, were ordered to refrain from entering Pakistani airspace and had to attack targets in Pakistani Kashmir from the Indian side, which significantly complicated the operation.[58] It is therefore not surprising that Musharraf also did not reach the nuclear brink and continued to authorize an assertive foreign policy. He contrasted his belief that the Kargil War was "controlled and localized" with his belief that the ten-month crisis in 2001–2 exhibited a greater danger of nuclear escalation.[59]

The 2001–2002 Crisis

On December 13, 2001, militants attacked the Indian Parliament building in New Delhi. No politicians were killed, but several security personnel lost their lives and the episode, occurring two months after the 9/11 attacks in the United States, caused great concern about Pakistani revisionism in India.[60] It is unclear if Musharraf authorized or was aware of planning for the attack, but he had certainly long nurtured the group that carried out the operation. In response, India mobilized almost eight hundred thousand troops along the LoC and international border and engaged in its own coercive diplomacy. As Paul Kapur has noted, Delhi "demanded that Pakistan surrender twenty criminals, renounce terrorism and shut down terrorist training camps based in Pakistan and stop the flow of militant infiltration into Jammu and Kashmir."[61]

Consistent with the ALF model, Atal Vajpayee and his associates appear to have learned much more about nuclear weapons and foreign policy from the Kargil War than the historical record (see chapter 5). Army chief Malik has since noted that "Kargil showed the way. If Pakistan could do Kargil, India could do something similar."[62] The Indian leader planned to respond to Pakistani defiance with a strike on terrorist training camps in Pakistan and through the seizure of some of Pakistan-controlled Kashmir. However, Pakistan responded with a mobilization of its own before Indian troops had reached their forward positions, resulting in over one million troops being mobilized across the LoC and international border.

According to the most authoritative study on Indian policy during the crisis, within five days of the Parliament attack Prime Minister Vajpayee apparently called the army, air force, and navy chiefs and told them to prepare for war.[63] During the December-January period of the crisis Indian forces were primarily directed at the regions of Jammu and Kashmir. They were mobilized to engage in multiple shallow offensives into Pakistan-held Kashmir to prevent Pakistani infiltration into India Kashmir while also preventing Pakistan from opening second fronts to expand the war by mobilizing along the border.[64]

During the night of January 5–6 some elements of India's 2 Corps, poised opposite the Rajasthan sector, moved closer to the border. After Indian political leaders learned of the advance—apparently through US intelligence sources—the corps commander was immediately replaced by the army training command chief of staff.[65] Throughout this period US secretary of state Colin Powell and his deputy, Richard Armitage, engaged in shuttle diplomacy, communicating commitments from Musharraf to Vajpayee in the hope of reining in sponsorship of terrorism. In January Musharraf publically pledged to stop the bloodshed in Kashmir.

Several months later, on May 14, 2002, militants killed thirty-two people—mostly women and civilians—at an Indian Army camp at

Kaluchak in Jammu. In response, India's strike corps was deployed to a highly offensive formation in the Rajasthan sector. Throughout the earlier period of the crisis, India's 1 Corps had countered Pakistan's 1 Corps in the northern region, while India's 2 and 21 Corps moved to engage Pakistan's 2 Corps further south in Rajasthan.[66] Following the Jammu attack, the 1 Corps, which had traditionally filled a role in Kashmir, relocated to Rajasthan.

The Indian Army had now left Jammu and Kashmir vulnerable, but for the first time positioned its three offensive strike corps in the strategically vulnerable Thar desert. Rather than seeking multiple shallow intrusions into Pakistani Kashmir in order to contain infiltration into Indian Kashmir, the Indian Army was poised to cross the border into Pakistani territory. Pakistan's core military offensive force, the 2 Strike Corps, could have been quickly destroyed by the much larger Indian force prepared to capture territory in the Thar, which could have led to the seizure of the Sindh and Punjab provinces as well. This potential to slice Pakistan in two would have surfaced horrible memories of Pakistan's losses in the 1971 war. On May 23 the Indian prime minister visited troops near the LoC and told them that "the time has come for decisive battle."[67] According to Brajesh Mishra, India "almost went" in May.[68] India's air force and army mobilized for war and its navy moved five Eastern Fleet warships into the Arabian Sea toward Pakistan.[69]

Vajpayee ultimately decided not to strike Pakistan, however. The crisis atmosphere had ended by early June, and around this time Musharraf made a commitment to Armitage to end infiltration permanently.[70] By October Indian and Pakistani troops began to demobilize from the international border and LoC. Fatalities in Kashmir reached 3,000 in 2002 but decreased thereafter: in 2004 there were 2,000, which dropped to 540 by 2008 and by 2012 reached the 1989 level of approximately 100. Proliferation pessimists such as Paul Kapur have argued that this was caused by US pressure on the Pakistani government following 9/11 to rein in the insurgent groups that it had long sponsored.

The assassination attempts on Musharraf following his outlawing of the groups indeed caused the government to take further measures against the insurgents. But this argument suffers from several problems. The assumption that Presidents Bush and Obama successfully coerced Pakistani leaders to refrain from sponsoring the insurgency flies in the face of the long history of the US's failure to distance Pakistan from the insurgent groups in Kashmir and Afghanistan. There are few reasons to presume that US coercive diplomacy then worked after 2002.[71] After all, Washington's need for Pakistani territory to support the effort in Afghanistan left Pakistan with countercoercion capability. Moreover, if the US presence in Afghanistan was able to make coercive threats against Pakistan credible, this credibility should have eroded with Washington's drawing down from the region and caused sponsorship of the insurgency and Kashmir fatalities to increase. But Kashmir fatalities have never approached the peak number of fatalities in 2001.

Another explanation for the decline in Kashmir fatalities after 2002 would be the ALF model's prediction that Vajpayee's assertive riposte to Pakistani revisionism caused Musharraf to reach the nuclear brink. Two days after the Kaluchak attacks on May 16, Musharraf put his forces in the north of Pakistan on high alert (even though India's 1 Strike Corps had moved south).[72] Pakistan tested three short- and medium-range missiles on May 25, 26, and 28 to pressure the Indian leader to stop his apparently imminent invasion. As India deployed its short-range nuclear-capable ballistic missiles close to the border, Pakistan reciprocated and sent many signals to Delhi that any invasion of Pakistan would warrant a Pakistani nuclear response.[73]

During a May 28 televised address to the nation Musharraf offered no new steps to combat extremism, openly supported the "liberation struggle" in Kashmir, and claimed that "we'll shed our last drop of blood" if Indian forces entered Pakistan.[74] On May 30 he told Pakistani fighter pilots "to take the war into India" if India launched its threatened attack.[75] The United States and many other nations issued an evacuation advisory to citizens in India and Pakistan during the May crisis but had not done so during the January one. Unlike in January, the Indian armed forces were prepared and determined to launch major offensives in the desert sector in June on an unprecedented scale. In a *Time* magazine interview on January 14, shortly after the first height of the crisis, Musharraf claimed that "I never feel scared."[76] Between May 30 and June 1, 2002, however, Musharraf "hardly slept for several nights" and "feared nuclear war."[77] Musharraf's three missile tests and belligerent rhetoric had not caused the Indian Army, poised in a deeply offensive posture and ready to slice Pakistan in two for the second time in three decades, to stand down. Musharraf knew that any Indian invasion would have quickly triggered Pakistani nuclear escalation. By the end of May, Musharraf worried that nuclear war would engulf his country.

In the absence of archival records, the public speeches of Pervez Musharraf offer the clearest view of the evolution of his beliefs about the dilemma of nuclear assertion and the opportunities and dangers presented by nuclear weapons. Between the October 13, 1999, military coup and December 2004 he delivered over one hundred speeches, lectures, and public interviews—about one every three weeks—to Pakistani, Indian, and international audiences. The approximately thirty-month periods before and after May 30, 2002, exhibit striking differences in his attention to the dangers of nuclear escalation. His reference to the importance of the Kashmir dispute to Pakistan, its peaceful resolution, and the high resolve of the Pakistani armed forces to defend Pakistani territorial sovereignty are constant throughout. But following the May nuclear crisis he spoke many times of how close India and Pakistan had come to nuclear war that month, of how the perils of provocative policies could cause miscalculations and nuclear escalation, and the importance of shared understandings between leaders to moderate these dangers. These claims are consistent throughout speeches and interviews delivered to Pakistani, South Asian, US, and international audiences and were not forthcoming after the December 2001 crisis.

The forty-three speeches delivered between October 13, 1999, and May 14, 2002, contain very few references to the dangers of nuclear escalation. During this period Musharraf made six mostly vague references to the dangers of nuclear escalation. In the nearly three years between late May 2002 and December 2004 he made about twenty explicit references to nuclear escalation. Over three-fourths of Musharraf's public references to the dangers of nuclear escalation in the first five years of his presidency were made in the months after the late May crisis. These statements addressed the mechanisms of nuclear escalation in much more detail than the sketchy references to nuclear danger made before May 2002. Musharraf also more frequently claimed after May 2002 that military power was less important to realizing Pakistan's foreign policies than diplomacy and confidence-building measures. This variation in foreign policy preferences is precisely what the ALF model expects of a leader who has experienced fear of imminent nuclear war.

Pakistani and Indian forces were mobilized on the LoC for the first ten months of 2002. However, despite India's mobilization and coercive demands after the December 2001 attacks on Parliament, Musharraf made very few references to the danger of nuclear escalation before the end of May. He claimed in January and February 2002 that the standoff could be "very dangerous" and that "this is brinksmanship at its most dangerous."[78] He made many more references to the dangers of nuclear escalation at the end of May. On May 25 Musharraf told the *Washington Post* that "the situation is certainly tense and serious."[79] In his May 27 presidential address to Pakistan he claimed: "Pakistan is currently passing through a critical juncture. We are faced with a grave situation and we are standing at the cross road of history. Today's decision will have serious internal and external effects on our future. . . . Tension is at its height. The danger of war is not yet over . . . all these allegations with aggressive overtones increases the heat of war and creates war hysteria."[80] These remarks cannot be solely attributed to US and Indian pressure on Pakistan to rein in insurgent sponsorship, because the insurgency had been a constant since long before then. Musharraf's first public presentation following the May 30 crisis—a CNN interview on June 1—was his first articulation of a more-detailed argument for caution in the face of nuclear danger. He made several remarks about the strength and resolve of Pakistan's armed forces, but also, for the first time, integrated these claims with several references to the dangers of miscalculation and nuclear escalation: "Any sane individual cannot even think of going into this unconventional mode, whatever the pressures . . . if we make our minds that we cannot go to war, war is an expensive hobby for both sides . . . leadership on both sides must realize that this is a very dangerous situation. There should be no miscalculation on either side. And I would hope that I don't miscalculate."[81]

At the first Conference on Interaction and Confidence-Building Measures in Asia held in Kazakhstan two days later, Musharraf outlined the contours of a new foreign policy: "Tension along our borders with India and the Line of Control is high, stirring deep fears in South Asia and around the world over the real possibility of a conflict. We do not want war . . . the path of dialogue and negotiations is the only sane option in the dangerous environment of South Asia."[82] He described the May crisis as "very close" and "extremely tense because there were war clouds."[83] By August 14, in another presidential address to Pakistan, he repeated that "provocative rhetoric and war hysteria serve no purpose; instead they lead to inflexibility, confrontation and only complicate issues."[84] Very few of his speeches before May 2002 contain such explicit reference to the dangers of advertent or inadvertent nuclear escalation.

In September of that year Musharraf told a Harvard audience that "there is grave risk, yet nothing to be gained from military brinkmanship."[85] Fourteen months earlier he had equated nuclear power with "military muscle."[86] In January 2002 Musharraf typically claimed that "we are a powerful nation of 140 million people. We are militarily very strong."[87] But by September 2002 he proclaimed that nuclear weapons are "primarily designed to deter aggression."[88] He advised the United Nations General Assembly the next day that "peace in South Asia is hostage to one accident, one act of terrorism, one strategic miscalculation.[89]

Musharraf also spoke of nuclear dangers after Indian and Pakistani troops withdrew from the LoC in October 2002. Commemorating the one-year anniversary of the crisis in June 2003, he told an Indian interviewer that "Pakistan and India cannot go to war, must not go to war."[90] Nine days later he told the *Washington Post* that "two hundred percent, there won't be war" because of "the understanding of the leaders. We've fought three wars and we know the hazards of war."[91] Musharraf made no such assurances after the Kargil War and the December 2001 Parliament attacks. He told the *London Times* that "When a war starts [you don't know] what direction it will take because there are a lot of intangibles which then come in the way."[92] He claimed in an interview in *India Today* in 2004 that "The strategy of military coercion with numbers is inapplicable when an adversary, albeit weaker, is prepared to accept losses and inflict maximum retaliatory damage, which may be untenable to the other side."[93] He proclaimed to the United Nations General Assembly in 2005 that "The catastrophic consequences of a nuclear war make it imperative to prevent one from ever taking place."[94]

Musharraf's references to the limits of military power increased after May 2002. In 2006, at the National Security Workshop held at the National Defence University in Islamabad, he told one audience that "national security is not the domain of the military alone, it involves all the elements of national power . . . diplomacy is the first line of defence."[95]

And he told a Cornell University audience in September 2006 that "the military cannot deliver peace; the ultimate solution has to come through different means."[96] Such a foreign policy formulation was absent from his thinking before he had reached the nuclear brink. In short, Musharraf's many references to the dangers of nuclear escalation after May 2002, though he rarely made reference to it before then, corroborates the interview evidence that he experienced fear of imminent nuclear war at the end of May 2002.

P. R. Chari, Pervez Cheema, and Stephen Cohen's index of major US, Indian, and Pakistani English-language newspaper coverage during the years of the South Asian crisis suggests that Musharraf experienced fear of imminent nuclear war at the end of May 2002.[97] The crisis captured much more Pakistani than Indian or American attention. Pakistani newspaper coverage of the crisis during the last week of May was about eight times greater than Pakistani coverage in December 2001 when the Indian Parliament was attacked. Indian coverage at the end of May 2002 was about half that of Pakistan's and roughly equal to Indian coverage of the first height of the crisis. Coverage in the United States during these periods was still smaller: between one-half and one-fourth that of India. Pakistani coverage during the last week of May 2002 was about three-fourths of Pakistani coverage of the Kargil War between mid June and mid July 1999, when the Indian Army began assaults on Pakistani positions, killed hundreds of Pakistani troops, and recaptured occupied territory.[98] The fact that Pakistani coverage in May 2002 was almost as much as when hundreds of Pakistani troops were being killed in Kashmir during the first Indo-Pakistani war in almost three decades suggests that the May crisis also captured much more national attention than the December-January phase of the crisis.

Musharraf's experience of fear of imminent nuclear war surely caused him to authorize a restrained foreign policy in Kashmir. An estimation of Pakistani sponsorship of the Kashmir insurgency after 2002 based on Kashmir fatality data is complicated by the fact that several attacks were directed against the Pakistani government itself. But the fact is, violence and fatalities in Kashmir steadily declined from 2002. By 2009 the number of fatalities was 375, only a third of the 1990 level. The ALF model explains why Musharraf authorized an assertive foreign policy after

Kargil and 2001 but substantially toned down his revisionism in Kashmir after experiencing fear of imminent nuclear war in May 2002. His time at the nuclear brink was likely necessary for him to turn from assertive threats and pursue his revisionist goals in Kashmir through confidence-building measures and diplomacy instead. US pressure on Musharraf after the September 11 attacks may also have made a cessation of Kashmir fatalities after 2001 overdetermined, but if this argument is correct, fatalities in Kashmir should have increased as the United States left Afghanistan. It is likely that Musharraf's experience of fear would have moderated Pakistani assertion in Kashmir absent US pressure.

By 2003 October, Musharraf conditionally accepted India's twelve confidence-building measures and added an additional one.[99] One month later a formal cease-fire was announced. The following June Pakistani foreign secretaries met with their Indian counterparts to discuss the Kashmir dispute, and by October Musharraf released his "three points" as the basis for resolving the Kashmir dispute; he dropped both his demand for a plebiscite in Kashmir and his insistence that progress on Kashmir was necessary for Pakistani cooperation on other issues.

After India reciprocated with a counterproposal in November, Musharraf continued to use talks at the prime minister, foreign minister, and foreign secretary levels to pursue his Kashmir objectives throughout 2007. This was a stark change from the nuclear assertion of five years earlier. Musharraf indeed authorized a paradigm shift in his approach to Kashmir: Pakistani representatives met with their Indian counterparts in hotel rooms in Bangkok, Dubai, and London to establish a "deniable but detailed" Kashmir deal.[100] Khurshid Kasuri, Pakistani former foreign minister, recalled by early 2007 that the talks had become "so advanced that we'd come to semicolons."[101] Though these agreements picked up where earlier negotiations a decade earlier had left off, they indicate a fundamentally different strategy to achieve the same Pakistani goals in Kashmir from what Musharraf had authorized between 1999 and 2002. It is unlikely that US threats caused him to change course. As one scholar has noted, "nuclear learning" caused the Pakistani leader to take steps to defuse military crises and resolve the Kashmir dispute through dialogue.[102]

The 2008 Mumbai Attacks and Alternative Explanations

One might argue that the 2008 Mumbai attacks, which came long after Musharraf experienced fear, falsify the ALF model because they were sponsored by the Pakistani Army and led to an Indo-Pakistani crisis. They occurred shortly after Ashfaq Kayani had succeeded Musharraf as army general and Musharraf had fled Pakistan. It is not clear if Kayani experienced fear of imminent nuclear war in May 2002. But it also is not clear that Lashkar-e-Taiba, the group responsible for the attacks, had the support of the army or the ISI. Those responsible for training and recruiting the attackers appear to have been retired ISI and army officials.[103] It is likely that the original government-sponsored plan for the attack was for a much smaller operation but was then undermined by Lakshar such that the army and ISI lost operational control of it.[104]

The resulting Indo-Pakistani crisis was much less dangerous than the one in 2001–2. The earlier crisis witnessed military mobilizations and public statements of resolve by Indian and Pakistani leaders; the 2008 crisis did not. Rather, India's prime minister, Manmohan Singh, privately requested that Pakistan's prime minister, Yousuf Raza Gilani, send the head of the ISI, Shuja Pasha, to Delhi. Gilani seems to have agreed, but Pasha declined and sent a representative instead. Singh made a vague public statement that "We will take up strongly with our neighbors that the use of their territory for launching attacks on us will not be tolerated, and that there would be a cost if suitable measures are not taken by them."[105]

Singh subsequently demanded that Pakistan hand over suspected terrorists and take strong action against militant groups alleged to be involved but did little after Pakistan did not comply.[106] Thus an Indian defense analyst compared the 2001–2 crisis with the aftermath of the 2008 attacks and concluded that "no such tension exists now."[107] Much of the crisis atmosphere in 2008 arose when one of the organizers of the attacks called Pakistani president Asif Zardari and Army General Kayani from prison. He claimed to be India's minister of external affairs and threatened them with an imminent military response.[108] It is likely that one of the motives for the Lakshar attacks was to stall progress in Indo-Pakistani peace talks.[109]

Many scholars have pointed toward Pakistan's nuclear doctrine as evidence of an aggressive or coercive posture or policy that increases the probability of Indo-Pakistani conflict.[110] Vipin Narang has shown that since 1998, Pakistan has had an "asymmetric escalation" posture that attempts to deter not only nuclear but conventional conflict by threatening strategic or tactical nuclear first-use.[111] According to Narang, this posture is "the most aggressive option available to nuclear states: it involves fielding both tactical and strategic capabilities that can be mobilized and launched quickly, often through pre-delegated authority in the event of conventional conflict."[112] Pakistan is also substantially beefing up its nuclear arsenal with two new plutonium reactors soon to be built, as well as more nuclear weapons fuel and new delivery systems. Its nuclear weapons stockpile could reach 150–200 warheads by 2020.[113]

This alarmism, however, misses a key point. Asymmetric escalation postures can be used to support both assertive and restrained foreign policies. Pakistan's nuclear posture is designed to deter both conventional aggression against Pakistan and retaliation against Pakistani aggression. While it is designed to deter Indian retaliation to Pakistani sponsorship of terrorism, it is also designed to deter Indian aggression in the aftermath of attacks by terrorist groups that Pakistan no longer controls.[114] Thus, while Pakistan has had an asymmetric escalation doctrine since 1998, it was used to support an assertive foreign policy through 2002 and a restrained one thereafter. Pakistan's reliance on nuclear weapons is growing, but it may well be for deterrence rather than assertion. One recent analysis concludes that Pakistan is concerned, "above all with countering India's growing superiority in conventional weaponry, deterring punitive or disarming conventional strikes by India, and preventing defeat if a major war were to occur . . . a key objective of Pakistan's nuclear program is to deter India from retaliating in the event of another major terrorist attack traced back to Pakistan."[115]

Is Pakistan's foreign policy since 1990 best explained by its strategic culture? Fair has argued that it lies at the root of Pakistani revisionism. The Pakistani Army, having long called all major foreign policy shots, perceives an existential threat from conventionally superior and nuclear-armed India. But strategic culture alone does not explain key variation in Pakistan's foreign policy and nuclear strategy choices. Narang argues that if strategic culture is the unmoved mover, Pakistan should have authorized an asymmetric escalation posture much earlier than 1998.[116] Ever threatened by India and unable to continue for more than a few weeks in any conflict with Delhi, Pakistan should have, according to a strategic culture argument, developed and operationalized tactical nuclear weapons into its conventional doctrine and posture in order to deter conventional aggression at the outset of its nuclear journey. In the realm of foreign policy, a strategic-culture argument would not expect Pakistani assertion in Kashmir to taper off after 2001 when Pakistani ambitions in that disputed territory remained unrealized and US interests in Afghanistan had begun to wind down. As Fair has argued, the Pakistan Army's strategic culture commits the nation to eternally take the fight to India as the defeats pile up and the political and economic costs accumulate. A strategic-culture argument would expect a fully fledged revisionist stance by Pakistan and cannot come to terms with its restrained foreign policy actions in Kashmir after 2003, especially after such persistent nuclear assertion in the previous decade. The ALF model is necessary to explain this variation.

Has Pakistani foreign policy been caused by civil-military or even military-military tensions? The Pakistani military has a long history of strongly influencing Pakistani foreign policy toward India.[117] The 1999 intrusion into the Kargil sector of Kashmir, however, was likely planned and controlled by General Musharraf. Only three other members of the military were informed of the logistical details of the operation.[118] Prime Minister Sharif seems to have signed off on the plan even though he remained unaware of its operational and tactical details.[119] Sharif's order to retreat from Kargil once the identity of the troops became known only exacerbated civil-military tensions and was followed months later by a military coup.

Summary

Table 4.2 summarizes the different learning models' ability to explain how Pakistani leaders have come to terms with the fundamental dilemma of nuclear coercion and foreign policy. The Waltzian model would expect Pakistani leaders to learn that nuclear assertion rarely works and thus to authorize a restrained foreign policy. It cannot explain the evidence,

Table 4.2. Nuclear Learning Models: Pakistan, 1998–2003

	Waltzian	Rational-Signaling	ALF Two-Stage
Assertion in 1990s Kashmir insurgency	✗	✓	✓
Assertion in 1999 Kargil War	✗	✓	✓
Assertion in 2001–2002 crisis	✗	✗	✓
Restrained foreign policy in Kashmir, 2003–	✓	✓	✓

which shows that Musharraf was emboldened by Pakistan's new nuclear capability and sponsored the Kashmir insurgency and infiltration deep into the Kargil sector of Kashmir in 1999. The rational-signaling model can explain Pakistani assertion through the 1990s but cannot explain its persistence after India's costly signal of resolve to stand its ground in Kashmir in 1999. Nor can it explain the evidence that Musharraf authorized nuclear assertion through 2001 and the first half of 2002. The ALF model, however, can explain why Musharraf authorized a restrained foreign policy in Kashmir once he experienced fear of imminent nuclear war in May 2002. All three learning models can explain Musharraf's eventual authorization of a restrained foreign policy in Kashmir in 2003 but cannot explain why it took several years, a costly Kashmir insurgency, a war, and a nuclear crisis to get there.

The ALF model resolves three puzzles associated with Pakistan's experience as a new nuclear power. It explains why the 1990–2002 period exhibited much more danger than the post-2003 period: Musharraf's experience of fear of imminent nuclear war. This experience, caused by Vajpayee's offensive deployment in May 2002, led him to abandon the nuclear assertion that had been the foundation of Pakistani policy in Kashmir since it developed nuclear weapons. Indian costly signals were unable to effect this change in strategy. Musharraf's experience of fear of imminent nuclear war also explains why he pushed so hard to revise the Kashmir status quo through the use of force but then tacitly accepted it in 2003 when the situation remained inherently unfavorable.

The ALF model also explains why Musharraf seems to have learned so little about the trade-offs associated with the fundamental issues of nuclear assertion from the Cold War. Despite the high incentives for Musharraf to have learned from Khrushchev's experience, those events would not have been cognitively accessible to the Pakistani leader. Despite high incentives and presumably the resources needed to authorize a relevant study, Musharraf instead learned only from his own cognitively accessible successes with Pakistani nuclear weapons. The dangerous pathologies of availability had a similar effect in both the USSR and Pakistan cases.

Musharraf's interview admissions and the striking variation in his public speeches and newspaper reports strongly suggest that Musharraf reached the nuclear brink in May 2002 and that this caused Pakistani revisionism in Kashmir to subsequently taper off. India's costly signal at Kargil was insufficient to deter Pakistani assertion. As his many public speeches suggest, Musharraf appears to have developed a much more sophisticated understanding of the dangers associated with nuclear assertion after late May 2002. Leaders do not stay in power forever, and the fact that the Mumbai attacks occurred barely three months after he left office beg the question of what his successor, Army general Ashfaq Kayani, learned from the crisis. But as of early 2017 neither Kayani nor his successor, Raheel Sharif, have overseen assertiveness in Kashmir that even approximates what Musharraf and his predecessors orchestrated in the 1990s and the early 2000s. The Mumbai attacks were not as brazen as the December 2001 or May 2002 attacks that targeted Indian politicians and family members of the armed forces, and they did not pose the same nuclear escalation risk. The Pakistani Army and ISI no doubt maintain allegiance to a swathe of insurgent groups despite the threat they pose to Pakistan. But the fact is, Pakistani foreign policy in Kashmir has been much less assertive since 2003.

The Indo-Pakistani dyad differs from that of the Cold War superpowers in many ways. Pakistan developed a much less sophisticated command-and-control system and a smaller and less-diversified nuclear arsenal. US leaders attempted to deter Soviet challenges on the allies as well as on the mainland: with the possible exception of Afghanistan today, India has not attempted to defend its allies from Pakistani challenges. Unlike the superpower relationship, the revisionist power in South Asia has sponsored insurgent groups in their attacks on military and civilian targets inside India.

India and Pakistan are territorially contiguous and exhibit a historical animosity that predates either's development of nuclear weapons. Yet the

Soviet and Pakistani experiences with nuclear weapons in 1959–1962 and 1999–2002 have much in common. Leaders in both states desired changes to a central tenet of the status quo but lacked conventional military power to sustain such revisions over the long run. In both cases the dangers and opportunities that nuclear weapons presented arose from the choices that leaders made when confronting the fundamental nuclear assertion dilemma. Khrushchev claimed in his memoirs that "anyone dealing with rocket technology for the first time was just as ignorant."[120] Pakistan's experience with nuclear weapons, a full five decades into the nuclear age and long after the Cold War had ended, is strikingly similar. The powerful effects of availability and fear on the foreign policy of nuclear powers are not confined to the superpowers. Nuclear proliferation by Pakistan became dangerous when Pervez Musharraf learned that nuclear assertion is safe, but it became safe when he learned that it is dangerous.

Notes

1. Peter Popham, "'The World's Most Dangerous Place' Is Already at War," *The Independent* (Asia), March 18, 2000; and Clinton, *My Life*, 597. Also see Riedel, *American Diplomacy and the 1999 Kargil Summit*, 3–4; and Talbott, *Engaging India*, 157.

2. Nayak and Krepon, "U.S. Crisis Management," 23n50.

3. Ibid.

4. *Wall Street Journal*, April 6, 2010, 11.

5. Crail, Horner, and Kimball, "Pursuing the Prague Agenda."

6. Kapur, "Revisionist Ambitions" and "Ten Years of Instability"; Ganguly, "Nuclear Stability in South Asia."

7. Narang, *Nuclear Strategy in the Modern Era*, 1.

8. Jervis, "Kargil, Deterrence, and International Relations," 377.

9. Fair, *Fighting to the End*, 18.

10. Kapur and Ganguly, "The Jihad Paradox," 115–16; Jalal, *State of Martial Rule* and *Democracy and Authoritarianism*; Haqqani, *Pakistan*; and Shaikh, *Making Sense of Pakistan*.

11. Kapur and Ganguly, "Jihad Paradox."

12. Cohen, *India*, 212–13; Talbot, *Pakistan*, 114.

13. Ganguly, *Crisis in Kashmir*; Kapur, "India and Pakistan's Unstable Peace"; Cohen, *India*, 215; Talbot, *Pakistan*, 114; and Wirsing, *India, Pakistan, and the Kashmir Dispute*, 125.

14. Talbot, *Pakistan*, 113; Wirsing, *India, Pakistan, and the Kashmir Dispute*; and Cohen, *India*, 217, 220. For the argument that the sources of Indo-Pakistani conflict run much deeper than Kashmir, see Fair, *Fighting to the End*.

15. Ganguly, *Crisis in Kashmir*, 10.

16. K. J. M. Varma, "Pak Not Ready to Sideline Kashmir: Musharraf," *Press Trust of India*, June 17, 2003.

17. Celia W. Dugger and Thom Shanker, "India Sees Hope as Pakistan Halts Kashmir Militants," *New York Times*, June 9, 2002, 1.

18. Narang, *Nuclear Strategy in the Modern Era*.

19. Jones et al., *Tracking Nuclear Proliferation*, 132n140.

20. Perkovich, *India's Nuclear Bomb*, 293–97. However, also see Kampani, "New Delhi's Long Nuclear Journey.

21. Kapur, "Revisionist Ambitions," 195.

22. Ibid., 196.

23. Malik, "Lessons from Kargil," 197, 225.

24. Kargil Review Committee, *From Surprise to Reckoning*, 241.

25. Nawaz, *Crossed Swords*, 500–518; and Shah, *Army and Democracy*, 179–81.

26. Musharraf, *In the Line of Fire*.

27. "India Should Remember What Happened in East Pakistan: Musharraf," *Pakistan Today*, March 14, 2003. For a similar statement, see the interview of Musharraf by Neena Gopal, "LoC Is the Problem, Not the Solution," July 13, 2001, http://www.outlookindia.com/article.aspx?212597; and "Pervez Musharraf 'Crossed LoC before Kargil War,' V. K. Singh Praises Ex-Pak Army Chief's Courage," *Times of India*, February 1, 2013.

28. "Kargil Was Musharraf's Disaster: General Aziz," *Pakistan Today*, January 16, 2013.

29. Ansar Abbasi, "Kargil: The Gang of Four Kept Even GHQ out of Loop," *News International*, October 29, 2013, http://www.thenews.com.pk/Todays-News-13–26338-Kargil-The-Gang-of-Four-kept-even-GHQ-out-of-loop.

30. Raghavan, *Siachen*, 56; Chari, Cheema, and Cohen, *Four Crises and a Peace Process*, 21; and Qadir, "Analysis of the Kargil Conflict 1999."

31. Raghavan, *Siachen*, 92–93.

32. Press Trust of India, "When Benazir Opposed a Kargil-Type Operation," *Times of India*, June 25, 2015, http://timesofindia.indiatimes.com/india/When-Benazir-opposed-a-Kargil-typeoperation/articleshow/47815259.cms.

33. Ganguly and Hagerty, *Fearful Symmetry*, 153. India's defenses were particularly sparse because Vajpayee and his associates did not expect a Kargil-like challenge. Brajesh Mishra discussion with the author, New Delhi, April 2009.

34. Kapur, *Dangerous Deterrent*, 123n44.

35. Khan, Lavoy, and Clary, "Pakistan's Motivations and Calculations," 90.

36. Malik, *Kargil*, 272.

37. Khan, Lavoy, and Clary, "Pakistan's Motivations," 77–79; Raghavan, *Siachen*, 92–93; and Ganguly and Hagerty, *Fearful Symmetry*, 193.

38. Kapur, "Ten Years of Instability," 75–76.

39. Ibid., 76.

40. Raghavan, "Limited War," 88.

41. Ibid.

42. Ganguly and Hagerty, *Fearful Symmetry*, 28–32, 160; and Raghavan, "Limited War," 91.

43. Chari, Cheema, and Cohen, *Four Crises and a Peace Process*.

44. Riedel, *American Diplomacy*, 3–4.

45. Raj Chengappa, "Pakistan Tried Nuclear Blackmail," *Newspaper Today*, January 12, 2000.

46. "Pakistan Has to Stop Aggression: Indian FM," *Agence France Press*, June 1, 1999.

47. "Vajpayee Stood Firm during Kargil Conflict: Clinton Aide," *Times of India*, May 19, 2002.

48. C. Raja Mohan, "Fernandes Unveils 'Limited War' Doctrine," *Hindu*, January 25, 2000.

49. Musharraf, *In the Line of Fire*, 299; and Pervez Musharraf, discussion with the author, Seattle, March 14, 2010. The summit made no progress on Kashmir, and most of Vajpayee's cabinet committee on security advised the prime minister not to attend.

50. Musharraf , "Wrong Attitude."

51. Pervez Musharraf, discussion with the author, Seattle, March 14, 2010.

52. Tellis, Fair, and Medby, *Limited Conflicts*, 7, 30.

53. Ibid., 21; and "Kargil Was Musharraf's Disaster," *Pakistan Today*, January 16, 2013.

54. C. Christine Fair, discussion with the author, Seattle, September 1, 2011.

55. Kargil Review Committee, *From Surprise to Reckoning*, 236. This conclusion is strikingly similar to Israel's assessment of Sadat's motives for starting the 1973 war.

56. Khan, *Eating Grass*, 253, 257.

57. Kapur, "Ten Years of Instability," 77–80; and Brajesh Mishra, discussion with the author, New Delhi, April 2009.

58. Chari, Cheema, and Cohen, *Four Crises and a Peace Process*, 139.

59. Pervez Musharraf, discussion with the author, Seattle, March 14, 2010. Musharraf may have incentives to deny the fear he experienced at Kargil. However, he admitted to the fear of imminent nuclear war that he experienced during the ten-month crisis. Moreover, almost all other South Asian commentators agree that the Kargil War did not exhibit the danger of nuclear escalation that the ten-month crisis did.

60. For a more detailed treatment of this crisis, see Ganguly and Kraig, "2001–2002 Indo-Pakistani Crisis."

61. Kapur, "Ten Years of Instability."

62. Kapur, *Dangerous Deterrent*, 134.

63. Sood and Sawhney, *Operation Parakram*, 62.

64. Ibid., 73–83.

65. Ibid., 80.

66. Ibid., 81.

67. Rama Lakshmi and Rajiv Chandrasekaran, "Indian Leader Steps up War Rhetoric," *Washington Post*, May 23, 2002, A16.

68. Steve Coll, "The Stand-Off: How Jihadi Groups Helped Provoke the Twenty-First Century's First Nuclear Crisis," *New Yorker*, February 13, 2006.

69. Khan, *Eating Grass*, 281; and Josy Joseph, "The Mood Is for War," *India Abroad*, May 31, 2002.

70. Dugger and Shanker, "India Sees Hope."

71. For more-detailed studies of Pakistan's sponsorship of terrorism, see Kapur and Ganguly, "Jihad Paradox," Rashid, *Descent into Chaos*; Hussain, *Frontline Pakistan*; and Shaikh, *Making Sense of Pakistan*. For an assessment of coercive diplomacy, see Art, "Coercive Diplomacy"; and George and Simons, "Findings and Conclusions," 287.

72. Karl Vick and Kamran Khan, "Pakistan Puts Some Forces on High Alert as India Plans Reprisal," *Washington Post*, May 17, 2002.

73. Khan called these missile tests a new norm for signaling deterrence; see Khan, *Eating Grass*, 282; and Narang, *Nuclear Strategy in the Modern Era*, 275.

74. "Pakistan's Stark Warning," *Guardian* (London), May 28, 2002, 1.

75. David Williams, "Pakistan 'Will Take War to India,'" *Daily Mail* (London), May 30, 2002.

76. "Time Magazine Interviews Pervez Musharraf," *Time*, January 14, 2002.

77. Pervez Musharraf, discussion with the author, Seattle, March 14, 2010.

78. President of Pakistan General Pervez Musharraf's address to the Ulema and Mashaikh conference, Islamabad, January 18 2002 (Islamabad: Directorate General of Films and Publications, 2002); and B. Muralidhar Reddy, "Kashmir Cannot Be Sidestepped: Musharraf," *Hindu*, February 6, 2002, 1, http://www.hindu.com/2002/02/06/stories/2002020603020100.htm.

79. "President General Pervez Musharraf's Interview," *Washington Post*, May 25, 2002, at South Asia Terrorism Portal, http://www.satp.org/satporgtp /countries/pakistan/document/papers/Pervez_interview.htm.

80. President Pervez Musharraf, May 27, 2002 Presidential Address http:// www.satp.org/satporgtp/countries/pakistan/document/papers/Pervez _May272002.htm. For another reference by Musharraf to a "turning point" see Lally Weymouth, "Here's What I'll Do: The Pakistani President's Interview with Lally Weymouth," *The Washington Post*, June 23, 2002.

81. Tom Mintier's CNN interview with Musharraf, posted June 2, 2002, http://asia.cnn.com/2002/WORLD/asiapcf/south/06/01/musharraf.transcript/.

82. President Pervez Musharraf's Speech at the Conference on Interaction and Confidence Building Measures in Asia (CICA) Almaty, Kazakhstan, June 3, 2002, http://www.satp.org/satporgtp/countries/pakistan/document/papers/Almaty.htm.

83. Musharraf, "Here's What I'll Do"; and "Interview with Pervez Musharraf," *Christian Science Monitor,* September 10, 2002, http://www.csmonitor.com/2002/0910/p25s02-wosc.html.

84. Address to the Nation by the President of Pakistan, General Pervez Musharraf, on the occasion of 55th Independence Day, August 14, 2002, http://www.satp.org/satporgtp/countries/pakistan/document/papers/pervez_14Aug2002.htm.

85. "Musharraf Pledges Support for US," *BBC News, World Edition,* September 9, 2002, http://news.bbc.co.uk/2/hi/south_asia/2245565.stm.

86. Address by President Musharraf to the Twenty-Fifth National Seerat Conference, Islamabad, June 5, 2001, http://ipripak.org/journal/summer2001/document10.shtml.

87. "Time Interviews Pervez Musharraf," January 14, 2002.

88. Noreen Ahmed-Ullah, "Al Qaeda Is on the Run, Pakistan's Leader Declares," *Chicago Tribune,* September 11, 2002, http://articles.chicagotribune.com/2002–09–11/news/0209110261_1_al-qaeda-pakistani-leader-gen-musharraf; see also "Interview with Pervez Musharraf," *Christian Science Monitor.*

89. Address by H. E. General Pervez Musharraf President of Pakistan at the 57th Session of the UN General Assembly, September 12, 2002, http://www.un.org/webcast/ga/57/statements/020912pakistanE.htm.

90. "Before Kargil . . . Kashmir . . . Was A Dead Issue:" NDTV Prannoy Roy's interview with Pervez Musharraf, June 16 2003: http://www.outlookindia.com/article.aspx?220438.

91. "Two Hundred Percent, There Won't Be War," excerpts from Pervez Musharraf's interview with *Washington Post* editors and reporters, June 25, 2003, http://www.outlookindia.com/article.aspx?220543. For a similar claim with explicit reference to the "dangerous confrontation of 2002," see Musharraf, "Address to the Fifty-Ninth Session of UN General Assembly."

92. Michael Evans and Bronwen Maddox, "Nuclear Arms Our Last Hope, Says Pakistan Leader," *Times* (London), June 19, 2003, 18.

93. Interview of President General Pervez Musharraf to *The India Today Conclave,* March 13, 2004, http://ipripak.org/journal/summer2004/doc12.shtml.

94. President Pervez Musharraf address to United Nations General Assembly, September 15, 2005, http://www.satp.org/satporgtp/countries/pak

istan/document/papers/Text_of_Musharraf_speech_at_UN_General _Assembly.htm.

95. President Musharraf's speech, National Security Workshop, National Defence College, March 2, 2006, http://presidentmusharraf.wordpress.com /2005/01/09/6th-national-security-2006/.

96. A Conversation with Pervez Musharraf, September 26, 2006, http:// weill.cornell.edu/news/news/2006/10/a-conversation-with-pervez-musharraf .html.

97. Their index of coverage reviewed the *Hindu,* the *Times of India,* the *Nation, Dawn,* the *New York Times,* and the *Washington Post.* Chari, Cheema, and Cohen, *Four Crises and a Peace Process,* 180, 224.

98. Ibid., 146.

99. Ibid., 36–37.

100. Coll, "The Back Channel."

101. Ibid.

102. Mistry, "Complexity of Deterrence," 184.

103. Karin Brulliard, "Infiltrators Worry Pakistani Military," *Washington Post,* May 28, 2011, http://www.highbeam.com/doc/1P2–28783666.html; Jane Perlez and Salman Masood, "Terror Ties Run Deep in Pakistan, Case Shows," *New York Times,* July 27, 2009, http://www.nytimes.com/2009/07/27 /world/asia/27pstan.html?_r=0; Manoj Joshi, "No Closure as Yet on Mumbai," *Mail Today,* November 24, 2010; "26/11 Attacks: Lakhvi, Shah 'Believed to Have Confessed,'" *Indian Express,* July 29, 2009, http://www.indianexpress .com/news/2611-attacks-lakhvi-shah-believed-to-haveconfessed/495653/; and "Headley an ISI Spy, Groomed for 26/11 Operation," *New Indian Express,* January 3, 2011, http://newindianexpress.com/world/article402442.ece?ser vice=print.

104. Tellis et al., "Lessons of Mumbai," 26; Jason Burke, "Mumbai Spy Says He Worked for Terrorists—Then Briefed Pakistan," *Guardian,* October 19, 2010; and "A Monster We Can't Control: Pakistan's Secret Agents Tell of Links with Militants," *Times* (London), December 22, 2008.

105. Keith Bradsher and Somini Sengupta, "Troops Battle Remaining Militants; Indian Officials Accuse Pakistan in Attacks; Toll Nears 150 Dead," *International Herald Tribune,* November 29, 2008, 1.

106. Bruce Loudon, "India Poised to Strike Terror Base: Military Chiefs Urge Raid inside Pakistan," *Australian,* December 3, 2008, 10.

107. "BBC Monitoring South Asia."

108. "Hoax Caller Who Brought India, Pak on Verge of War Post 26/11 Was Pearl's Alleged Assassin," *Asian News International,* November 26, 2009, http://m.mumbaimirror.com/index.aspx?Page=article&sectname=News%20 -%20World&sectid=4&contentid=20091127200911270214296875599241
7; and "Army, PAF Put on High Alert after Indian Threats," *Nation (AsiaNet),* November 29, 2008, http://www.nation.com.pk/pakistan-news-newspaper

-daily-english-online/politics/30-Nov-2008/Army-PAF-put-on-high-alert -after-Indian-threats.

109. Coll, "The Back Channel."

110. Recent work on Pakistan's nuclear doctrine includes Narang, *Nuclear Strategy in the Modern Era*; Khan and Lavoy, "Pakistan"; and Hoyt, "Pakistan's Nuclear Posture."

111. Narang, *Nuclear Strategy in the Modern Era*, 77–78.

112. Ibid.

113. Robert Norris and Hans Kristensen, "Nuclear Notebook: Pakistan's Nuclear Forces 2011," *Bulletin of the Atomic Scientists* (July/Aug.). Available at http://bos.sagepub.com/content/67/4/91.full.pdf+html.

114. Rodney W. Jones, "Pakistan's Answer to Cold Start?," *Friday Times*, May 13–19, 2011, http://www.thefridaytimes.com/13052011/page7.shtml.

115. Meyerle, Gause, Ostovar, "Nuclear Weapons and Coercive Escalation."

116. Narang, *Nuclear Strategy in the Modern Era*, 91.

117. Shah, *Army and Democracy*.

118. Sameer Arshad, "Musharraf Had Planned Kargil Operation with 3 Confidants: Retired Pak General Shahid Aziz," *Times of India*, February 1, 2013.

119. Nawaz, *Crossed Swords*, 500–518.

120. Khrushchev, *Memoirs*, 3:456.

5

I Thought It Was My Last Meal: Kennedy, Vajpayee, Nixon, and Mao

HOW FAR do the psychological mechanisms in the ALF nuclear-learning model travel beyond the Soviet and Pakistani cases? The nuclear learning models are tested on four further cases here: that of US president John Kennedy in the 1960s, India's prime minister Atal Vajpayee from 1999 to 2003, US president Richard Nixon from 1969–1974, and China's leader Mao Zedong in 1969–1970.

The United States of the early 1960s was not a new nuclear power, but President Kennedy authorized an assertive policy to address Nikita Khrushchev's revisionism in Berlin and Cuba. In 1998, India was a fairly new nuclear power when Prime Minister Atal Vajpayee authorized an assertive foreign policy to address Pakistani revisionism. The effects of availability and fear are not limited to leaders of new nuclear powers. If leaders in experienced nuclear powers learn that nuclear assertion is safe and effective, nuclear proliferation becomes dangerous. The case of Richard Nixon is probative for this discussion because he had learned that nuclear assertion is powerful from a cognitively available episode during his time as vice president in the early 1950s. The learning models should therefore be able to explain Nixon's assertive foreign policy in 1969 and 1973. The comparable effects of the 1969 war scare on Mao Zedong's foreign policy suggest that the effect of fear of imminent nuclear war that was observed of Khrushchev and Musharraf cannot be

159

written off to chance or something particular to their cases. When he believed that nuclear war was imminent, Mao authorized a restrained foreign policy toward the Soviet Union after 1970. Taken together these four cases furnish more empirical support for the ALF nuclear-learning model.

The United States, 1961–1963

Kennedy authorized a mostly restrained foreign policy in his first year as president. He did not issue any assertive threats to Khrushchev, and his Berlin policy throughout 1961 centered on deterring Soviet challenges and ensuring that Khrushchev would not miscalculate US resolve. Kennedy's remarks to Khrushchev at the Vienna summit were likely aimed at both deterring Soviet challenges and making clear the US's commitment to resisting any Soviet revisions. As Kennedy claimed at Vienna, "When we are talking about West Berlin, we are talking about Western Europe" and "it will be a cold winter." His June 25, 1961, speech and subsequent funding requests from Congress were costly signals, but they nonetheless left much unclear about how he would respond to a Soviet challenge in West Berlin.[1] Kennedy went so far as to tell Khrushchev that he believed that the balance of military power was about equal when he knew that he possessed many more nuclear weapons than the Soviet Union.

Given Khrushchev's resolve to eject Kennedy from West Berlin and his conviction that nuclear assertion held the key to unlocking this geopolitical imperative, it is perhaps not surprising that Kennedy's costly signal did not deter further Soviet challenges. Costly signaling models assume, after all, that the perceiver can always understand the sender's message. A psychological model, on the other hand, would assume that Khrushchev's beliefs are a better predictor of his behavior. The pathologies of availability explain why Khrushchev's still vivid lessons from Suez caused him to persist with nuclear assertion: he had not yet reached the nuclear brink.

After Khrushchev outlined his second Berlin ultimatum, Kennedy authorized Deputy Secretary of Defense Roswell Gilpatric to proclaim that Washington was aware of the true nuclear balance of power:

This nation has a nuclear retaliatory force of such lethal power that an enemy move which brought it into play would be an act of self-destruction on his part. . . . In short, we have a second strike capability which is at least as extensive as what the Soviets can deliver by striking first. There-fore we are confident that the Soviets will not provoke a major nuclear conflict.[2]

Aleksandr Fursenko and Timothy Naftali note that Gilpatric's com-ments were partly meant to address a domestic audience: Kennedy wanted to calm American fears and resist calls for further weapons pro-curement being made by the US armed services and their congressional allies.[3] But the purpose of the speech was also surely to stop Soviet nuclear assertion without a costly US coercive response. When this failed, Kennedy raised the ante by announcing increased defense expen-ditures and further troop call-ups but without issuing any explicit coer-cive demands of Moscow. All three nuclear learning models can explain this behavior: the Waltzian model because it cannot be considered nuclear assertion; the rational-signaling model because it was a US attempt to establish resolve in West Berlin in the face of a Soviet challenge; and the ALF model because Kennedy was the leader of an experienced nuclear power but had not experienced imminent nuclear escalation.

After learning of the existence of Soviet missiles in Cuba, Kennedy fairly quickly decided against an attack and ordered a blockade to prevent any further Soviet weapons from reaching Cuba. His coercive threat on October 27 must be coded as an assertive foreign policy. He sent his brother Robert to inform Soviet ambassador Dobrynin that if Moscow removed the nuclear missiles from Cuba, the US would pledge to not attack the island and should be able to secretly remove the Jupiter mis-siles based in Turkey within six months but also that he would attack Cuba if Khrushchev did not accept that offer within twenty-four hours.[4] Kennedy also raised the nuclear alert status to DEFCON 2. The block-ade should be viewed as both deterrence and a restrained foreign policy: it was designed to prevent the additional missiles from reaching Cuba and to maintain the status quo between the two superpowers.

Kennedy's assertive nuclear threat was issued in the face of Soviet nuclear assertion and faced an atypical number of advantages. Because

Khrushchev had lived with the status quos in Berlin and Cuba for so long, coercive threats to revise them under the risk of nuclear escalation were not credible. Kennedy's threats were aimed directly at restoring a status quo that Khrushchev had taken great pains to undermine. Moreover, Kennedy possessed both nuclear and conventional superiority over the Soviet Union in Cuba (but not in West Berlin) and he was arguably more resolved to remove the missiles from Cuban soil than Khrushchev was to keep them there. Khrushchev had, after all, hinted that he would be willing to trade the Cuban nuclear missile base for concessions on Berlin. Such a confluence of circumstances is rarely found, so it is therefore unsurprising that Kennedy's assertive threat is a rare case of success. But because nuclear assertion tends to be effective only when it is attempting to stop other nuclear assertion, this should not be surprising.

The Waltzian learning model explains this episode poorly. It would expect Khrushchev to have not authorized nuclear assertion, and not expect Kennedy to have authorized nuclear assertion in response. It is not surprising that a model that expects leaders to only use nuclear weapons for deterrence cannot explain how Soviet and US nuclear assertion caused the Cuban Missile Crisis.

The rational-signaling model does not do much better. While it would expect leaders to authorize nuclear assertion to display their resolve, Khrushchev already had very publicly displayed his resolve to keep the missiles in Cuba. Soviet ultimatums regarding Berlin were a costly signal, and Kennedy should have rationally understood Khrushchev's resolve and the limits of nuclear assertion, thereafter abstained from US nuclear assertion, and accepted the Soviet nuclear missiles in Cuba. After Khrushchev issued his demands at the Vienna summit, including a December 31 deadline for a settlement on East Berlin, he distributed a copy of the demands to foreign communist leaders and Soviet and international newspapers, and then repeated his threat on Soviet television a week later. Khrushchev remarked at an event commemorating the surprise 1941 German attack that those who tested Soviet resolve on Berlin would "share the fate of Hitler."[5] The following July he announced a one-third increase in the Soviet defense budget and a suspension of planned reductions in the armed forces.[6] By September 11, 1962, Soviet forces went on their highest alert level since 1945.[7] The Kremlin also publicized its concern that Kennedy's desire to call up reserve troops implied that an attack on Cuba was imminent.[8] Another more-limited alert occurred on October 15, and following Kennedy's national address Soviet forces went on another very high state of alert.[9]

The rational-signaling model would expect Kennedy to have accepted the new Cuban status quo. It badly misses the mark because it focuses on the sender rather than on the perceiver of costly signals. Kennedy had staked his political reputation on standing firm in Berlin and not accepting Soviet nuclear missiles in Cuba. It is not surprising, then, that a theory that expects a public display of resolve to be able to extract submission on such core issues would fail to explain US policy in this case. The limitations of a costly signaling approach regarding two states that are edging toward a nuclear crisis are severe. The model would expect that the crisis should effectively end when both produce costly signals; these costly signals objectively display resolve. But perceptions are king in international affairs, and there is no reason to expect that a costly signal will deter an emboldened or resolved leader from edging closer to the nuclear brink. For Khrushchev, the pathology of availability trumped his perception of Kennedy's costly signal. Nor would any amount of Soviet posturing likely have forced Kennedy to back down. The subjective experience of fear, not the objective display of resolve, de-escalated the crisis.

The ALF model's predictions depend on knowing what Kennedy found cognitively available. It would expect him to authorize an assertive strategy once he learned (exclusively from Soviet actions) that assertion was a worthwhile and effective strategy and given what he perceived Khrushchev to possibly gain from assertion. It would not expect him to develop a policy based on lessons from history. The ALF model's expectations regarding Kennedy's 1962 coercive threat are therefore unclear: the extent to which he consulted historical research on the causes of World War I—that is, by reading Barbara Tuchman's *The Guns of August*— to formulate his policy remain vague.[10]

Attention to the historical record is precisely what the ALF model does not expect to occur. Members of Kennedy's executive committee later recalled that Kennedy made extensive reference to Tuchman's study throughout the crisis, often remarking how inflexible war plans had caused the war and may have led to nuclear escalation in 1962.[11] But it is equally likely that Kennedy had already learned about the dangers posed by military advisers with inflexible war plans through his own cognitively available personal experiences: his extensive European travels, his military service in the Pacific (where his own PT boat was broken in half by a Japanese destroyer), and the failed Bay of Pigs invasion of 1961. Together these may well have taught him of the limits of military power long before he picked up Tuchman's study.[12]

Historian Michael Beschloss claims that "there was not a sentence in Kennedy's American University speech proclaiming the dangers of nuclear war with which he would have privately disagreed in 1960."[13] Kennedy's national security adviser, McGeorge Bundy, once claimed that Kennedy "may well have believed the key elements of his American University speech before 1963, but he did not feel that he could say them publicly."[14] The ALF model's expectations and ability to explain Kennedy's 1962 coercive threat are unclear: Kennedy issued a nuclear threat on October 27 at a time when he seems to have believed that nuclear war was imminent. This is exactly what the ALF model does not expect.

Since Kennedy prevailed in the Cuban Missile Crisis, why did he not continue with an assertive foreign policy to extract further Soviet concessions? ALF explains Kennedy's otherwise odd authorization of a restrained foreign policy after coercing Khrushchev to remove Soviet nuclear missiles and other weapons from Cuba: he experienced fear of imminent nuclear war during the Cuban Missile Crisis. When the blockade was about to take effect, Kennedy told the executive committee that "what we are doing is throwing down a card on the table in a game which we don't know the ending of."[15]

Robert Kennedy, the president's most intimate adviser, referred to the moment when the president experienced "greatest worry"—on the same day that Sergei Khrushchev claims that a change took place in his father's thinking regarding Khrushchev's response to the American blockade of Cuba. Secretary of Defense Robert McNamara informed Kennedy on October 24 that because Soviet submarines were unable to receive orders from Moscow, McNamara had unilaterally changed the rules of engagement for the US destroyers trailing them. He had deviated from standard international practice in authorizing depth charges that could hit but not destroy submarines, using them as warning notices and instructions for unidentified submarines to surface.[16] But Soviet submarine captains could not know of this new procedure and that the warning depth charges hitting their submarine were not meant to destroy them.[17] Kennedy likely worried about the submarine captains' immediate response to the charges. He responded to McNamara that "we don't want to have the first thing we attack [be] a Soviet submarine."[18] Robert Kennedy referred to this as "the time of greatest worry by the President." The president's hand "went up to his face and covered his mouth and he closed his fist. His eyes were tense, almost grey," and, Kennedy noted, "we just stared at each other across the table."[19]

Kennedy's usual routine involved dispatching his wife and children to the family vacation home in Florida every Friday, then spending Friday evening with one of his mistresses in Washington and joining his family in Florida the next day. But on Friday, October 26, he deviated from this routine and kept his family with him in Washington. The subsequent Friday they went to Florida without him.[20] Kennedy's longtime mistress Mimi Alford recalled that when she saw the president on the twenty-sixth,

> his expression was grave. Normally, he would have put his Presidential duties behind him, had a drink, and done his best to light up the room and put everyone at ease. But not on this night. Even his quips had a half-hearted, funereal tone. At one point, after leaving the room to take another urgent phone call, he came back shaking his head and said to me "I'd rather my children be red than dead." . . . Although our get-togethers were usually quite sexually charged, it wasn't to be on this occasion.[21]

When the president told his aide Dave Powers that "the way you're eating up all that chicken and drinking up all my wine, anybody would think it was your last meal," Powers responded, "The way Bobby's been talking, I thought it was my last meal."[22] Khrushchev claimed in his memoirs that Ambassador Dobrynin described Robert Kennedy at the climax of the crisis as "very tired; his eyes were very red; it was obvious that he hadn't slept all night."[23]

President Kennedy told the Soviet ambassador that "the situation might get out of control, with irreversible consequences."[24] He did not wait to see whether Khrushchev might withdraw the missiles in return for the no-invasion pledge before immediately sending his brother to meet with Ambassador Dobrynin, to sweeten the deal with the strictly secret removal of the Turkish Jupiter missiles. By this point Kennedy likely feared that he had almost lost control of the crisis.[25] He famously said afterward that he believed that the probability of nuclear escalation was between one in three and even. As Ambassador to the Soviet Union Llewellyn Thompson had warned earlier, "Danger arises from the fact that that if K[hrushchev] carries out his declared intentions and we carry out ours, the situation will likely get out of control."[26]

Kennedy told Khrushchev that resolving the crisis was a top priority because "developments were approaching a point where events could have become unmanageable."[27] Kennedy surely experienced fear of imminent nuclear war between October 24 and October 26, and it does not appear he experienced fear of imminent nuclear war before then.[28] McGeorge Bundy reported on November 21, 1961, about a presentation of the Net Evaluation Subcommittee to the National Security Council on the impact of US-Soviet nuclear war: Kennedy did not sit "as though transfixed" or show "great stress."[29]

Kennedy excluded the State and Defense Departments from weighing in on his important and sincere 1963 American University speech preparation to ensure that its impact was not undermined.[30] After the Cuban Missile Crisis he secretly authorized one US official to have deniable but intensive talks with Castro with the aim of improving relations with Havana. From a rational perspective it is unclear why Kennedy both authorized a restrained foreign policy toward the Soviet Union (especially regarding West Berlin) and did not continue to attempt to undermine Castro's regime after he prevailed in Cuba. The ALF model can explain this anomaly: while he authorized nuclear assertion only as a response to Soviet assertiveness, the experience of fear caused him to subsequently avoid assertive foreign policies that he associated with ones that had precipitated the crisis. He would have perceived nuclear assertion and the undermining of Castro's regime as too risky and too likely to bring him back to the nuclear abyss of October 1962. He preferred the less-risky options of a restrained foreign policy and tacit cooperation with Khrushchev and Castro.

One November 1961 government directive states that the United States planned to "help the people of Cuba overthrow the Communist regime from within Cuba and institute a new government with which the United States can live at peace."[31] By early 1962 US policy was limited to isolating Cuba and limiting Cuban influence. A March 1962 update added that "the U.S. will make use of indigenous resources, internal and external, but recognizes that final success will require decisive U.S. military intervention."[32] The president and his brother authorized the military services to prepare for possible intervention. By the end of April Kennedy refused to set up training camps for a new landing attempt or say anything that would encourage hope that he would eventually approve an armed invasion.

In early November 1963 Kennedy allowed an official to go to Havana for secret talks to improve relations with Washington but only if official involvement could be plausibly denied. Kennedy was apparently "very interested" in "thinking along more flexible lines" with Castro.[33] Domestic politics alone cannot explain this turnaround in US policy toward Havana. After being threatened by Soviet missiles in Cuba in 1962, domestic political pressures would predict Kennedy to tow a harder line on Havana. Public pressure may explain why Kennedy pursued rappochement with Havana in secret, but it cannot explain why he made such a fundamental turnaround in US policy.

Table 5.1 summarizes the ability of the learning models to explain Kennedy's foreign policy toward the Soviet Union. All three models predict Kennedy's 1961 costly signal and the embargo of Cuba in 1962 as displays of resolve in the face of nuclear assertion. But none of the models explain Kennedy's 1962 coercive threat. The Waltzian model expects Khrushchev and Kennedy to have never authorized nuclear assertion. The rational-signaling model would expect Kennedy to have accepted

Table 5.1. Nuclear Learning Models, United States, 1961–1963

	Waltzian	Rational-Signaling	ALF Two-Stage
Response to second Berlin threat, 1961	✓	✓	✓
Embargo following Cuban missile deployment, 1962	✓	✓	✓
Coercive threat after Cuban missile deployment, 1962	✗	✗	✗
Acceptance of Castro regime, 1963	✓	✓	✓

the Soviet missile base on Cuba once Soviet costly signals displayed Khrushchev's resolve to revise the status quo. The ALF model cannot explain Kennedy's actions either: to the extent that it was informed by his attention to the historical record, a coercive threat is unexpected when he believed that nuclear war was imminent. Kennedy's apparent attention to the lessons of World War I and to his direct experiences and assertion when he was at the nuclear brink are anomalous. All three models can explain Kennedy's gradual opening to Cuba in 1963, but the ALF model best explains why he needed to go through the Cuban Missile Crisis rather than Soviet costly signals to get there.

India, 1999–2002

The Pakistani challenge at Kargil and subsequent terrorist attacks all surprised Prime Minister Vajpayee and his group of senior advisers, the Cabinet Committee on Security. Events forced them to confront the dilemma of how they could defend their position in Kashmir in the face of both an emboldened nuclear Pakistan plus insurgent groups that had grown somewhat autonomous from the Pakistani military. Before the summer of 1999 Vajpayee and his colleagues believed that Indian and Pakistani nuclear weapons would promote peace. As Rajesh Basrur has pointed out, following the nuclear tests many believed that Pakistan would "no longer risk a conflict in Kashmir, the strategic status quo would remain stable and that India would be able to address the Kashmir insurgency as an internal matter."[34]

Two months before the Kargil intruders were discovered, Vajpayee proclaimed: "The nuclear weapon is not an offensive weapon."[35] After the Pakistani nuclear test and the increase in the number of attacks by insurgents in Kashmir, Vajpayee increased troop deployments there and authorized a conference of the All Parties Hurriyat to address local Kashmiri concerns. Nevertheless, he continued to believe that more ambitious Pakistani revisionism would not occur.[36] Army general V. P. Malik pointed out to Vajpayee and his colleagues that the winter months would permit the Pakistani Army to stage an operation to occupy large parts of India-held Kashmir. As Malik stated later, "not many people took [my] statement seriously until Kargil happened."[37] According to Brajesh Mishra,

Vajpayee's national security adviser at the time, the discovery of the Kargil intruders and their Pakistani identity deeply shocked all of the civilian leadership.[38]

The ALF model expects new nuclear powers to authorize assertive foreign policies. It would not expect the restraint shown by India in Kashmir throughout the 1990s, especially in the face of increasingly assertive Pakistani sponsorship of the Kashmir insurgency. However, some other cognitively accessible developments may have trumped the effects of Indian nuclear tests and suggested that Pakistani aggression would not result: the confidence-building measures of 1998 and 1999, the exchanged lists of nuclear installations and facilities, the February 1999 Lahore declaration committing India and Pakistan to peaceful conflict resolution, and the initiation of the New Delhi–Lahore bus service. Vajpayee was personally involved in most of these agreements, which all pointed toward Pakistani moderation in Kashmir. The ALF model thus has a mixed performance in explaining Indian foreign policy throughout the 1990s: as a new nuclear power it was not assertive. But the model is wrong for the right reasons: Vajpayee and his associates learned from other cognitively available data points that nuclear restraint would be more effective than nuclear assertion in managing Pakistani revisionism.

What caused Vajpayee and the Cabinet Committee on Security members to change their minds about nuclear assertion? They learned that "there is a strategic space to fight limited conventional war below the strategic threshold."[39] This learning did not come from the historical record; rather, it emanated from the cognitively accessible events of Pakistan's intrusion at Kargil. Shortly after the second Indian test but before the Pakistani tests, Home Minister L. K. Advani claimed that India's tests would make Islamabad "roll back its anti-India policy, especially with regard to Kashmir."[40] But in January 2000, several months after Kargil, Defence Minister George Fernandes proclaimed that nuclear weapons "can deter only the use of nuclear weapons, but not all and any war; Indian forces can fight and win a limited war at a time and place chosen by the aggressor."[41] General Malik more explicitly pointed to the source of these lessons: "Kargil showed the way: if Pakistan could do Kargil, India could do something similar."[42] Thus Basrur claimed that Vajpayee and his associates learned more from their personal experiences about India's rivalry with Pakistan than from the historical record.[43] Even so, the ALF model expects these lessons to have caused Indian policy to become assertive.

The Waltzian model can explain Indian restraint throughout the 1990s in the face of Pakistani nuclear emboldenment and increasing aggression in Kashmir, but it does not expect Delhi to have taken a leaf from the Pakistani nuclear assertion playbook. The rational-signaling model can explain Delhi's assertiveness in 1999 to demonstrate its resolve to stay the course in Kashmir, but it cannot explain why it took eight years of progressively more dangerous Pakistani sponsorship of the Kashmir insurgency to do it. The rational-signaling model would expect Indian assertion to have occurred closer to 1990, when Pakistani revisionism in Kashmir intensified. India's responses to Pakistan's assertion throughout the 1990s were defensive: Vajpayee worried that taking the battle onto Pakistani soil would cause nuclear escalation.[44] He aimed only to restore the status quo and sought no further gains in Kashmir. Indian policy effected by Operation Parakram in 2001 and 2002 was unprecedented in its assertiveness. The Indian leader authorized the mobilization of eight hundred thousand troops and in May deployed the strike corps to an inherently offensive posture that threatened to occupy large swaths of Pakistan and possibly slice the country in two (again). Vajpayee demanded that Pakistan arrest and extradite twenty alleged terror suspects, permanently eliminate all terrorist training camps, and end sponsorship of the insurgency in Kashmir.[45]

How effective were the 2001–2002 coercive threats by India? US secretary of state Colin Powell had assured Vajpayee that Musharraf was committed to combatting extremism in Pakistan and that he might extradite some alleged criminals, so the Indian prime minister believed that his threat had compelled Musharraf's concessions.[46] However, while Musharraf incarcerated some of the criminals on Vajpayee's list, he refused to extradite them and did little to dismantle training camps. In fact, he publically vowed to continue Pakistani support of the Kashmir insurgency. The insurgency tapered off in early 2002 because the heavy snowfall of the winter months prohibited infiltration through the Himalayan mountain passes. By the summer it had increased again.[47] Only after Musharraf believed that nuclear war was imminent did fatalities in Kashmir decline.

The Waltzian model can explain Vajpayee's response to the Kargil War but cannot explain India's assertion and coercive demands in the 2001–2002 crisis. The rational-signaling model can explain India's demonstrations of resolve but not following Pakistan's costly signals. As discussed earlier, the rational-signaling model breaks down when two states are coercing each other and edging toward the nuclear brink; it expects them to learn of their adversaries' resolve from costly signals. Pakistani aggression in Kargil and the countermobilization in 2001 were two costly signals from which Vajpayee should have learned about Pakistani resolve and thereafter accepted Pakistani challenges. But after such provocative attacks on Indian territory the Indian leader's hand was never going to be stayed by a Pakistani costly signal. If the rational-signaling model is correct, Pakistan and India should have come to terms after Kargil; the 2001–2 crisis should not have occurred. But Pakistan mobilized half a million troops and Musharraf made several public commitments to both support the insurgency and defend his country from an Indian invasion. After US deputy secretary of state Richard Armitage extracted a promise from Musharraf in early June 2002 to permanently end infiltration and terrorist acts subsequently decreased, Vajpayee and his associates concluded that their coercive demands had caused the desired outcome.[48]

The ALF model produces mixed results regarding Indian policy toward Pakistan in the 1990s, but it does explain why Indian policy became assertive once the most provocative aggression in the two nations' history in 1999 had left no doubt that nuclear proliferation opened up a large possibility for limited conflict. If ever there was a data point that Vajpayee and his associates would learn from about the possibilities of nuclear assertion, this was it. They learned from Pakistan's policy, rather than from history, that nuclear assertion could yield useful dividends. Twice India made unsuccessful coercive demands of Musharraf. It is clear that Vajpayee and his advisers did not experience fear of imminent war through early 2002, so the ALF model expects them to have persisted with nuclear assertion.[49] It is unclear whether they experienced fear of imminent nuclear war during May 2002. So the ALF model's performance in explaining the subsequent Indian conventional doctrine—which itself remains somewhat elusive—is also unclear.

Delhi's recent "Cold Start" doctrine is designed to enable a more rapid large-scale attack that inflicts serious damage on Pakistani forces stationed below the nuclear "red line" before they can mobilize, defend, or counter attack.[50] The deployment of Indian troops in 2001 required relocating troops from the border with China, it took several weeks, and it denied Delhi the advantage of surprise. When the mobilization was completed Pakistani troops were ready and waiting. Cold Start is currently a work in progress. As Walter Ladwig has pointed out, "Indian planners will have to overcome a number of organizational, bureaucratic, and resource-related obstacles before they can fully implement it."[51] Whether this undermines the ALF model depends on whether Vajpayee and his successors experienced fear of imminent nuclear war in May 2002: it would be undermined if they experienced fear of imminent nuclear war yet continued to believe that the Cold Start doctrine would better enable India to compel Pakistan to not sponsor insurgent groups, but it would not be undermined if they did not experience fear of imminent nuclear war and believe in Cold Start's efficacy.

More recently, on September 29, 2016, Indian special forces crossed the LoC and apparently successfully targeted border posts that had been used by groups such as Jaish-e-Mohammad to attack an Indian police and air force station the previous year. This strike, however, does not suggest that the Cold Start doctrine is now operational. It involved a small special forces group penetrating at most several kilometers inside Pakistani Kashmir with a limited mission and duration. Pakistan Army personnel seem to have not been targeted. By justifying the attack on the grounds that "some terrorist units had positioned themselves to infiltrate," the Indian director general for military operations apparently called his Pakistani counterpart to inform him of the operation and reduced the pressure on Pakistan to retaliate.[52] This is a far cry from the deeper, larger, and more-ambitious and risk-acceptant covert operations that the Cold Start doctrine envisions.

Table 5.2 summarizes the ability of the nuclear learning models to explain Indian foreign policies toward Pakistan between 1998 and 2002. The Waltzian model explains Indian restraint throughout the 1990s but, as ever, cannot explain cases of nuclear assertion. Indian nuclear assertion likely increased the probability that Musharraf would be pushed to the nuclear brink but then back down in Kashmir; but the Waltzian model expects neither country to move toward nuclear assertion. The rational-signaling model does little better. It cannot explain why Vajpayee

Table 5.2. Nuclear Learning Models: India, 1998–2002

	Waltzian	Rational-Signaling	ALF Two-Stage
Restraint, 1990s	✓	✗	✗
Restraint, 1999 Kargil War	✓	✓	✓
Assertion, 2001–2002 crisis	✗	✗	✓
"Cold Start" doctrine, 2003–	?	?	?

did not respond more forcefully to Pakistani revisionism in Kashmir in the 1990s, and it does not explain Indian coercion in the face of multiple Pakistani costly signals. The ALF model does somewhat better in explaining Indian policy in the 1990s and correctly explains the onset of Indian assertion after Kargil: the Indians had not experienced fear of imminent nuclear war, so they persisted with assertive policies throughout the 2001–2 crisis, but then Vajpayee and his associates eventually learned from not the historical record but Pakistan's much more cognitively available intrusion at Kargil. All the models are ambiguous in explaining Indian policy, and specifically the Cold Start doctrine after 2003, because it is unclear whether they experienced fear of imminent nuclear war early in May 2002 or if they have from the current operational status of Cold Start.

United States, 1969–1973

In 1969 Richard Nixon inherited a costly and deteriorating position in the Vietnam War. He believed that US travails in this conflict were a symptom of the decline in postwar US hegemony and a threat to Washington's credibility on many issues of interest to Moscow and Beijing. He was strongly resolved to turn the tide. The conflict had proved to be difficult to end on American terms. Lyndon Johnson had aimed to defend Saigon from North Vietnamese attacks, take the fight to the North, and prevent North Vietnamese forces from overrunning the South. But the weak, unpopular, and corrupt US-sponsored South Vietnamese government could not survive the North's onslaughts. Nixon was backed into a corner: public opinion and his political standing at home demanded an acceleration of US troop withdrawals from Southeast Asia. However, such a withdrawal threatened to discourage Saigon, encourage Hanoi, and weaken the US position at the Paris peace negotiations. As the members were aware, Vietnam was the Nixon administration's "foreign policy problem number one."[53]

The president embarked on a complex plan to end US involvement in Vietnam through a strategy that involved the gradual withdrawal of US troops, a strengthening of South Vietnamese troops, continued US military efforts against North Vietnamese guerilla forces, negotiations with the North Vietnamese government, and détente with the Soviets. Central to Nixon's plan was the belief that Moscow exerted real influence on Hanoi and that US nuclear "saber rattling" would extract Soviet concessions there. As he explained to Charles de Gaulle, "The Soviets have great influence on the North Vietnamese" because "eighty-five percent of their weapons came from the Soviet Union."[54] Both assumptions proved incorrect. While the "de-Americanization" of the conflict inevitably strengthened Hanoi and undermined Saigon, at the time Nixon oddly believed that nuclear threats, "linkage" politics, and "Vietnamization" would embolden Saigon, deter Hanoi, and appease the US public.

It is important to note that Nixon's foreign policy toward the Soviet Union was often restrained: he actively pursued détente and agreed to the SALT I and ABM treaties as well as other confidence-building measures like the Basic Principles Agreement. But when it came to staving off a declining position in Vietnam—as well as the 1973 Arab-Israeli War—he and Henry Kissinger were often inherently assertive. Central to his foreign policy was what Nixon referred to as the "principle of the threat of excessive force" that he believed facilitated linkage politics with the Soviets and would realize a long-elusive resolution to the Vietnam quagmire. He outlined this "madman" logic to his chief of staff in 1968:

I want the North Vietnamese to believe that I've reached the point that I might do anything to stop the war. . . . We'll just slip the word to them that, for God's sake, you know Nixon is obsessed about communism. We can't restrain him when he is angry—and he has his hand on the nuclear button—and Ho Chi Minh himself will be in Paris in two days begging for peace.[55]

The madman theory, well documented by William Burr, Jeffrey Kimball, Scott Sagan, and Jeremi Suri, was key to Nixon's hopes for coercing the North Vietnamese and Soviets into complying with his ambitious demands.[56] According to Kimball, Nixon believed that nuclear coercion was an essential component of diplomacy and would be especially potent "if his opponents could be convinced that he was capable of or intent upon using extreme force, since this would suggest that he possessed one or more of the interrelated qualities of madness."[57]

Frank Gavin has shown that Nixon's beliefs about nuclear weapons should not be written off to his personality or to Henry Kissinger; rather, they represent a theoretically coherent and serious "philosophy of the nuclear age."[58] Thus after barely one week into his presidency, Nixon met with Kissinger, Secretary of Defense Melvin Laird, and Chairman of the Joint Chiefs of Staff Earle Wheeler to explore "a program of potential military actions which might jar the North Vietnamese into being more forthcoming."[59] Nixon explained in 1970 that "the real possibility of irrational American action is essential to the Soviet relationship."[60] Kissinger weighed in on a debate about responding to a downed US reconnaissance plane: "If we strike back . . . they will say, this guy is becoming irrational and we'd better settle with him."[61]

Nixon and Kissinger had initially advocated a Vietnam strategy that was much more aggressive than just Vietnamization.[62] In September 1969 Nixon had contemplated a major escalation, code-named Duck Hook, that involved extensive bombing of Hanoi, mining the waters near Haiphong, increased ground operations in the demilitarized zone, attacks on Cambodian supply routes, and bombing of North Vietnam's transport and communication infrastructure (including of the northern river dikes and the country's various connections to China). He threatened to authorize it all on November 1 unless Hanoi accepted his terms at the Paris negotiations. Eventually he put them all aside and decided on a nuclear alert and military measures that were designed to signal his resolve on Vietnam and were "discernible to Moscow but not threatening in themselves."[63] Nixon hoped that Moscow and therefore Hanoi would believe that he would unleash Duck Hook after the alert and be willing to make important concessions.

According to Kissinger's military aide Alexander Haig, on October 6, 1969, Nixon asked Laird to authorize US strategic and tactical nuclear forces to take a "series of increased alert measures designed to convey to the Soviets an increasing readiness by U.S. strategic forces."[64] As Burr and Kimball have documented,

> one week later, U.S. strategic and tactical nuclear forces in the United States, Europe, and Asia began a stand down of training flights to raise operational readiness. The Strategic Air Command (SAC) increased the numbers of its bombers and tankers on ground alert and the operational readiness of selected overseas units was heightened. On October 25 the readiness of nuclear bombers was increased, and two days later B-52s undertook a show of force alert over Alaska for the first time since the 1968 Thule nuclear accident.[65]

Eighteen B-52 bombers took off from California and Western Washington bases and flew in eighteen-hour vigils to and from the Soviet Union.[66] Nixon later referred to this move as "irresistible military pressure."[67]

H. R. Haldeman, Nixon's chief of staff, noted in his diary on October 17 that "signal type activity going on around the world to try to jar the Soviets and NVN . . . appears to be working because Dobrynin asked for early meeting."[68] According to Haldeman, "K(issinger) thinks this is good chance of being the big break, but that it will come in stages. P(resident Nixon) is more skeptical."[69] Nixon told Sir Robert Thompson, the head of the British Advisory Mission to South Vietnam, that while "the USSR was not presently exercising its influence," Moscow might do so if there were incentives on the "negative side."[70] The next day Kissinger sent Nixon briefing papers that linked the nuclear alert with a vague warning to Soviet ambassador Dobrynin, something akin to the "train leaving the station." He reminded Nixon that in their forthcoming October 20 meeting, which they believed the nuclear alert brought about, "Your basic purpose will be to keep the Soviets concerned about what we might do around November 1: our main concern with the Soviets at present is their support of Hanoi's intransigence."[71] Kissinger also said: "Your comments might just give them ammunition to use in Hanoi in lobbying for a more flexible position."[72]

Nixon's 1969 nuclear alert was implicit nuclear assertion: he never made explicit threats to use nuclear weapons but nonetheless believed that his nuclear signaling would compel Moscow to engineer North

Vietnamese concessions. But Moscow may not have made any mental connection between the US military readiness measures, the vague references to the "train leaving the station," and the situation in Vietnam. US military intelligence found no evidence of a Soviet reaction.[73] If Brezhnev had connected the dots, he would surely have viewed the opaque nuclear threat—over a conflict that Moscow had little control over—as an incredible bluff. As Scott Sagan and Jeremi Suri ask, "How would the sight of nuclear-armed B-52s flying toward Siberia convince the Soviets to procure concessions [from Hanoi] for the United States in Southeast Asia?"[74] In conversations between Dobrynin, Kissinger, and Thompson shortly after the alert ended on October 30, Dobrynin did not mention the recent US military moves and reaffirmed Moscow's hostility toward Nixon's Vietnam linkage strategy. As Thompson aptly put it, "They could not get us out of a war into which we had gotten ourselves."[75]

Laird later admitted that he "never saw a curtailment of Russian support" and "couldn't see that they would cut down a bit because of the operation."[76] Kissinger had told the National Security Council that in the nuclear age, bluff is "taken seriously."[77] However, the North Vietnamese seemed to see through Nixon's madman strategy. Rose McDermott has pointed out that Nixon's adversaries believed he was "crazy like a fox and not simply crazy."[78] In a reply to Nixon's earlier threatening letter of August, Ho Chi Minh rejected Nixon's terms, proposed his own, and called Nixon's bluff on threats to use highly destructive levels of military force.[79] A top aide to Le Duc Tho who was in negotiations with Kissinger later claimed that he "can surprise . . . but this backfired on Nixon because we saw that Nixon could not have a big stick because of the step-by-step withdrawal of American forces."[80]

Aleksandr Kislov, a Soviet official, noted that "Mr. Nixon used to exaggerate his intentions regularly. He used alerts and leaks to do this."[81] Nixon's worldwide nuclear readiness test was never going to help the US gain Soviet or North Vietnamese concessions in Vietnam. Dean Acheson's comment about Nixon's ill-fated invasion of Cambodia on April 30, 1970, also applied to Nixon's nuclear assertion: Nixon was "the only horse he knew who would run back into a burning barn."[82] The president nevertheless believed that the threat of intensive nuclear or conventional bombing added a veil of credibility to his otherwise outlandish coercive demands. He often brought up the use of nuclear weapons in discussions and surely believed throughout his presidency that they would help realize otherwise elusive concessions.

During the 1970 crisis in the Middle East, Nixon admitted in a private briefing to newspaper editors in Chicago that it might be advantageous to the United States were Brezhnev and his associates to believe that the administration was capable of "irrational or unpredictable" action.[83] Kissinger also expressed to Nixon his belief that assertive behavior "broke the India-Pakistan situation last year."[84] Nixon threatened massive retaliation and appeared willing to scuttle the Moscow summit after the 1972 North Vietnamese spring offensive. In October 1972 he authorized the infamous Linebacker II operation that bombed around Hanoi to compel North Vietnam to adhere to his proposed peace treaty. He emphasized the importance of demonstrating this "brutal unpredictability": "The Russians and the Chinese might think they were dealing with a madman and so [they] had better force North Vietnam into a settlement before the whole world was consumed into a larger war."[85] Earlier in the year Nixon had instructed his associates to make the impending attack "the finest damn thing that's ever been done . . . I don't think anybody realizes how far I am prepared to go to save this . . . whatever is necessary to stop this thing has to be done."[86] In one debate with Kissinger he infamously mentioned using nuclear weapons to kill two hundred thousand people by destroying North Vietnamese dikes: "A nuclear bomb? Does that bother you? I just want you to think big, Henry."[87] Two weeks later he clarified his thinking to members of the National Security Council: "Obviously we are not going to use nuclear weapons but we should leave it hanging over them."[88]

By October 1973 Kissinger, near the height of his power, had authorized a DEFCON 3 nuclear alert when Nixon was engaged with Watergate and apparently drunk, although the president must have been aware of and signed off on the approval. Kissinger believed the October surprise Egyptian and Syrian offensive was part of a Soviet gambit for greater influence in the Middle East.[89] His proposed cease-fire was designed to smoke out Soviet involvement: "If they want the fighting stopped this will stop it fast. If they refuse to do this then we have to assume some collusion."[90] After Kissinger delayed the deadline of the agreed-on cease-fire and stalled on increasing aid to Israel, Israeli forces made further gains and trapped the Egyptian Third Army on the banks of the Suez Canal with minimal supplies and in need of rapid assistance. Brezhnev sent Nixon a brief letter noting that Israel had violated the agreement, and called for joint military contingents to implement and enforce the cease-fire. The letter closed with a threat of "taking appropriate steps unilaterally" if US cooperation was not forthcoming.[91] While Brezhnev likely contemplated using about 250 observers to monitor the cease-fire, Kissinger took Brezhnev to be threatening the deployment of combat troops and, given his strong desire to undermine and contain Soviet influence in the region, decided to raise the readiness level of US nuclear forces.[92]

Kissinger told the Washington Special Actions Group that "he had learned, finally, that when you decide to use force you must use plenty of it."[93] By leaving open both the possibility of joint action under the auspices of the Security Council and ongoing diplomatic efforts that gave Moscow access to the conflicting parties, Kissinger hoped to provide Brezhnev with large enough incentives that the nuclear threats would elicit cooperation on US terms. But the nuclear alert was never going to cause Soviet accession. As Eric Grynaviski has shown, the Americans and Soviets had profoundly different ideas about their respective roles in the resolution of the crisis.[94] Since Nixon and Kissinger took no other menacing steps, it is not clear that Brezhnev and his associates learned of the alert until it almost ended. Moscow likely never intended to deploy troops, and, as Lebow and Stein explain, "Many Soviet officials saw the alert as so inconsistent with the ongoing negotiations and the frequent communication between the two capitals that they could find no explanation other than Watergate."[95]

Brezhnev chose to ignore the alert: "What about not responding at all to the American nuclear alert? Nixon is too nervous—let's cool him down."[96] The crisis ended quickly when UN Security Council Resolution 340 created an emergency force without US or Soviet troops to promptly monitor the cease-fire, obviate the need for joint superpower intervention, and end the crisis. Nuclear assertion by Nixon and Kissinger had failed again.

Why did Nixon persist with an assertive foreign policy for five years despite repeated failures to realize any concessions? Nixon's nuclear assertion is anomalous, as experienced nuclear powers tend to authorize restrained foreign policies. Nixon may have wanted to continue the fight in Vietnam, but he should not have rationally believed that nuclear weapons would provide any assistance to such a goal. The ALF model can explain his persistence in the face of Soviet and North Vietnamese costly signals: he seems to have learned from a few cognitively accessible experiences as vice president that nuclear weapons offer significant assertive power. Brezhnev had authorized a restrained foreign policy throughout Nixon's presidency, so it is unsurprising that Nixon did not experience fear of imminent nuclear war.

The Waltzian model cannot explain Nixon's authorization of assertive foreign policies or nuclear alerts that would be unlikely to bring about North Vietnamese or Soviet concessions in Vietnam or the Middle East. The model expects him to have authorized a restrained foreign policy that involved fighting in Vietnam but which would have restricted the use of nuclear weapons as a deterrent to Soviet challenges on other core US interests. It cannot explain his use of nuclear alerts to coerce the Soviet Union into reining in their North Vietnamese and Egyptian clients or compel the North Vietnamese to accept his terms.

The rational-signaling model can explain Nixon's nuclear assertion as a display of resolve but not after costly signals had demonstrated that the US's adversaries were willing to stand their ground. North Vietnam's continued fight against the US-sponsored South in the face of very heavy US bombing was a costly signal of Hanoi's resolve; the rational-signaling model cannot explain Nixon's subsequent assertive policies or nuclear alerts in the face of this. The North Vietnamese had long demonstrated their resolve to fight to the end. The rational-signaling model does better in explaining Nixon's nuclear assertion to Moscow because Brezhnev did not produce a costly signal. The invasion of Czechoslovakia was a costly signal but was directed at foreign interference in communist states; it said little about Moscow's resolve in Vietnam and the Middle East. But because Nixon tried to coerce both Hanoi and Moscow, the rational-signaling model's usefulness is ambiguous. The ALF model explains Nixon's nuclear assertion because Nixon learned from some cognitively available experiences in 1953—eight years after the United States first developed nuclear weapons—that nuclear assertion can turn the tide. It thus would expect him to have authorized nuclear assertion when he became president.

Before addressing the lessons Nixon learned about nuclear assertion from his time as vice president, one must consider the lessons he learned about bluffing from his poker experiences when he was a navy lieutenant serving in the South Pacific in 1944. Bluffing in poker and nuclear assertion in international politics are obviously enormously different contexts, but both involve the art of making a credible commitment to make a move that could be very costly. Nixon's poker successes may have influenced his subsequent lessons about nuclear assertion. Stephen Ambrose concludes that for Nixon, the Pacific War was "above all a learning experience: he learned the ways of the world, and a great deal more about his own potentials as a leader."[97] Nixon admitted in his biography that he found playing poker "instructive and profitable."[98] According to Ambrose, after learning to raise only if he "was convinced he had the best hand," he played nightly and apparently became adept at the use of bluffing. His estimated winnings range from three to ten thousand dollars.[99] Another player claimed that Nixon was "as good a poker player as anyone we had ever seen." Although "sometimes the stakes were pretty big, Nick [Nixon] had daring and a flair for knowing what to do." According to Ambrose, his poker experiences were instructive because he learned "when he could bluff the man with the strongest hand into an ignominious retreat . . . and when to fold his own hand."[100]

There is little evidence that Nixon learned about nuclear assertion from his poker successes. But in closed door remarks at the Republican National Convention in Miami in 1968, he partly explained his strategy to end the Vietnam War with an analogy from his cognitively accessible poker experiences: "I played a little poker when I was in the Navy. . . . I learned something. . . . When a guy didn't have the cards, he talked awfully big. But when he had the cards, he just sat there—had that cold look in his eyes. Now we've got the cards. . . . What we've got to do is walk softly and carry a big stick and we can have peace in this world. And that is what we are going to do."[101]

Nixon also likely learned about nuclear assertion from his cognitively accessible Korean War experiences in 1953. In May of that year, John Foster Dulles had sent a message to Russian and Chinese leaders that Washington might use nuclear weapons if the war was not quickly resolved. The Panmunjom Peace Treaty established an armistice in late July. However, Dulles's threat almost certainly did *not* end the war:

conditions for a cease-fire were already ripe by the time Dulles issued the threat.[102] Stalin, whom Beijing and Pyongyang were heavily dependent on for war supplies, had hinted that he might welcome summit talks in December 1952. His death gave new life to the prospect of de-escalation and ending the conflict. Moreover, Beijing's potential willingness to accept POW repatriation moved the parties still closer to a negotiated settlement. American public opinion was also highly supportive of a negotiated solution.[103] Although Dulles's threat was likely unnecessary to end the Korean War, it was much more cognitively accessible to Richard Nixon in 1953 than were the changes in the Soviet and Chinese bargaining positions. It is unclear if Nixon was aware of these other factors in causing the end of the Korean War, but the ALF model explains why then–vice president Nixon overlearned about nuclear assertion from Dulles's cognitively available and apparently successful assertive threat.

Several instances reveal Nixon's belief about Eisenhower's successful nuclear assertion, beginning with a comment to Kissinger in October 1969.[104] Eighteen months later Kissinger referred to vague threats to use nuclear weapons as Nixon's use of "the Dulles ploy."[105] And seven years after that, Haldeman wrote that Nixon saw a parallel between Eisenhower's coercive threat to "end . . . the Korean War" and his own plans to resolve the Vietnam War.[106] Melvin Laird claimed in 2001 that Nixon "was influenced by Ike . . . particularly as it related to his getting a settlement with Korea."[107] Nixon recounted in 1985 that although the Chinese and Russians were weary of war, "it was the bomb that did it."[108]

Nixon may well have seen many similarities between Eisenhower's policies in 1953 and his own plans for Vietnam. In both cases, leaders came to power facing a drawn-out conflict that they wanted to end on their own terms. Eisenhower's threat was followed quickly by Chinese concessions; Nixon likely learned that nuclear assertion ended the Korean War and would work in Vietnam. Throughout April 1954 Nixon strongly encouraged Eisenhower to authorize an air strike that may have involved nuclear weapons to stave off the overrunning of the French garrison at Dien Bien Phu and the end of Western influence in Vietnam.[109] In the face of strong domestic opposition, Eisenhower, Dulles, and Nixon made a series of speeches that declared that the United States could not afford a communist victory in Vietnam and the country should be prepared for possible intervention.[110] The Chinese made concessions in the form of forcing the North Vietnamese to accept a temporary partition at the Geneva negotiations, but they were responding to the Korean War rather than to US nuclear threats.[111] Nixon, however, mistakenly learned that the nuclear threat caused the concessions.

The ALF model would be falsified if Nixon had experienced fear of imminent nuclear war but still subsequently authorized nuclear assertion. There is no evidence in the extensive archival records and secondary literature that he did so. Brezhnev never authorized an assertive policy toward him, and he did not reach the nuclear brink in 1969 or 1973. During the Cuban Missile Crisis—another episode when Nixon may have learned of the dangers of nuclear assertion and inadvertent escalation—Nixon was focused on his (ultimately unsuccessful) campaign to become governor of California. The crisis itself is barely mentioned in his memoirs.[112] If he did experience fear of imminent nuclear war in October 1962, he would have correctly believed that he had no control over it.

Under these kinds of conditions, fear has little effect on one's risk acceptance. The ALF model therefore explains Nixon's nuclear assertion. Had Brezhnev responded more assertively and dragged Nixon into a nuclear crisis, he would have been more likely to experience fear of imminent nuclear war and authorize a more restrained foreign policy in Vietnam, the Middle East, and elsewhere.

Table 5.3 summarizes the ability of each model to explain Richard Nixon's implementation of his madman theory. The Waltzian model fails. A theory that expects leaders to use nuclear weapons only for deterrence cannot explain Nixon's and Kissinger's frequent recourse to nuclear alerts and assertive demands in Vietnam and the Middle East. The rational-signaling model cannot explain Nixon's assertion to the North Vietnamese, even though it can explain his assertive signaling to Moscow. The ALF model can explain why Nixon made an inferential move similar to one Khrushchev would make three years later, and why he incorrectly believed that nuclear assertion had turned the tide. It explains

Table 5.3. Nuclear Learning Models: United States, 1969–1973

	Waltzian	Rational-Signaling	ALF Two-Stage
Assertion, 1969–1973	✗	?	✓

his persistence with nuclear assertion throughout his presidency in the face of North Vietnamese costly signals: he had never experienced fear of imminent nuclear war.

Arguments rooted in domestic politics and strategic culture fare poorly in this case because the public's demand for getting out of Vietnam was so strong. Coercive demands backed by nuclear alerts to maintain a fading status quo in Vietnam went against the will of a large majority of Americans. Arguments rooted in strategic culture thinking must confront the fact that Nixon had centralized his foreign policy making to such an extent—the State Department, for example, was very much out of the loop—that he and Kissinger alone were the strategic culture.

China, 1969–1970

Five years after China acquired nuclear weapons in 1964, Chinese troops found themselves fighting Soviet patrols on the disputed yet small, uninhabited, and submerged at high tide Zhenbao Island on the Ussuri River.[113] Skirmishes on the island had regularly occurred since Sino-Soviet tensions were exacerbated in the early 1960s. But the use of fatal military force hadn't occurred until 1969.

There is little data on Mao Zedong's beliefs about nuclear assertion or deterrence, or about China's territorial status quo.[114] Thus it is far from clear that the Chinese leader had revisionist ideas about regional territorial boundaries: his revisionist preferences during the Cultural Revolution—regarding the institutions and leadership of the Communist Party and government bureaucracy—were arguably more important to him than concerns over territorial disputes with the Soviet Union. The Great Leap Forward and Cultural Revolution involved greater effort, more risk, and many, many more Chinese casualties than Mao's regional foreign policy initiatives. Ultimately, the degree to which Mao was emboldened in 1969 by nuclear weapons in order to revise disputed borders versus the relative importance of the fatal domestic reforms cannot yet be established.

Some scholars have argued that in 1968 Mao "began preparations to create a small war on the border."[115] While his nuclear weapons may

have emboldened him to authorize minor challenges over disputed territory, a Soviet military buildup made his acts appear at least partly defensive. Brezhnev had authorized a military buildup in Siberia, in the Far
East, and in Mongolia during the mid-1960s, and by August 1968 proclaimed his right to intervene in the affairs of other communist states
through the power of the Brezhnev doctrine, which was marked by the
Soviet invasion of Czechoslovakia. The move deeply alarmed Mao and
caused him to question the extent of Soviet ambitions.[116] At the time, a
People's Liberation Army reference to "counterattack for the purpose of
self-defense" was partly accurate.[117]

Moreover, the Cultural Revolution, in full swing by 1969, reinforced
Mao's authority and created a strong political incentive to scapegoat the
Soviets as a unified external threat. Yang Kuisong, for example, finds
that the increasingly militarized dispute resulted mostly from Mao's
domestic mobilization strategies. The Chinese leader had told Zhou
Enlai that "we should let them come in, which will help us in our mobilization."[118] Then, at a tense September 11 Beijing airport meeting, Zhou
informed Alexei Kosygin: "We have very many domestic problems to
deal with. How can you believe that we want to go to war?"[119] Polish
leader Wladyslaw Gomulka claimed to Brezhnev in March 1969 that
"the recent events on the Sino-Soviet border can be examined through
the prism of China's internal needs and can be connected with the CCP
congress."[120] As Taylor Fravel argues, China has

> participated in twenty-three distinct territorial disputes on land and at
> sea between 1949 and 2005, it has pursued compromise and offered con-
> cessions in seventeen of them. China has usually offered to accept less
> than half of the contested territory in any final settlement. These compro-
> mises have resulted in boundary agreements in which China has aban-
> doned potential irredentist claims to more than 3.4 million square
> kilometers of land that had been part of the Qing empire at its early
> nineteenth century height. China has contested only 7 percent of territory
> once part of the Qing. Where China has used force, it has rarely seized
> land that it did not control before the outbreak of hostilities.[121]

Given the current lack of available data to conclusively determine the
sources of Mao's emboldenment in 1969, two questions can still be

addressed: Did Mao experience fear of imminent nuclear war during the winter of 1969–1970? Did this influence his foreign policies toward the Soviet Union on the Ussuri River and elsewhere?

In 1969, after several cases of Soviet heavy-handedness against Chinese patrols, Mao authorized Chinese troops to lure Soviet forces into a trap that resulted in heavy Soviet casualties. Brezhnev replied with his only assertive nuclear threat during eighteen years in power: he authorized retaliation that resulted in heavy Chinese casualties and issued an implicit threat to attack China's nuclear facilities. By the winter of 1969–1970 Mao had reached the nuclear brink. He sincerely worried that Brezhnev would authorize a preventive nuclear or conventional strike on his nascent nuclear arsenal or major Chinese cities.

After Mao engaged in comprehensive boundary talks with the Soviet Union in February 1964, the two sides reached a draft agreement in May that is strikingly similar to the one they reached twenty-seven years later.[122] However, that summer the talks collapsed. By August Moscow suggested that the two sides resume negotiations in mid-October, but negotiations ground to halt once Khrushchev was ousted on October 14 and China tested a nuclear bomb two days later. According to Taylor Fravel, both of the territorial disputes that China engaged in within five years of developing nuclear weapons involved China's use of force rather than concessions and compromise. There is, however, no evidence that these actions resulted from Mao's beliefs about nuclear assertion. Both events occurred within a shifting context: declining local Chinese military power, increased border deployments and an assertive forward-patrolling posture into disputed areas by the Soviets, and the 1968 Brezhnev doctrine that specified the right of Moscow to intervene in socialist states.[123]

Although the 1964 draft agreement allocated to China roughly half of the disputed islands on the Ussuri River, between 1968 and 1969 Soviet border guards brutally evicted Chinese patrols from them. Moscow and Beijing had accepted a tacit rule against shooting and had limited confrontations in the area to shouting, shoving, and clubbing. Attacks grew more frequent in the late 1960s, and between December 27, 1968, and February 25, 1969, Soviet border guards beat twenty-eight Chinese soldiers in nine different incidents.[124]

Then, on March 2, 1969, two Chinese patrols ambushed Soviet patrols on Zhenbao Island after a group of about twenty-five Chinese border guards marched toward the island chanting Maoist slogans. Soviet border guards inevitably arrived to engage and evict them. According to Thomas Robinson, "The Chinese patrols arranged themselves in two rows with the first row apparently unarmed. When the Soviets followed the standard practice of approaching the Chinese to demand they leave, the first row quickly scattered to reveal a heavily armed second row that quickly opened fire."[125] A Soviet reprisal of heavy artillery and rockets occurred two weeks later and caused ninety-one Chinese fatalities.[126] Moscow then threatened Mao with nuclear escalation.[127] However, as Harry Gelman notes, Brezhnev issued these nuclear threats in a "gingerly fashion, conveying the message primarily by innuendo, by implication, through occasional statements in non-authoritative Soviet sources and, above all, by manipulating and encouraging a crescendo of Western speculations and assertions."[128] Brezhnev even went so far as to publically deny any nuclear threats while discreetly encouraging Beijing to ignore his denials.[129]

A month before his removal, Khrushchev warned Mao that Moscow would use "all means at its disposal" to defend its borders, including up-to-date weapons of mass destruction."[130] A Soviet radio statement broadcasted immediately after the Soviet reprisal to the March 1969 ambush proclaimed: "The destruction range of these rockets is practically unlimited . . . thus if Mao Tse-tung and his group were to meet the Soviet Union in a contest of strength they would certainly end up in utter defeat."[131] On March 29 a further warning came that Chinese provocations would be met with "military counterattack," and the Soviet military continued to publically assert that negotiations could begin only when "the Chinese have been punished through a preemptive Soviet strike."[132] When a US State Department staffer asked Second Secretary Yuri Linkov if Moscow planned to attack China, the Russian admitted that Moscow "had to prepare for any contingency."[133] Linkov justified Soviet defiance with the warning that "the Chinese had to be shown that they couldn't continue to get away with these acts."[134]

As William Burr documents, by August US intelligence had detected "a stand-down in the Soviet air forces in the Far East." Moreover, "Soviet forces were making mock attacks on targets made to resemble the Chinese nuclear facilities."[135] On August 18, KGB officer Doris Davydov asked State Department staffer William Stearman how the US government "would react to a Soviet strike against Beijing's nuclear weapons facilities."[136] The Russian told Stearman that Moscow wanted to know possible US reactions to "a number of contingency plans."[137] It is unclear if Davydov had instructions from a higher authority in Moscow, whether other Soviet officials were posing similar questions to others, and how close Moscow was to attacking. Secretary of State William Rogers reported these Soviet overtures as a "first move" in a "probing operation" with the probability of attack "substantially less than fifty-fifty."[138] On August 28 the director of the Central Intelligence Agency revealed to journalists that Moscow had been consulting with other communist states about a potential China strike.[139]

The Soviet military subsequently threatened "crushing nuclear retaliation" on China by using "nuclear-armed missiles with unlimited destruction."[140] On September 16 Soviet agent Victor Louis published an article in the *London Evening News* that warned that "well-informed sources in Moscow" were asserting that "Russian nuclear installations stand aimed at Chinese nuclear facilities" and that the Soviets "plan to launch an air attack on Lop Nor."[141] Apparently Andrei Grechko, the Soviet defense minister who had planned the 1968 invasion of Czechoslovakia under the pretext of Warsaw Pact training exercises, had threatened to punish China with a nuclear assault or strike on Chinese nuclear facilities.[142] According to Arkady Shevchenko,

> the Soviet leadership had come close to using nuclear arms on China. . . . A Foreign Ministry colleague who had been present at the Politburo discussion told me that Marshal Andrei Grechko, the Defence Minister, advocated a plan to "once and for all get rid of the Chinese threat." He called for unrestricted use of multi-megaton bombs. . . . One of Grechko's colleagues, Nikolai Ogarkov (proposed) the alternative . . . to use a limited number of nuclear weapons in a kind of "surgical operation" to intimidate the Chinese and destroy their nuclear facilities.[143]

Some evidence suggests that Washington was able to stay Brezhnev's hand. Stearman had told Doris Davydov that Nixon could not accept a

Soviet attack, and according to Shevchenko, Dobrynin relayed to Moscow that "the United States would not be passive."[144]

The Soviet leadership likely concluded that a credible threat to attack China's nuclear and missile facilities would at the very least compel Mao to back down in Zhenbao. When US intelligence picked up signals of Soviet military preparations, Moscow may have "authorized leaks about a strike to East European governments and US intelligence in the hope that they would reach the Chinese."[145] Dobrynin continually probed the White House for Washington's reactions to a Soviet strike, and other sources warned of an attack on Chinese nuclear facilities.[146] The French foreign minister suggested to Nixon on September 18 that Moscow was using the Australian communist party to "scare China stiff" and "let the Chinese know that the Russians meant business."[147] It is worth repeating that Brezhnev's nuclear threat to China was his only such threat in seventeen years in power and was issued in response to the Chinese surprise attack at Zhenbao. Brezhnev authorized an assertive policy to Mao in 1969, but his foreign policy for the previous four and subsequent thirteen years was mostly restrained.

This Soviet assertive response caused Mao to believe that he had reached the nuclear brink. In November 1957 Mao had famously proclaimed: "I'm not afraid of nuclear war . . . China has a population of six hundred million; even if half of them are killed, there are still three hundred million people left." One month after China's first nuclear test, Mao had approved a report to relocate some key industrial and research facilities to China's interior, far out of range of Soviet bombers.[148] In 1966 Mao had told several People's Liberation Army (PLA) marshalls that Moscow would attack China within two years.[149] The 1969 Soviet threat reinforced fears resulting from the aggressive Soviet Zhenbao patrols and the knowledge that the Brezhnev doctrine could mean a preemptive and possibly nuclear attack against China was imminent.[150]

In March 1969 Mao called for readiness to "fight a great war, an early war, and even a nuclear war."[151] A Chinese defector referred to "genuine concern over cooperation between Moscow and Washington."[152] Although Moscow and Beijing had "cooperated in escalation control" at Zhenbao, Mao confided to his personal nurse that "China and the Soviet Union are now at war."[153] On March 15 he told the Central Cultural Revolution Group that "when the war breaks out, it will not be enough to rely upon the annual conscription . . . we are now confronted with a formidable enemy . . . our nuclear bases should be prepared, be prepared for the enemy's air bombardment."[154] Beginning in May, Chinese announcements made frequent reference to Soviet nuclear threats and potential surprise attacks.[155] By June, after Mao had informed the Central Military Commission administrative group not to worry if the Soviet Union struck China with nuclear weapons because "we, too, have atomic bombs," the general staff scrambled its communications unit to construct an emergency underground cable network."[156] On August 1, Henry Kissinger learned from the Pakistani chief of staff that Zhou Enlai "feared a preemptive attack on China" and that Zhou had "spent great time on Chicom fear and mistrust of the Soviets."[157] State Department analysts reported that Chinese propaganda statements reflected "genuine concern over encirclement."[158]

Mao's doctor recalled the August relocation of millions from the city to the country: "Remaining city residents were mobilized to 'dig tunnels deep' in preparation for aerial, possibly nuclear, attack" and to "be fully prepared to fight a war against aggression."[159] On August 28 Mao issued an urgent instruction to protect many more key installations from a sudden nuclear strike and greater military discipline.[160] Even though Mao's skeptical generals reported to him that an attack "was not very likely," Mao concluded that "it is not good for all central officials to assemble in Beijing" because "even one atomic bomb will kill many of us." By mid-September the influential four generals whom Mao had authorized to study international affairs concluded that the Soviets "intend to wage a war of aggression."[161] One specifically reported that Mao had authorized efforts to relocate some nuclear facilities to Tibet.[162] Mao then authorized two nuclear tests on September 23 and 29 to signal his resolve to make any war with Moscow a "total war."

After Brezhnev agreed to send Premier Alexei Kosygin to the Beijing airport to restart negotiations, Mao feared that Kosygin's incoming flight also carried special forces that would attack Beijing just as the August 1968 training exercise had turned into an attack on Prague.[163] Mao ordered military units to be placed on alert before Kosygin landed and moved several battalions of elite troops to the airport.[164] War preparations continued throughout September and October for a perceived imminent Soviet invasion. Mao denounced wars of aggression where "atom bombs are used as weapons."[165] At a meeting of generals to address readiness, the term most often heard was apparently "the coming Soviet surprise attack."[166] Aircraft in the Beijing area were evacuated, and Mao's deputy Lin Biao believed that the three huge reservoirs outside Beijing could flood the city and its outskirts if their dams were destroyed; he told local authorities to release their water.[167] With Mao's approval, Lin also placed all PLA units on their highest state of alert.[168] Premier Zhou Enlai however objected to and canceled this order.[169] When Zhou received Kosygin's letter stating that Soviet negotiators would arrive by October 20, Mao believed that this was when the Soviet surprise attack would come.[170] Rumors from Moscow suggested that the aircraft that was to carry the Soviet delegation to Beijing was retrofitted with nuclear-tipped air-to-surface missiles. Mao directed most of the central leaders and PLA generals to depart Beijing before the Soviet delegation's expected arrival.[171]

On October 18 Lin's famous "No. 1 order" warned of surprise attacks and ordered China's strategic missile force, the Second Artillery, on full alert for the immediate launch of nuclear missiles; all PLA units were to reach a state of total readiness.[172] This was the first and only time Chinese strategic forces were ordered to highest alert status. On October 19 Lin remained fixated on the Soviet aircraft that was carrying the Soviet delegation to Beijing, demanded intelligence updates every few minutes, and delayed his usual afternoon nap until the Soviet delegates had departed Beijing.[173] China's top leaders fled the capital shortly thereafter.[174] During the crisis Mao authorized the relocation of almost one million soldiers, thousands of aircraft, and hundreds of ships in preparation for war.[175] It is clear that panic had struck the Chinese leadership during this period; the expectation of imminent (and possibly nuclear) conflict explains Mao's erratic directives.

By early February 1970 the Soviet troops had withdrawn from many disputed islands and refrained from aggressive forward patrolling.[176] However, Chinese troops and heavy weapons were only allowed to stand down in late April.[177] Mao's concern about Soviet intentions, fueled by the Soviet invasion of Czechoslovakia and the implicit messages of an imminent strike on China, led him to view rapprochement with Washington as a means offsetting the pressure from Moscow and overcoming domestic opposition.[178] In January 1969 the French general consul in

Hong Kong had noted "a certain thaw in the Chinese policy of the great powers that have direct interests in Asia."[179] Concern about Soviet aggression and the need to contain Soviet influence in East Asia led the initially tentative Nixon to grow warmer to rapprochement with a nuclear China.[180] As Gelman notes, Moscow's "display of anxiety about China in their communications with the United States was itself stimulating the very U.S. efforts to exploit the China issue that Moscow wished to head off."[181]

Although Soviet troop deployments in the contested region continued after March 1969—with several small clashes occurring on the China-Mongolia border throughout the summer of 1969 and into the 1970s—China never again threatened or used force on the Ussuri River or in any dispute with the Soviet Union. After the October 1969 Zhou-Kosygin talks, Moscow and Beijing proposed and agreed to conflict-prevention and escalation-reducing measures.[182]

By 1970 the local military balance had become more favorable to Beijing. Almost no subsequent uses of force by China occurred until nearly ten years later—after 1979—and were directed at territorial disputes with Vietnam and the Philippines.[183] Mao's experience of fear of imminent nuclear war caused him to minimize escalatory risk in Chinese foreign policy toward the Soviet Union and to refrain from further challenging Soviet patrols in Zhenbao. When contemplating subsequent policies toward Moscow, his cognitive association of fear, as experienced in 1969 and 1970 from his policy of challenging Soviet troops on Zhenbao, likely caused his emotional brain to automatically prefer cooperation to challenge.

It is not clear if Chinese challenges on Zhenbao were nuclear assertion: Mao never issued any implicit or explicit nuclear threats, and he only warned Brezhnev that any Soviet attacks would lead to total war with China. The three nuclear learning models are therefore indeterminate regarding Mao's 1969 ambush. The Waltzian model would be falsified had Mao believed that nuclear weapons enabled him to challenge forward Soviet patrols in a manner that had earlier been considered untenable; it could explain Mao's restraint after 1970 because it expects leaders to abstain from nuclear assertion. The rational-signaling model might explain Mao's attack as a display of resolve: in the face of domestic unrest, a vulnerable nuclear arsenal, and resolved and far superior Soviet conventional military forces, Mao needed to demonstrate his resolve to stop brutally aggressive Soviet patrols.[184] However, the rational-signaling model might not be able to account for Mao's attack in the face of Brezhnev's costly signal at Czechoslovakia, which demonstrated Brezhnev's resolve to interfere in other communist states. Exactly which types of provocations the Soviet costly signal should rationally have deterred is not clear. Thus the rational-signaling model might expect Mao to have accepted the Soviet challenges but not reacted so provocatively in 1969. It could explain his restraint toward the Soviet Union after 1970, but it may not be able to explain the earlier challenge.

The ALF model is also indeterminate regarding Mao's challenges at Zhenbao because it is not clear that the policies were nuclear assertion. It can, however, explain China's foreign policy toward the Soviet Union after Mao's 1969–1970 experience of fear of imminent nuclear war. From a rational perspective, it is unclear why Mao would refrain from challenging Soviet positions after experiencing fear when he had earlier been so willing to confront the Soviet patrols. Equally puzzling is his moderation in all territorial disputes with Moscow after reaching the nuclear brink earlier that winter.

One might argue that worsening relations with the Soviet Union combined with the possibility of détente with the United States explain Mao's moderate foreign policy toward the Soviet Union after 1970. Perhaps Mao's experience of fear at the nuclear brink was not necessary to change Chinese foreign policy toward the Soviet Union in 1970. But if improved relations with Washington were the principal cause of the policy shift toward Moscow, why did he refrain from challenging Soviet positions after his relations with Washington actually had improved? Détente with Washington might have emboldened Mao to take a harder line on territorial disputes with Moscow. Any explanation of the Chinese policy change in 1970 that is based on the balance of power and Sino-US détente must also explain why Mao challenged Soviet positions on Zhenbao in 1969 but refrained from challenging any Soviet forces after détente with Washington substantially improved his position vis-à-vis Moscow. Finally, one can challenge the learning models on the grounds that Chinese foreign policy was influenced by many leaders or Chinese strategic culture. But Mao dominated all aspects of Chinese politics and foreign policy.[185]

Table 5.4. Nuclear Learning Models: China, 1969–1970

	Waltzian	Rational-Signaling	ALF Two-Stage
Zhenbao ambush, 1969	?	?	?
Zhenbao restraint, 1970–	✓	✓	✓

Conclusion

The Waltzian model cannot explain John Kennedy's, Atul Vajpayee's, or Richard Nixon's nuclear assertion, the first two of which resulted from Khrushchev's and Musharraf's nuclear assertion, respectively. The Waltzian model also cannot explain Mao's aggression in 1969, if indeed his actions were nuclear emboldenment. Any theory that expects leaders to use nuclear weapons only for deterrence runs into problems, not only when leaders in new nuclear powers authorize nuclear assertion but when their adversaries respond with assertive policies.

If the Waltzian nuclear learning model is correct, the most dangerous crises of the nuclear age should not have occurred. The rational-signaling model does not explain events any better: it expects leaders facing an assertive new nuclear power who has authorized a costly signal (such as Khrushchev and Musharraf) to respond with restrained foreign policy even when they have strong incentives to authorize an assertive policy in order to stem an adversary's assertion. The rational-signaling model is also indeterminate in the case of Richard Nixon: it can explain Nixon's assertiveness to Moscow, but it cannot explain his assertion with Hanoi.

Costly signals are an insufficient means for deterring nuclear assertion. Rational-signaling predictions are particularly erroneous in the cases of Kennedy and Vajpayee: two leaders edging toward a nuclear crisis who compelled their adversaries to cease their revisionism. The rational-signaling model would expect them both to have just accepted his adversary's revisionism because they had authorized a costly signal. The ALF model does not explain all the cases described in this chapter. Most damningly, it incorrectly predicts that India should have authorized an assertive foreign policy to Pakistan in 1990 when this did not occur until 1998 (an omission that the Waltzian model does explain). It cannot explain Kennedy's possible learning from World War I plus his coercive threat when he surely believed that nuclear war was imminent. But neither of the other models explains this case either. Kennedy's potential attention to the historical record in formulating his foreign policy during the Cuban Missile Crisis is deeply anomalous. Even so, the ALF model outperforms the others in correctly predicting Nixon's nuclear assertion throughout his presidency, and it explains Kennedy's restraint after the crisis in Cuba. ALF outperforms the others in predicting India's assertion in 2001–2 and also, like the other two models, explains Mao's restraint after 1970. Insufficient data prevents a definitive test of the models in the cases of Mao's aggression in 1969 and India's Cold Start doctrine since 2003.

In short, the ALF model explains much of the variation in the foreign policies authorized by US, Chinese, and Indian leaders. In the cases of Kennedy, Vajpayee, and Nixon, nuclear proliferation became dangerous when these leaders learned that nuclear assertion was safe or at least worthwhile. In the cases of Kennedy and Mao, nuclear proliferation became safe when they learned that nuclear assertion was dangerous. The case of Nixon shows that the ALF model also applies to leaders of experienced nuclear powers: when they learn that nuclear assertion is safe they tend to authorize dangerously assertive foreign policies that increase the risk of nuclear escalation.

While the Waltzian and rational-signaling models cannot explain nuclear assertion or its persistence after a costly signal, the ALF model predicts the variation in foreign policies that follows leaders facing fear of imminent nuclear escalation. The ALF model substantially outperforms the others and correctly explains how leaders have approached the fundamental dilemma of nuclear assertion from the onset of mutually assured destruction facing the United States in the late 1950s and early 1960s and the nuclear histories of India and China. Over four decades the leaders in these three countries authorized restrained foreign policies when they stumbled to the nuclear brink. There can be little doubt that Kennedy and Mao experienced fear of imminent nuclear war and that it caused, especially in Mao's case, important policy changes. These effects cannot be attributed to strategic culture or domestic politics since most of the leaders described here had substantial independent control over foreign policy, and the policies they devised and authorized—especially coercive threats—would not have received public approval. While nuclear coercion worked in the cases of Kennedy, Vajpayee, and Brezhnev, it did so only because the objective was always to prevent further nuclear assertion. Precisely because nuclear assertion is a poor instrument for revising a status quo, it can compel leaders to adopt more restrained foreign policies.

Notes

1. *FRUS*, 1961–1963, Vol. 5, Docs. 87–89.

2. "Address by Roswell G. Gilpatric, Deputy Secretary of Defense, Before the Business Council at the Homestead, Hot Springs, Virginia, Saturday, October 21, 1961, 9pm," *The National Security Archive*, The George Washington University, http://www2.gwu.edu/~nsarchiv/NSAEBB/NSAE BB56/BerlinC6.pdf.

3. Fursenko and Naftali, *Khrushchev's Cold War*, 409.

4. May and Zelikow, *Kennedy Tapes*, 390.

5. Slusser, *Berlin Crisis of 1961*, 5–15; and Fursenko and Naftali, *Khrushchev's Cold War*, 365.

6. Slusser, *Berlin Crisis of 1961*, 51–57.

7. Johnson, *American Cryptology during the Cold War*, 289–494.

8. Seymour Topping, "Kennedy Assailed," *New York Times*, September 12, 1962.

9. Johnson, *American Cryptology during the Cold War*, 331.

10. Tuchman, *Guns of August*. Tuchman's book was published a few months before the Cuban Missile Crisis.

11. Kennedy, *Thirteen Days*; M. Taylor, *Swords and Ploughshares*; and Sorensen, *Kennedy*.

12. May and Zelikow, *Kennedy Tapes*, xlii–xliv, 62; Cohen, "Live and Learn."

13. Beschloss, *Crisis Years*, 600.

14. Fursenko and Naftali, *Khrushchev's Cold War*, 523n114.

15. May and Zelikow, *Kennedy Tapes*, 197.

16. Ibid., 229.

17. For one participant's retrospective account to this effect, see Peterson, *Cuban Missile Crisis*.

18. May and Zelikow, *Kennedy Tapes*, 230.

19. Schlesinger, *Robert Kennedy and His Times*, 514.

20. I thank Tim Naftali for this point.

21. Alford, *Once upon a Secret*, 93–95.

22. Ibid., 94.

23. Khrushchev, *Memoirs*, 3:338.

24. "Cold War Crises," *Cold War International History Project Bulletin* 5 (Spring 1995): 79.

25. Bundy, *Danger and Survival*, 426.

26. *FRUS*, 1961–1963, Vol. 14 (microfiche supplement), "Telegram from Embassy in Soviet Union to Department of State, May 27, 1961."

27. *FRUS*, 1961–1963, Vol. 6, Doc. 69.

28. The sources used to make this claim, in addition to sources that address Khrushchev's experience of fear of imminent nuclear war, are Dallek, *An Unfinished Life*; Schlesinger, *A Thousand Days*; Reeves, *President Kennedy*; Guthman and Shulman, eds., *Robert Kennedy in His Own Words*; O'Donnell, Powers, and McCarthy, *Johnny, We Hardly Knew Ye*; Nash, "Bear Any Burden?"; Sorensen, *Kennedy*; Freedman, *Kennedy's Wars*; O'Brien, *Kennedy: A Biography*; and Bundy, *Danger and Survival*.

29. "Papers of John F. Kennedy, Presidential Papers, National Security Files, Meetings and Memoranda, National Security Council Meetings, 1961: No. 489, 20 July 1961," John F. Kennedy Presidential Library and Museum, http://www.jfklibrary.org/Asset-Viewer/Archives/JFKNSF-313-016.aspx. See also Dean Rusk, *As I Saw It* (New York: W. W. Norton & Company, 1990), 246–47.

30. Sorensen, *Counselor*, 326.

31. Chang and Kornbluh, *Cuban Missile Crisis, 1962*, 351.

32. Ibid., chaps. 5 and 6.

33. "Memorandum for the Record, Subject: Mr. Donovan's Trip to Cuba, March 4, 1963," Cuba Files, Kennedy and Castro: The Secret History, *The National Security Archive*, The George Washington University, http://www.gwu.edu/~nsarchiv/NSAEBB/NSAEBB103/630304.pdf.

34. Basrur, *Minimum Deterrence*, 82.

35. Prime Minister A. B. Vajpayee, Statement of March 15, 1999, cited in Prakash Karat, "Kargil and Beyond," *Frontline*.

36. Brajesh Mishra, discussion with the author, New Delhi, April 2009.

37. Malik, "Lessons from Kargil."

38. Brajesh Mishra, discussion with the author, New Delhi, April 2009.

39. Kapur, *Dangerous Deterrent*, 129n66, 133n82.

40. "India Ratchets Up Rhetoric against Pakistan and China," *Agence France Presse*, May 18, 1998, cited in Perkovich, *India's Nuclear Bomb*, 423n102.

41. C. Raja Mohan, "Fernandes Unveils 'Limited War' Doctrine," *Hindu*, January 25, 2000.

42. Kapur, *Dangerous Deterrent*.

43. Basrur, "Lessons of Kargil," 311.

44. Narang, *Nuclear Strategy in the Modern Era*, 271–73.

45. Ganguly and Kraig, "2001–2002 Indo-Pakistani Crisis," 298.

46. Brajesh Mishra, discussion with the author, New Delhi, April 2009.

47. Ganguly and Kraig, "2001–2002 Indo-Pakistani Crisis," 299–302.

48. Brajesh Mishra, discussion with the author, New Delhi, April 2009. See also Sood and Sawhney, *Operation Parakram,* 60; and Kapur, "Ten Years of Instability," 82.

49. Brajesh Mishra, discussion with the author, New Delhi, April 2009.

50. Ladwig, "A Cold Start?"

51. Ladwig, "A Cold Start?," 175–90.

52. "India Strikes Terror Launch Pads along LoC," *Indian Express,* October 14, 2016; Annie Gowen and Shaiq Hussain, "India Claims 'Surgical Strikes' against Militants in Pakistan-Controlled Kashmir," *Washington Post,* September 29, 2016.

53. "Dobrynin to Politburo, Report on Meeting with Kissinger, July 12, 1969," Communist Party of the Soviet Union Central Committee Archive, *Cold War International History Project Bulletin* 3 (Fall 1993): 62–67.

54. "Memorandum of Conversation, Nixon and De Gaulle Feb. 28, 1969," cited in Burr and Kimball, "Nixon's Secret Nuclear Alert."

55. Haldeman, *Ends of Power,* 82–83, 97–98.

56. Burr and Kimball, "Nixon's Secret Nuclear Alert," 113–56; and Sagan and Jeremi Suri, "Madman Nuclear Alert."

57. Kimball, *Vietnam War Files,* 15.

58. Gavin, *Nuclear Statecraft,* 118.

59. "Memo, Haig to Kissinger, March 2, 1969," cited in Burr and Kimball, "Nixon's Secret Nuclear Alert."

60. Ibid., note 14.

61. Nixon, *Memoirs,* 384.

62. Kimball, *Vietnam War Files,* chap. 1.

63. Burr and Kimball, "Nixon's Secret Nuclear Alert," 121–29.

64. "Memorandum, Haig to Kissinger, October 14, 1969," ibid.

65. Ibid., 113.

66. Sagan and Suri, "Madman Nuclear Alert"; Burr and Kimball, "Nixon's Secret Nuclear Alert."

67. Nixon, *No More Vietnams,* 101–7.

68. "Diary Entry, October 17, 1969," H. R. Haldeman Diaries, Nixon Presidential Library, cited in Burr and Kimball, "Nixon's Secret Nuclear Alert."

69. Ibid.

70. "Memorandum of Conversation between Nixon, Kissinger, and Thompson, October 17, 1969," Box 1023, National Security Council Files, Nixon Presidential Library, cited in Burr and Kimball, "Nixon's Secret Nuclear Alert."

71. "Memo, Kissinger to Nixon, October 18, 1969," ibid. For the reference to the train leaving the station, see "Memo, Kissinger to Nixon, October 1, 1969, 'Conversation with Soviet Ambassador Dobrynin,'" attached to memorandum of conversation, Kissinger and Dobrynin, September 27, 1969, Box 489, Burr and Kimball, "Nixon's Secret Nuclear Alert"; Nixon, *Memoirs,* 400; and Kissinger, *White House Years,* 304.

72. "Memo, Kissinger to Nixon, October 21, 1969," cited in Burr and Kimball, "Nixon's Secret Nuclear Alert."

73. Ibid., 144–45.

74. Sagan and Suri, "Madman Nuclear Alert," 158.

75. "Llewellyn Thompson to Secretary of State Rogers, November 5, 1969, RG 59," Subject-Numeric Files, 1970–73, POL US-USSR, box 489, Dobrynin/Kissinger 1969 (Part II), National Security Council Files, Nixon Presidential Library, cited in Burr and Kimball, "Nixon's Secret Nuclear Alert."

76. Kimball, *Vietnam War Files*, 115–16.

77. Gavin, *Nuclear Statecraft*, 114.

78. McDermott, *Presidential Leadership*, 188.

79. "Letter, Ho to Nixon, August 25, 1969 (Top Secret: Sensitive)," folder: Mister "S," vol. 1, box 106, Country Files: Far East–Vietnam Negotiations, National Security Council Files, Nixon Presidential Library, cited in Burr and Kimball, "Nixon's Secret Nuclear Alert."

80. Kimball, *Vietnam War Files*, 286.

81. Lebow and Stein, *We All Lost the Cold War*, 488n37.

82. Kimball, *Vietnam War Files*, 641.

83. Brandon, *Retreat of American Power*, 134.

84. *FRUS*, 1969–1976, Vol. 14, Doc. 82. For a chilling account of how Kissinger encouraged "a tough stand with the Soviets" where "we may have to go on alert and put forces in" to ensure "we're coming off like men," see Bass, *Blood Telegram*, 305–9.

85. Kimball, *Vietnam War Files*, 32; and Kissinger, *White House Years*, 665–66.

86. Randolph, *Powerful and Brutal Weapons*, 86, 93, 158, 161, 183, 198–99.

87. Kimball, *Vietnam War Files*, 217.

88. Burr and Kimball, "Nixon's Secret Nuclear Alert," 188n17.

89. *FRUS*, 1969–1976, Vol. 25, Docs. 100–112, esp. 104, 108–109. Brezhnev had actually attempted to prevent Sadat from attacking on at least four occasions. See Garthoff, *Détente and Confrontation*, 207.

90. *FRUS*, 1969–1976, Vol. 25, Doc. 106.

91. *FRUS*, 1969–1976, Vol. 25, Doc. 146.

92. Lebow and Stein, *We All Lost the Cold War*, 236–37, 246–47; *FRUS*, 1969–1976, Vol. 25, Docs. 254–278.

93. *FRUS*, 1969–1976, Vol. 25, Doc. 269.

94. Grynaviski, *Constructive Illusions*, 73–85.

95. Lebow and Stein, *We All Lost the Cold War*, 266–68.

96. Ibid.; and Israelyan, *Inside the Kremlin*, 179–83.

97. Ambrose, *Nixon*, 106, 115.

98. Nixon, *Memoirs*, 29.

99. Ambrose, *Nixon*, 106–14.

100. Ibid., 111, 114.

101. Kimball, *Vietnam War Files*, 65.

102. Dingman, "Atomic Diplomacy," 50–91; Foot, "Nuclear Coercion," 92–112; and Keefer, "President Dwight D. Eisenhower," 267–89.

103. Dingman, "Atomic Diplomacy," 81; and Foot, "Nuclear Coercion."

104. Burr and Kimball, "Nixon's Secret Nuclear Alert."

105. *FRUS*, 1969–1976, Vol. 7, Doc. 190.

106. Haldeman, *Ends of Power*, 83.

107. Kimball, *Vietnam War Files*, 115.

108. "A Nation Coming into Its Own," *Time* 126, no. 4 (July 29, 1985): 48–59.

109. Ambrose, *Nixon*, 343–46.

110. Logevall, *Embers of War*, 459–61; John Foster Dulles, "The Threat of a Red Asia," remarks made before the Overseas Press Club in New York, March 29, 1954, *Department of State Bulletin* (April 12, 1954): 539–40; and Ambrose, *Nixon*, 344–45.

111. Logevall, *Embers of War*, 612. See also Yang Kuisong, "Changes in Mao Zedong's Attitude toward the Indochina War, 1949–1973," Cold War International History Project Working Paper 34 (February 2002): 7–12;" and Jian, "China and the First Indo-China War," 105.

112. Nixon, *Memoirs*, 244.

113. Maxwell, "Chinese Account," 731.

114. Fravel and Medeiros, "China's Search for Assured Retaliation," 52, 55–67.

115. Cited in Goldstein, *Preventive Attack*, 77–78.

116. Chen Jian and David L. Wilson, "All under the Heaven Is Great Chaos: Beijing, The Sino-Soviet Border Clashes, and the Turn toward Sino-American Rapprochement, 1968–69," *Cold War International History Project Bulletin* 11 (Winter 1998): 155–61.

117. Kuisong, "Sino-Soviet Border Clash of 1969," 28n20. See also Scobell, *China's Use of Military Force*, 15.

118. Kuisong, "Sino-Soviet Border Clash," 30n23.

119. Ibid., 38n56.

120. "Polish-Soviet Talks in Moscow," March 1, 1969, Cold War International History Project, http://digitalarchive.wilsoncenter.org/document/112937.

121. Fravel, *Strong Borders, Secure Nation*, 1–2.

122. Ibid., 122n239.

123. Robinson, "China Confronts the Soviet Union," 250; Richard Wich, *Sino-Soviet Crisis Politics*, 5, 57; Garthoff, *Détente and Confrontation*, 228; and Fravel, *Strong Borders, Secure Nation*.

124. Fravel, *Strong Borders, Secure Nation*, 208–9.

125. T. W. Robinson, "Sino-Soviet Border Dispute," 1188–89.

126. Fravel, *Strong Borders, Secure Nation*, 202; Kuisong, "Sino-Soviet Border Clash"; Goldstein, "Return to Zhenbao Island"; Gurtov and Hwang, *China under Threat*; and Robinson, "Sino-Soviet Border Conflict."

127. Gelman, *Soviet Far East Buildup*, ix.

128. Gelman, *Soviet Far East Buildup*, 37–38.

129. "Moscow Denies Any Atom Threat," *New York Times*, March 23, 1969.

130. *Pravda*, September 15, 1964, cited in Gelman, *Soviet Far East Buildup*, 17.

131. Cited in Gerson, *Sino-Soviet Border Conflict*, 29; and Wich, *Sino-Soviet Crisis Politics*, 106.

132. Kuisong, "Sino-Soviet Border Clash," 32.

133. Goldstein, *Preventive Attack*, 82; Burr, "Sino-American Relations, 1969," 82; and Garthoff, *Détente and Confrontation*, 209.

134. Burr, "Sino-American Relations," 86n41.

135. Ibid., 86n42, 89n53.

136. Kissinger, *White House Years*, 183–85; Garthoff, *Détente and Confrontation*, 237; Tyler, *A Great Wall*, 66–67; Gobarev, "Soviet Policy toward China," 46; and Shevchenko, *Breaking with Moscow*, 165–66.

137. Gobarev, "Soviet Policy toward China," 46; Shevchenko, *Breaking with Moscow*, 165–66; and Tyler, *A Great Wall*, 65–67.

138. Burr, "Sino-American Relations," 89n54.

139. Kissinger, *White House Years*, 184. See, for example, "Russia Reported Eyeing Strikes at China A-Sites," *Washington Post*, August 28, 1969; "Western Envoys Differ on Soviet Threat to China," *Washington Post*, August 29, 1969; "U.S. Doubts Soviet Will Bomb China," *New York Times*, August 29, 1969.

140. Cited in Lewis and Litai, *Imagined Enemies*, 52n54.

141. Victor Louis, "Will Russia Czech-Mate China?," *London Evening News*, September 16, 1969.

142. Christian Osterman, "East German Documents on the Border Conflict," *Cold War International History Project Bulletin* 6–7 (1995–96): 187; Kuisong, "Sino-Soviet Border Clash," 32; and Lewis and Litai, *Imagined Enemies*, 56n79.

143. Shevchenko, *Breaking with Moscow*, 165; and Goldstein, *Preventive Attack*, 82.

144. Burr, "Sino-American Relations," 88n48; Shevchenko, *Breaking with Moscow*, 166; and Tyler, *A Great Wall*, 69.

145. Burr, "Sino-American Relations," 87; and Lewis and Litai, *Imagined Enemies*, 56.

146. Burr and Richelson, "Whether to 'Strangle the Baby,'" 97.

147. Burr, "Sino-American Relations," 92n60; and Kissinger, *White House Years*, 186.

148. Lewis and Litai, *Imagined Enemies*, 46; and Kuisong, "Sino-Soviet Border Clash."

149. Lewis and Litai, *Imagined Enemies*, 48n25.

150. Ibid., 52n55, 55n76.

151. Kuisong, "Sino-Soviet Border Clash," 31.

152. Cited in Burr, "Sino-American Relations," 79–80n19.

153. Lewis and Litai, *Imagined Enemies*, 40, 50n36.

154. "Mao Zedong's Talk at a Meeting of the Central Cultural Revolution Group," March 15, 1969, *Cold War International History Project Bulletin* 11 (Winter 1998): 162.

155. Gelman, *Soviet Far East Buildup*, 43n19.

156. Lewis and Litai, *Imagined Enemies*, 53n62.

157. Burr, "Sino-American Relations," 86–87n44.

158. Ibid., 80n21.

159. Lewis and Litai, *Imagined Enemies*, 54n70; "The CCP Central Committee's Order for General Mobilisation in Border Provinces and Regions," August 28, 1969, Cold War International History Project *Bulletin* 11 (Winter 1998): 168–69.

160. Kuisong, "Sino-Soviet Border Clash," 37; Burr, "Sino-American Relations," 92n61; and Sutter, *China Watch*, 86–87.

161. Jian and Wilson, "All under the Heaven," 170–71; and Kuisong, "Sino-Soviet Border Clash," 35–37.

162. Sydney H. Schanberg, "China Said to Be Moving Nuclear Plant to Tibet," *New York Times*, September 13, 1969, 5.

163. Stanley Karnow, "Soviet Attack Coming, Peking Tells Its People," *Washington Post*, September 11, 1969, A12. For details on the visit, see Osterman, "East German Documents," 186–93, 191–93; and Jian and Wilson, "All under the Heaven," 171–72.

164. Lewis and Litai, *Imagined Enemies*, 58n93.

165. Ibid., 59n104.

166. Ibid., 60.

167. Kuisong, "Sino-Soviet Border Clash," 40.

168. Report by four Chinese Marshals—Chen Yi, Ye Jianying, Nie Rongzhen and Xu Xiangqian—to the CCP Central Committee, "Our Views about the Current Situation, September 17, 1969," *Cold War International History Project Bulletin* 11 (Winter 1998): 170; and Kuisong, "Sino-Soviet Border Clash," 40–41.

169. Lewis and Litai, *Imagined Enemies*, 61n110.

170. Kuisong, "Sino-Soviet Border Clash," 40; Lewis and Litai, *Imagined Enemies*, 61n116; and MacFarquhar and Schoenhals, *Mao's Last Revolution*, 317.

171. Lewis and Litai, *Imagined Enemies*, 62n120.

172. Kuisong, "Sino-Soviet Border Clash," 40; and Lewis and Litai, *Imagined Enemies*, 64.

173. Lewis and Litai, *Imagined Enemies*, 69n146.

174. Kuisong, "Sino-Soviet Border Clash," 36n49; Lewis and Litai, *Imagined Enemies*, 57n88; and MacFarquhar and Schoenhals, *Mao's Last Revolution*, 313–14.

175. Kuisong, "Sino-Soviet Border Clash," 40–41.

176. Fravel, *Strong Borders, Secure Nation*, 216n174.

177. Lewis and Litai, *Imagined Enemies*, 72n160.

178. Luthi, *Sino-Soviet Split*.

179. "Gerard de la Villesbrunne to the New Foreign Minister, 'New Interest of Western Diplomacy towards China: Hopes and Illusions,'" January 30, 1969, Cold War International History Project, http://digitalarchive.wilsoncenter.org/document/116449.

180. See, for example, Burr, "Sino-American Relations."

181. Gelman, *Soviet Far East Buildup*, 47.

182. Fravel, *Strong Borders, Secure Nation*, 216n173.

183. Ibid., 64–65.

184. On China's small nuclear arsenal see, for example, Goldstein, *Preventive Attack*, 86–88.

185. See MacFarquhar and Schoenhals, *Mao's Last Revolution*; and Short, *Mao: A Life*.

6

If You Can Get through This Period: When Proliferation Causes Peace

DOES THE POSSESSION of nuclear weapons prevent or promote interstate conflict? Scholars have debated this question since the beginning of the nuclear age and have amassed extensive evidence that supports a variety of conclusions. Policymakers coming to terms with the consequences of nuclear weapon development by states such as North Korea and Iran face contradictory policy prescriptions, all with robust empirical support. John Lewis Gaddis and Kenneth Waltz have shown that nuclear weapons stabilize international relations because they diminish the tendency of nations to take risks.[1] Scott Sagan influentially has shown that while accidental detonations and accidental war have thus far been avoided, nuclear arsenals are not yet secure from accident.[2] Paul Kapur has shown that nuclear weapons make the world dangerous because Iranian and North Korean leaders with nuclear weapons may see them as a shield behind which they can engage in coercion and aggression.[3] Staking out a third position, John Mueller argues that nuclear weapons have had little impact on international politics because war between the major powers has become obsolete since 1945.[4] Other evidence supports Mueller's thesis and shows that nuclear weapons do not influence the conflict propensity of states, because states that develop nuclear weapons are already highly conflict prone.[5] These three positions represent competing orthodoxies regarding how nuclear weapons have influenced international politics since the end of World War II. They all are, however, either wrong or incomplete.

Current thinking about nuclear weapons and international conflict neglects a state's experience with nuclear weapons and, more specifically, the effect of fear of imminent nuclear escalation on a leader's foreign policy. Nuclear weapons have had positive, negative, and neutral effects on international conflict depending on where one chooses to look. Leaders in new nuclear powers tend to authorize assertive foreign policies that cause conflict and nuclear crises. But these same leaders, if they have experienced fear of imminent nuclear war, tend to authorize restrained foreign policies toward their primary adversaries and often to other states that in the end reduces the danger of conflict and nuclear escalation. These stabilizing and destabilizing effects cancel each other out over the long run.[6]

The choices that leaders have made when facing the dilemma of nuclear assertion have largely driven the challenges and opportunities that nuclear weapons present. Waltz, Sagan, and Mueller are all partly correct: new nuclear powers tend to be dangerous. But the experience of fear in a nuclear crisis leaves these nuclear powers nearly as conflict prone as they were before they developed nuclear weapons. Thus Nikita Khrushchev's claim in 1958 was accurate: "The possibility of a nuclear war is always there, but the moments of greatest risk are in the first shock of new events. If you can get through this period all right, you will be safe."[7] Scholars and commentators who want to address the dangers posed by nuclear powers can no longer cherry-pick historical episodes to support their prior policy preferences. They must be attentive to the specific leader's personal experience with nuclear weapons and whether that leader has endured a nuclear crisis.

Restricting one's analysis to new or experienced nuclear powers or studying nuclear crises or costly signals and neglecting the effect of fear overlooks its systematic effect on a leader's foreign policy and conflict propensity and their change over time. The pathologies of availability and fear have made the spread of nuclear weapons exert a profound but counterintuitive effect on international relations. Proliferation optimists cannot easily explain the high conflict propensity of new nuclear powers. Proliferation pessimists cannot easily explain why most nuclear powers exhibit restrained foreign policies most of the time. Without a coherent theory that explains the changing behaviors of nuclear powers over time, all that is left is a grab bag from which policymakers and scholars can select whichever ideas best fit their preexisting policy predictions; each theory has extensive empirical support.

Because proliferation pessimism can explain the most undesirable and costly consequences of nuclear proliferation, it has become the orthodox wisdom among policymakers and most scholars. As Richard Betts notes, though "Waltz's argument that 'more may be better' cannot simply be brushed off, surprisingly few academic strategists have tried to refute it in detail."[8] Even at seventy years into the nuclear age we still lack empirically supported explanations of variation in the foreign policies of new and experienced nuclear powers.

Other literature has addressed nuclear postures and conceptualized and attempted to quantitatively measure nuclear learning. The argument put forth here offers the first comparative theory of new nuclear power foreign policy. It explains the core foreign policy choices that leaders of new and experienced nuclear powers must make regarding the central dilemma of nuclear assertion. The psychology of availability and fear has shaped the challenges and opportunities that nuclear weapons present. Nuclear proliferation has been dangerous when leaders have learned that nuclear assertion is safe, but it has become safe when leaders have learned that nuclear assertion is dangerous.

The ALF model developed and tested here resolves three puzzles associated with nuclear weapons and international conflict. Why are some nuclear powers more conflict prone than others? The ALF model shows why new nuclear powers tend to exhibit dangerous assertive foreign policies whereas the same nuclear powers, once they gained experience, tend to exhibit restrained foreign policies. The experience of fear of imminent nuclear war causes leaders in new nuclear powers to abandon nuclear assertion. Why do leaders in new nuclear powers seem to not learn from the historical record when formulating their foreign policies despite the high incentive to do so? The ALF model explains why leaders tend to learn from their country's successes with nuclear weapons development rather than from the historical record overall: their own experiences are much more cognitively available than the historical record, and their own experiences tend to lead them to authorize nuclear assertion.

Why do leaders of new nuclear powers push so hard to revise unsatisfactory security environments and accept the risk of nuclear escalation but then accept the unsatisfactory environment when the underlying status quo remains unchanged? The ALF model explains why the experience of fear of imminent nuclear war, brought about by an adversary's assertive foreign policies, causes a leader to authorize restrained foreign policies and address security threats through diplomacy and confidence-building measures, even after having relied on coercive threats and military force. Defenders of the status quo, whether new or experienced nuclear powers, also tend to learn from an adversary that nuclear assertion can stop nuclear assertion. The nuclear brink disabuses leaders of both states from placing excessive faith in this coercive move.

The Waltzian model cannot explain why leaders in new nuclear powers and occasionally experienced nuclear powers authorize nuclear assertion. It correctly predicts the rational tendency for beliefs to "eventually converge around reality," but it does not specify when or how this occurs.[9] This is no minor misprediction: the Waltzian model cannot explain the onset of the most dangerous nuclear crises of the last seven decades. Leaders in new nuclear powers have tended to authorize nuclear assertion, which plunges their regions into nuclear crises, and the critics of proliferation optimism are correct to lambast the theory for failing to satisfactorily come to terms with reality. It does a poor job of specifying the causal mechanism whereby the spread of nuclear weapons has the pacifying effects that they expect. The rational-signaling model does only a little better: it expects leaders in new nuclear powers to display assertive foreign policies but also expects that an adversary's costly signals quickly disabuses them of the folly of the policy. The rational-signaling model would predict that the Cold War crisis years would have ended in 1961 and the South Asian crisis years would have ended in 1999. Like the Waltzian model, it cannot explain the two most dangerous interstate crises that nuclear weapons have caused. It struggles to explain why subjective perceptions, feelings, and beliefs tend to be more robust causes of foreign policy change than the objective costly signals. Perceptions are king at the nuclear brink.

Findings and Implications

This ALF model is a theoretically rigorous and empirically falsifiable theory that predicts whether leaders in nuclear powers will authorize assertive or restrained foreign policies. It explains the fundamental foreign policy choices made by new and experienced nuclear powers by drawing on two core insights from decades of psychological research—the availability heuristic and fear. It contributes to the literature on nuclear proliferation and international conflict by specifying the conditions when nuclear powers are likely to be emboldened to authorize assertive policies and when they are likely to authorize more restrained policies.

Leaders in new nuclear powers learn about nuclear assertion from their cognitively accessible successes with nuclear weapon development, and they tend to authorize assertive foreign policies. They will persist with them until they experience fear of imminent nuclear war, which will in turn cause them to authorize restrained foreign policies. An adversary's authorization of an assertive foreign policy is usually necessary for a new nuclear power to experience fear of imminent nuclear war, although it can take days (e.g., Khrushchev) or months (Mao and Musharraf) for the leader to reach the nuclear brink. Leaders do not learn about the trade-offs of nuclear assertion from the historical record or from an adversary's costly signals; a personal experience of fear at the nuclear brink is necessary for an emboldened nuclear power to authorize a restrained foreign policy.

The ALF model was tested against Waltzian realist and rational-choice-signaling approaches in the major foreign policy choices of six leaders in five nuclear powers over five decades. The analysis showed that the model performs better than the Waltzian and rational-signaling alternatives, as it is attentive to the key psychological pressures that drive the formation of and change in a leader's response to the nuclear dilemma of coercion or deterrence.

Table 6.1 summarizes the relative explanatory power of the Waltzian, rational-signaling, and ALF nuclear learning models against the US, Soviet, Chinese, Indian, and Pakistani nuclear experiences between the onset of the missile age in the Cold War and the early twenty-first century. The ALF model comfortably outperforms the alternatives across

Table 6.1. Summary of the Nuclear Learning Models

Case	Waltzian	Rational-Signaling	ALF Two-Stage
Soviet Union: Assertion, 1956–1962	✗	✗	✓
Soviet Union: Restraint, 1963–	✓	✓	✓
Pakistan: Assertion, 1990–2002	✗	✗	✓
Pakistan: Restraint, 2003–	✓	✓	✓
United States: Assertion, 1962	✗	✗	✗
United States: Restraint, 1963	✓	✓	✓
India: Restraint, 1990–2000	✓	✗	✗
India: Assertion, 2001–2002	✗	✗	✓
India: 2003–	?	?	?
United States: Assertion, 1969–1973	✗	?	✓
China: 1969	?	?	?
China: Restraint, 1970–	✓	✓	✓
Successful Predictions	5–7	4–7	8–10

the experiences of the five nuclear powers examined here. It accurately predicts between eight and ten of the twelve foreign policy choices: a success rate of between 66 and 83 percent. The Waltzian and rational-signaling models explain between 33 and 58 percent of them. Of the cases where available data permits a competitive probe of the three nuclear learning models, the ALF model explains 80 percent of foreign policy choices, while the Waltzian and rational-signaling models explain 50 and 40 percent, respectively.

In a third of the cases the ALF model correctly explains cases that the other models either mispredict or are unable to determine. In another third of the cases the ALF model is not the only explanation that accurately predicts a nuclear power's foreign policy. Two of the four missed cases are due to the lack of currently available data; none of the models explain them. The Waltzian model outperforms the ALF model in one case—Indian restraint in Kashmir in the 1990s—although the ALF model explains the more assertive Indian policy in that disputed region and outperforms the Waltzian model from the aftermath of the Kargil War.[10]

The ALF model's only major misprediction is Kennedy's assertive foreign policy when he was at the nuclear brink. But none of the models explain Kennedy's actions. His incorporation of personal lessons from his scholarly study of the First World War into the policymaking process during the Cuban Missile Crisis and US nuclear assertion in the face of Soviet costly signals is strikingly anomalous. Leaders of new nuclear powers tend to authorize assertive foreign policies in the face of costly signals, and the Waltzian and rational-signaling models do not explain or predict this. One could tautologically claim that some other rational model could do as good a job as the ALF model in predicting behavior. But while one could specify the utility and probability of nuclear assertion that explains the outcomes of these cases post hoc, there is no rational reason why leaders should learn of the limits of nuclear assertion from fear rather than from general danger.

All three models ultimately expect a nuclear power to exhibit a restrained foreign policy, but the ALF model does so by capturing the causal mechanisms that find the most support in the historical record. Nuclear powers simply do not automatically use nuclear weapons only for deterrence, as Kenneth Waltz has famously argued they should, and costly signals do not automatically temper the actions of a leader of a new nuclear power. In the eight cases that the ALF model correctly predicts, it is clear that the road to foreign policy restraint travels through a nuclear crisis. Leaders are not always averse to the risks of nuclear escalation, as Waltz predicts, and new nuclear powers generally need to be shaken by a nuclear crisis—not just a costly signal—to consistently behave as predicted. The successfully predicted ALF cases also provide strong grounds to be suspicious of theories of learning that emphasize the sender of a signal. The focus must be on the receiver herself in order to better predict what she will believe and what policies her lessons will cause. Rational-choice models should substantially relax assumptions about the origins of beliefs.[11]

The ALF model generally explains variation in the core aspects of most new nuclear powers' foreign policies and correctly identifies the decision-making processes that cause foreign policy change. Vipin Narang shows that his "posture optimization" theory is "the first broadly comparative theory for why states select the nuclear postures they do . . . and also provides a generalizable framework to predict when regional powers might *shift* their postures."[12] But posture is not policy, and the ALF model supplements Narang's research by developing and testing a comparative theory of nuclear power foreign policy that specifies both the foreign policies of new nuclear powers and the conditions when those policies will change. It is the first theory to explain the sources of and key variation in the nuclear weapon-induced foreign policy choices of the United States, Soviet Union, China, India, and Pakistan. While Narang's model is "a structural theory that predicts *outcome* and not necessarily *process*," the ALF model is also based on neoclassical realism but derives its explanatory power from leaders and their psychological biases. Therefore, it first and foremost predicts process which is usually necessary to explain policy change when structural factors do not vary.[13]

The nuclear crises on which the ALF model is based are caused by a new nuclear power's adversary abandoning foreign policy restraint in favor of assertion; because the adversary's policy is exogenous to the model, the ALF model does not fully specify when an emboldened new nuclear power will authorize a more restrained foreign policy. Nonetheless, the ALF model pinpoints exactly what it is about experience with nuclear weapons that tends to moderate a state's foreign policy.[14]

For too long the majority of scholars and policymakers who have assessed the dangers posed by the spread of nuclear weapons have either ignored variation in the foreign policies that nuclear powers exhibit or assumed that inexperience with nuclear weapons was theoretically intractable. The argument here has shown that attention to the psychological processes through which leaders come to terms with nuclear weapons and nuclear assertion over time yields high dividends. The ALF model explains the onset and resolution of the most dangerous episodes of the nuclear age through two psychological mechanisms that are largely measurable. During the Cold War, and in the more recent experiences in South Asia and East Asia, nuclear proliferation was dangerous when leaders learned that nuclear assertion is safe, but proliferation became safe when leaders learned that nuclear assertion is dangerous. Despite much talk that the end of the Cold War would usher in a "second (more safe) nuclear age," the differences between the present and the past have been, as Frank Gavin points out, vastly exaggerated.[15] The ALF model also offers predictions about the foreign policies that North Korea and

Iran will likely authorize if they develop nuclear weapons, and the best policies needed to meet these challenges.

Counterarguments

Skeptical readers might take issue with some of the key findings presented here. First, one might argue that because leaders do not stay in power forever, new leaders must experience fear of imminent nuclear war and stumble through a nuclear crisis personally in order for restrained foreign policies to continue into the longer run. The experiences of successors are beyond the scope of this book, but the rejoinder runs into the obvious problem that the successors to Khrushchev, Mao, and even Musharraf have not had to experience another nuclear crisis to maintain a more restrained foreign policy. There are at least two reasons for this. The first is regime type. In authoritarian regimes and personalist dictatorships, the successor to the leader is likely carefully groomed and therefore involved or at least closely aware of the foreign policy decisions that a leader has made. In non-democratic new nuclear powers, a leader's nuclear assertion will likely loom large to a successor, who likely also experienced fear of imminent nuclear escalation in the nation's nuclear crisis. There is, therefore, a strong chance that such a leader will also authorize a restrained foreign policy when he or she comes to power. The successors to Khrushchev, Musharraf, and Mao—Leonid Brezhnev, Ashfaq Kayani, and Deng Xiaoping—were in senior decision-making roles during their nuclear crises and likely experienced fear of imminent nuclear war as well.

Subsequent generations of leaders who come to power decades later in autocracies are more likely to authorize nuclear assertion because the earlier nuclear crisis will not be cognitively available to them. Thus, while much of Vladimir Putin's ongoing modernization of Russia's nuclear force is likely designed to increase survivability in the face of US nuclear primacy, Putin may also believe that a stronger nuclear force will increase his ability to revise undesirable territorial arrangements. This may explain Russia's frequent incursions into NATO member states' airspace and other limited but nonetheless significant signs of assertion. Putin was ten years old in 1962; we should not expect him to have learned the pacifying lessons of nuclear assertion from the Cuban Missile Crisis, because while that episode fundamentally shaped Khrushchev's views about nuclear assertion, it was not cognitively accessible to Putin. Prime Minister Dmitry Medvedev was born in 1965. But Putin's predecessor, Boris Yeltsin, was already thirty-one years old in 1962.

It is possible that one of the reasons that Xi Jinping has had little hesitation to throw his weight around the South China Sea when the Chinese armed forces and especially submarines are inherently vulnerable to US nuclear strikes is that the lessons of 1969 are not cognitively available to him. He was sixteen years old when Mao stumbled into a nuclear crisis at Zhenbao. But his predecessor, Hu Jintao, was twenty-seven in 1969. We may be witnessing the beginnings of Russian and Chinese nuclear assertion because Putin and Xi believe that nuclear assertion is safe.

In the most challenging contemporary cases of nuclear proliferation today, immediate successors to leaders that had experienced fear in a nuclear crisis will likely not need to stumble through a second nuclear crisis to authorize restrained foreign policies. But later generations of leaders may need this personal evidence, and future Russian and Chinese foreign policies may be probative if dangerous proof for this generational hypothesis. If Russian or Chinese leaders learn that nuclear assertion is safe, their foreign policies will become dangerous.

Democratic regimes involve higher leadership turnover, greater variation in foreign policy, and a greater probability of leaders coming to power who were not involved in previous nuclear crises. One might therefore conclude that experienced nuclear democracies have a greater likelihood of authorizing nuclear assertion. But Richard Nixon's actions are rare: the former president based his foreign policy on lessons learned during his vice presidency in the early years of the Cold War. It is hard to imagine a leader in the United States, Britain, France, Israel, or India basing his or her foreign policy on the probability that nuclear assertion will revise undesirable security arrangements. In the United States, for example, Ronald Reagan's experiences in the 1983 Able Archer Crisis seem to have been necessary for him to pursue a safer foreign policy toward the Soviet Union during his second term. On the other hand, the successors to Kennedy, Nixon, and Reagan—Lyndon Johnson, Gerald Ford, and George H. W. Bush—authorized restrained foreign policies or at least do not seem to have been emboldened by their nuclear weapons to authorize assertive foreign policies.

The most plausible case of democratic nuclear assertion is a future Indian leader authorizing nuclear assertion after another terrorist attack on Indian territory. But former prime minister Manmohan Singh was remarkably restrained in responding to the 2008 Mumbai attacks, and it is far from clear that his successor, Narendra Modi, would behave differently. Indian leaders seem to have learned that Pakistan's nuclear posture deters Indian coercion.[16] Singh and Modi were seventy and fifty-two years old, respectively, in 2002, and they presumably followed Indian and Pakistani policy in the crisis. But it remains unclear if any Indian leader or adviser experienced fear of imminent nuclear war at that time. Whether Indian policy changes as the Cold Start doctrine moves from theory to practice remains to be seen. Perhaps because democracies tend to have accepted most parts of their regional environments, most successors of leaders in democratic new nuclear powers will not need to stumble through another nuclear crisis to authorize restrained foreign policies.[17] Nuclear powers like India and perhaps a future nuclear South Korea will likely authorize assertive foreign policies only in response to very provocative Pakistani and North Korean revisionism.

The second reason that successors to leaders in new nuclear powers may not need to drag their countries through further nuclear crises is that leaders tend to forge agreements that increase the cost to their successors of taking a leaf from the earlier assertive playbook. After the Cuban Missile Crisis, Khrushchev signed both nuclear arms control agreements with the United States that led to the 1968 Non-Proliferation Treaty (NPT) and a spate of other agreements that were highly beneficial to Moscow and Washington. The NPT put a check on West German nuclear ambitions, and later nuclear arms control agreements prohibited a range of costly nuclear arms racing. Nuclear assertion by later Soviet leaders would have caused Washington to think twice about continuing to adhere to these agreements.

Later "inexperienced" Russian leaders may believe that the prevailing international order benefits Washington more than Moscow and feel uninhibited to make moves that threaten to undermine the global non-proliferation architecture. China and Russia have made substantial progress in resolving their Ussuri River boundary dispute. All else being equal, more institutionalized agreements should raise the cost and lower the probability of later nuclear assertion.

Since 2003 Pakistan and India made substantial progress in their Kashmir talks that would have been jeopardized by further state-sponsored or perhaps non-state-sponsored violence in India. Indeed, some have argued that the periodic warming of Indo-Pakistani relations has caused terrorist attacks that are designed to derail such accommodation. It is also possible that greater institutionalization—that ties democracies into the global economy—creates still further pressures to abstain from destabilizing actions like nuclear assertion and even greater costs from authorizing it. Todd Sechser and Matthew Fuhrmann, for example, find that most "compellence" threats by democracies since 1970 have been made against Serbia, Haiti, Iraq, and Afghanistan, where the stakes have been relatively low.

One can make a related criticism that although emotions are sometimes so powerful that humans have difficulty "shutting them off," even when they should, emotions do eventually lose potency. But Linda Skitka and her colleagues find that fear continues to influence people's tolerance levels several months after an event, and Leonie Huddy and her colleagues demonstrate that fear erodes support for broad civil liberties for "a year or more."[18] The genuine fear of imminent nuclear war should have much greater effects than those in Skitka's and Huddy's experiments, and these cannot not be replicated in the laboratory. Leaders in nuclear crises will be likely to experience far greater levels of fear than research subjects who are exposed to images of snakes or photos of the September 11 attacks. These leaders will also be more likely to believe that they have control over their nuclear crises. Lessons about nuclear assertion and foreign policy learned through fear at the nuclear brink will likely remain accessible throughout a leader's life.

One could argue that nuclear assertion is actually quite effective at sustaining revisions to the status quo because assertive foreign policies are necessary for leaders of new nuclear powers to experience fear of imminent nuclear war. This conclusion would be misleading because nuclear assertion is only successful at putting an end to a (new) nuclear power's nuclear assertion. Assertive foreign policies have been effective only in *restoring* a pre–nuclear assertion status quo. In no cases did weapons allow *revisions* to it; the effective outcomes were revisions to revisionism. The current argument thus supports the long-standing contention that nuclear weapons are a strong force for stability but a poor coercive tool. To the extent that the weapons cause short-term emboldenment that destabilize the status quo, they create greater negative feedback pressure to restore the status quo. When new nuclear power assertion becomes the status quo, as occurred in South Asia in the 1990s and likely will occur on the Korean Peninsula in the near future, nuclear assertion can revise it. But policymakers must remember that in such cases nuclear assertion is restoring a status quo that existed before the new nuclear power authorized coercive threats.

One might also argue that we cannot establish if or whether leaders actually experience fear of imminent nuclear war in a crisis. We cannot run experimental tests on past leaders that use experimental controls. Leaders certainly have incentives to misrepresent their preferences, and the experience of fear of imminent nuclear war rarely leaves a direct record, other than the policies that arise and leaders' later recollections of the crises. These criticisms are, however, misplaced. In a nuclear crisis leaders have obvious incentives to misrepresent their resolve to their adversaries, but fear of imminent nuclear war changes foreign policies and often makes leaders willing to reveal the source(s) of their new strategies. The experience of genuine fear of imminent nuclear war—as distinct from a healthy belief in the danger posed by nuclear weapons—is also something that leaders are unlikely to forget. Shortly after the end of the Cuban Missile Crisis, Nikita Khrushchev candidly revealed his fear to Norman Cousins, whom he knew would share the information with President Kennedy. As Khrushchev stated in his memoirs, "The essence of the matter stands out distinctly in my mind. I experienced this with great intensity and remember everything well."[19] Pervez Musharraf candidly revealed his experience of fear of imminent nuclear war eight years after the event, at a time when he was actively promoting his credentials for reentering Pakistani politics. There is no evidence from Mao himself that shows that he experienced fear of imminent nuclear war, but Mao and his colleagues' frantic and often erratic behavior during the winter of 1969–1970 is hard to understand if Mao did not fear imminent nuclear escalation.

Much evidence suggests that the leaders considered here experienced fear of imminent nuclear war. Thousands of pages of archival records, autobiographies, and secondary studies were reviewed, and no evidence was found that they experienced fear of imminent nuclear war earlier than their respective nuclear crises in 1962, 1969, and 2002. The evidence on Musharraf is thinner, but there is no reason to expect him to be disingenuous about his fear in late May 2002, especially when he compared the 2001–2 crisis with the Kargil War (which he believed posed little danger of nuclear escalation). The significant variation in Musharraf's public speeches and the regional newspaper coverage before and after May 2002 both suggest that he reached the nuclear brink when he said he did. All South Asian and most other commentators, as well as newspaper coverage at the time, viewed the May 2002 peak of the ten-month crisis as the most dangerous episode in South Asia's crisis years. The onus is now on future researchers to show that Khrushchev, Kennedy, Musharraf, and Mao did not experience fear of imminent nuclear war or that other factors caused them to authorize restrained foreign policies. Future research should address the source of Mao's aggression in 1969 and whether Vajpayee experienced fear of imminent nuclear war in May 2002.

Scott Sagan has argued that while "trials and errors" occur, learning from them is not an automatic process.[20] Feedback for organizations can be ambiguous, Sagan argues, because the nature of undesirable outcomes and their causes is not always clear. Leaders may only learn lessons that confirm preconceptions or attribute success to their own actions. Sagan argues that organizational learning often occurs in politicized environments, where assessments are not designed to promote learning but rather to protect powerful interests. Even when the environment provides relatively clear objective feedback, according to Sagan, inaccurate and incomplete reporting can impede accurate policy assessment. As he says, nuclear command organizations are primed to repeat serious errors.

None of these points, however, undermine this study's findings: leader learning about the fundamental dilemma of nuclear assertion and their learning within nuclear organizations exhibit important differences. Nuclear organizations often involve countless moving parts, so establishing cause and effect may be difficult. But the decision to authorize an assertive nuclear strategy is less complicated: either they attempt to revise major parts of the status quo or they do not. The resulting crises tend to occur within a few years of the assertive foreign policy, and the danger that they exhibit contrasts sharply with the earlier intolerable but peaceful status quo. In short, there is no reason to expect that the experience of fear of imminent nuclear war in a crisis provides ambiguous feedback about nuclear assertion. The human brain effectively deals with perceptions and feelings of danger and restraint associated with nuclear assertion and restraint.

The historical record strongly suggests that after leaders have learned that nuclear assertion is powerful they will attribute undesired outcomes to other factors and authorize a restrained foreign policy only when they have stumbled into a nuclear crisis. Thus, while learning about problems and solutions in nuclear organizations poses distinct challenges, learning about the dangers of nuclear assertion through fear of imminent nuclear war leads to the obvious, immediate, and simple solution of a restrained foreign policy.[21] The evidence presented here shows that, contrary to Sagan's findings regarding US nuclear organizations, the lessons leaders learned from their fear of imminent nuclear war did not confirm but rather *undermined* their earlier beliefs about nuclear assertion. Fear of imminent nuclear war caused leaders to attribute failure to their own actions.

While learning no doubt occurred in highly politicized environments, this did not prevent different leaders in different countries at different times from learning the same lesson from fear of imminent nuclear war. The quality of reporting cannot impede policy assessment, because the personal experience of fear requires no reporting to register. In short, the problems with nuclear learning that Sagan documented in US nuclear organizations are unlikely to apply to leader learning about nuclear assertion after the experience of fear of imminent nuclear war subsides.

There is a deeper problem with the atemporal arguments that claim that the organizational problems outlined by Sagan make nuclear proliferation more likely to cause nuclear over conventional war. Almost all of the cases of organizational problems that Sagan documents were associated with and followed cases of leaders authorizing assertive foreign policies. Absent the assertive foreign policies of Khrushchev, Kennedy, and Nixon in 1962 and 1973, most of the accidents and near-misses that Sagan documents may not have occurred. Nuclear crises, dangerous operating procedures of nuclear organizations, and nuclear accidents are obviously endogenous processes, so we cannot conclude that absent the former, the latter two would not have occurred. But it is surely more than coincidence that most of the cases of nuclear accidents that Sagan found occurred shortly after leaders authorized nuclear assertion. Scholars who have argued that the dangers that nuclear weapons pose emerge from accidents and organizational biases have been forced to puzzle at the seven decades of nuclear non-use.[22]

The ALF model developed here suggests that there is more to this than good luck. It shows that the episodes that Sagan and others have identified can usually be categorized by a theoretical model that explains variation in foreign policy of nuclear powers. Nuclear proliferation is dangerous when leaders learn that nuclear assertion is safe, but it becomes safe when they learn that nuclear assertion is dangerous.

Arguments about the dangers associated with preventive war motivations during a transition period and the challenge of making survivable arsenals are not immune from these charges.[23] Sagan has influentially argued that aspiring nuclear powers may become more conflict prone by inviting attacks by regional adversaries shortly before developing nuclear weapons, in order to prevent them from reaching the nuclear threshold. He has also argued that nuclear forces that cannot survive a surprise attack could either cause one or become highly vulnerable to one in a crisis. But, after almost seventy years of nuclear weapons, preventive motivations and unsurvivable arsenals have rarely led to strikes against states undergoing transition or to new nuclear powers, and those that occurred against Iraq and Syria did not escalate to war.

What constitutes a survivable arsenal is unclear: the correct question may be not how extensive and diversified an arsenal must be to survive a strike, but rather under what conditions another leader would risk her own country's destruction by striking. The requirements for survivability may mirror those of the US National Intelligence Estimate of 1970, which stated that it "cannot be objectively measured" and is "essentially a state of mind."[24] In short, the response of leaders to the trade-offs associated with the fundamental nuclear assertion dilemma has been a much more important historical force in shaping the dangers and stability that nuclear weapons present, rather than the preventive war motivations, non-survivable arsenals, and organizational biases that have existed at the same time.

One might also argue that this analysis tilts the scales against the rational-signaling model because in some cases what counts as a costly signal is unclear. Rational-choice theorists themselves have not satisfactorily addressed this concern; the rational-signaling model is based on the most influential scholarship in this tradition, but it fails to address what exactly constitutes a costly signal (that is, how public is the declaration and what commitment does it make). Who should be learning what about which issues from which signals is also often underspecified.[25]

Further clarification along the lines of audience cost theory would be beneficial and offer more concrete models that are amenable to empirical testing, such as focusing on signals that were threats to foreign adversaries or involved the use of military force and came through public statements that large portions of the domestic public were likely to hear. Among the cases studied here, these kinds of costly signals *never* caused nuclear powers to refrain from assertive foreign policies. This finding replicates other empirical research that has found that audience costs hardly ever influences the escalation and resolution of crises.[26]

A related problem is that alternative explanations were supplied here as part of the argument. However, those alternative explanations are transparently adapted from core insights of the most influential realist and rational-choice learning models. Perhaps realist and rational theory has led scholars to assume that leaders should not be emboldened by nuclear weapons to authorize assertive foreign policies, thus scholars have assumed that this prediction is accurate and not modeled how leaders actually confront the dilemma of nuclear assertion. But the evidence shows that this assumption is untenable. The criticism that the Waltzian and rational-signaling models developed here are straw men is unfounded.

One could argue that leaders rationally learn different lessons about costly signals from the ones specified here. For example, Musharraf should have rationally learned about the limits of nuclear assertion from Atal Bihari Vajpayee's costly signal at Kargil. But why couldn't Musharraf also rationally learn that an even more daring strategy might achieve the sustained revisions to the Kashmir status quo that the Kargil offensive failed to realize? The problem with this claim is that rational-learning models would assume that all leaders would learn the same lessons about Vajpayee's resolve and that these would cause everyone, Musharraf included, to choose a restrained foreign policy. Musharraf could hardly have rationally learned that a more daring strategy than Kargil might succeed: transgressing more than ten kilometers into India-held Kashmir territory with disguised Pakistani infantrymen who could not receive reinforcements to hold on to their positions atop freezing cold mountain peaks would always be considered a rather daring roll of the dice. It is a stretch to claim that Khrushchev, Musharraf, Nixon, or anyone should have *rationally* learned that more ambitious future attempts would succeed given the resources at hand and the elusive outcomes sought.

Finally, one can also argue that the tendency for leaders of new nuclear powers to experiment with nuclear assertion and then pull back in the face of danger is rational and consistent with the rational-signaling model developed. But this study has shown that from a rational perspective, it is not clear why leaders tend to learn from the deeply emotional experience of fear of imminent nuclear war rather than from general danger of the limits of coercive nuclear strategies. Rational models must incorporate utilities and probabilities based on this core psychological insight to explain the fundamental strategic choices and foreign policies of leaders of new nuclear powers.

North Korea

US National Intelligence director James R. Clapper intimated in 2016 that North Korea is at the top of his list of nuclear- and proliferation-related threats.[27] In October 2015 Adm. Harry Harris, commander of the US Pacific Fleet, declared that "the greatest threat I face on a day to day basis is North Korea."[28] Pyongyang has consolidated a global monopoly on nuclear tests in the twenty-first century and has conducted five nuclear tests in the decade since 2006. Three of these five tests, as well as many long- and short-range missile tests, have occurred under the leadership of Kim Jong Un. More will surely follow, as Kim Jong Un recently publically committed to improving North Korea's "nuclear attack capability" through further "nuclear explosion tests."[29] Kim is striving to develop the capability to target the United States with nuclear missiles. As of June 2016 his nuclear journey has been a struggle. The first 2016 nuclear test was unlikely to have been a hydrogen bomb, and Kim's initiative to field a more reliable sea-based deterrent has run into problems: multiple submarine-launched ballistic missiles appear to have failed, and at least one North Korean submarine recently sank.[30] Nevertheless, North Korea may soon possess more than twenty nuclear warheads and could realistically acquire the capability to target the United

States with them during US president Donald Trump's first term and before Kim turns forty. Costly signals from the United States, South Korea, and their allies have not been able to prevent periodic North Korean assertion. The theory and evidence presented here suggest a counterintuitive conclusion: a nuclear crisis that sufficiently rattles Kim to believe that nuclear assertion is dangerous and worth avoiding but which also does not lead him to believe that his dynasty and regime is over will be required for a turn to restraint.

In his 2015 New Year's Day address, Kim stated that "we were just[i-fied] in our efforts to firmly consolidate our self-reliant defence capability with the nuclear deterrent as its backbone and safeguard [of] our national sovereignty."[31] North Korea's current stockpile is estimated to consist of ten to sixteen weapons. The regime may have amassed enough enriched uranium to arm between four and eight nuclear weapons, and enough plutonium for an additional six to eight.[32] Pyongyang is making progress in its goal to develop the capability to target the United States with nuclear weapons.[33] The yield of the 2013 and 2016 tests was between 6–10 kilotons, much bigger than the 2006 (.9 kilotons) and 2009 (2–6 kilotons) tests. The 1945 Nagasaki bomb was 20 kilotons, but the 2013 device was smaller and lighter than those of earlier tests: Pyongyang may have come closer to its goal of miniaturizing a nuclear warhead to fit an ICBM, one of which the state recently used to successfully penetrate earth's atmosphere.[34]

Pyongyang currently faces two hurdles to its goal of being able to target the United States with nuclear weapons. The weight of the warhead has to be further reduced by as much as perhaps 50 percent, and it has not yet developed synthetic materials that can withstand significantly high temperatures to allow the missile's reentry into earth's atmosphere. These two steps could be accomplished in as little as four or five more years. Thus former US secretary of defense Robert Gates stated in January 2011 that the North Korean ICBM threat to the United States is not an "immediate threat" but also not a "five year threat."[35]

North Korea's military is large but is no match for that of South Korea or the United States. The operational readiness of Pyongyang's conventional capability is seriously undermined by an aging and in some cases obsolete weapons inventory, limited production of combat systems, a weak logistical system, and the deteriorating physical condition, limited training, and low morale of soldiers.[36] South Korea boasts one of the world's top militaries. While only half the size of North Korea's by number, it is better equipped and better trained. Seoul spends almost four times that of North Korea on defense expenditures, and unlike North Korea, it has a much larger GDP to make such expenditures sustainable. While Pyongyang would lose any conventional conflict very quickly, it nevertheless could inflict substantial damage on Seoul and South Korean and allied troops. North Korean artillery arrayed along the demilitarized zone is the largest such force in the world and consists of twenty-three hundred multiple rocket launchers, some of which may be armed with chemical weapons. Former US commander in Korea Gary Luck famously told President Clinton in 1994 that a second Korean war would kill one million people, cost the United States one hundred billion dollars, and cause one trillion dollars worth of industrial damage.[37]

North Korean motives surely include the survival and consolidation of the Kim Jong Un regime, especially in the aftermath of the death of Kim Jong Il. However, while the defense of Pyongyang from a foreign attack is clearly a defensive posture, the presence of several factors make regime survival and consolidation partly revisionist thinking. North Korea is arguably the most isolated state in the world. It is far removed from international flows of capital, technology, and ideas. The stability of the regime arguably depends on maintaining this status quo. But North Korean economic migrants work in China illegally and return home with news and souvenirs from outside.[38] Radio broadcasts by Voice of America and Radio Free Asia can be picked up in North Korea near the Chinese border. South Korean movies, videos, and music, the possession of which can be punishable by death, are constantly bought and smuggled into North Korea. Nongovernment organizations often float balloons into North Korea with packages of Chinese food, currency, and newspapers. North Korea has long desired a peace treaty with the United States to formally end the Korean War, its acceptance as a nuclear power (or at least as aspiring nuclear power), and the concomitant end to Pyongyang's political and economic isolation that would provide a cash boost to the Kim regime. These latter goals would require a revision to important aspects of the status quo on the Korean Peninsula, and many of these objectives are directed at the United States. It makes sense that much of Pyongyang's push is aimed at developing the capability to deliver nuclear payloads to Seoul and Washington. US president Barack Obama thus stated in February 2013 that North Korea's nuclear weapons and ballistic missile programs constitute a threat to US national security and undermine regional stability.[39]

Pyongyang's recent acts have been more dangerous than its earlier provocations, although the role of the leadership transition from Kim Jong Il to Kim Jong Un in causing them is unclear. The March 2010 sinking of the South Korean corvette *Cheonan* killed forty-six South Korean seamen, and the December 2010 firing of 180 artillery shells on the South Korean island of Yeonpyeong killed two South Korean marines and two local construction workers, injured nineteen civilians, and destroyed dozens of properties. These two strikes have constituted the most serious conventional military attack by North Korea on South Korea since an attempted commando raid on the South Korean presidential palace in 1968. Victor Cha has found that every North Korean provocation over the past thirty years has been followed within about six months by a period of dialogue and negotiations where Pyongyang has gained some concession from Washington, from Seoul, or from both.[40] The October 2006 first nuclear test led to international condemnation, UN Security Council sanctions, and long negotiations with the United States. When Pyongyang launched over Japan its three-stage Taepodong-I ICBM in 1998, the Clinton administration hosted missile talks in New York within two months. As the ALF model expects, Kim Jong Un has surely learned from these cognitively accessible successes with nuclear weapons that nuclear assertion will realize negotiations with the United States. Nuclear weapons have destabilized the Korean Peninsula because Kim and his associates have likely learned that nuclear assertion is safe. North Korean nuclear missiles able to target the United States will surely exacerbate regional instability.

If North Korea develops operational nuclear weapons, China's commitment to keeping Kim's regime afloat—which it holds to even in the face of its disdain for Pyongyang's truculence—would likely also further embolden him. He would probably believe that he could provoke Washington or Seoul and that Beijing would intervene to de-escalate any crisis. China ultimately wants to avoid the very outcomes that North Korean assertion might cause—more US influence in East Asia, or more Japanese and South Korean nuclear weapons—so it is not surprising that

Beijing's dissatisfaction with North Korea has recently grown. Kim likely understands and takes advantage of Beijing's strong preference to have an almost vassal state in North Korea on its border that sucks up so much US attention and resources even if North Korean behavior increases the long-term costs to China.

The ALF model would predict that if Kim develops the capability to target the United States with nuclear weapons, the cycles of provocation and negotiation will continue until a United States or South Korean assertive response causes Kim to experience fear of imminent nuclear war. If Kim believes that he has some control over whether nuclear war occurs, he will likely authorize a restrained foreign policy and accept major parts of the intolerable North Korean status quo. Nuclear proliferation on the Korean Peninsula will become safe when Kim learns that nuclear assertion is dangerous. But if Kim and his associates believe that they have no control over nuclear escalation in a nuclear crisis, he will persist with an assertive foreign policy and perhaps use nuclear weapons in a final bid to increase the costs to Washington and Seoul of regime change or to gamble for resurrection.

In the weeks after North Korea's third nuclear test, US B-52 and B-2 stealth bombers flew roundtrips over the Korean Peninsula to demonstrate US power by dropping inert munitions on a South Korean bombing range.[41] Pentagon officials referred to this as "a clear demonstration of the United States' ability to conduct long range, precision strikes quickly and at will." The US has assumed operational control over the South Korean military since the Korean War. While Seoul assumed peacetime control in 1994, the US is still obliged to lead South Korea's military in the event of war. South Korean president Park Geun-Hye claimed in October 2013 that she would seek high accuracy anti-weapons of mass destruction capabilities from the US or interoperability with US systems that enable preemptive strikes against North Korean missile and nuclear attacks.[42] The challenge facing the United States and South Korea regarding North Korea will be to deter challenges toward the US mainland and regional allies while assuring Kim that he has some control over nuclear escalation in a crisis.

The South's Combined Counter-Provocation Plan of March 22, 2013, is designed to "quickly and firmly punish any kind of provocations from North Korea" and may have tempered Pyongyang's belligerence."[43] Former

South Korean president Lee Myung-bak said that "prolonged endurance and tolerance will spawn nothing but more serious provocations."[44] The head of operations for South Korea's joint chiefs of staff recently warned that "if North Korea pushes ahead with provocations that would threaten the lives and safety of our citizens, our military will strongly and sternly punish the provocations' starting point."[45] Some reports suggest preemptive strikes on Pyongyang's nuclear and missile targets if Pyongyang appears to be preparing to use its nuclear weapons.[46] The challenge will lie in organizing conventional forces capable of making carefully calibrated responses to limited aggression and other North Korean assertive acts while also enabling Washington, Seoul, and their allies to credibly commit to live with a nuclear North Korea.[47]

Iran

The July 2015 Joint Comprehensive Plan of Action—commonly known as the Iranian nuclear deal—put a long-term staged freeze on known uranium enrichment and plutonium production and aims to resolve all outstanding questions on weaponization through IAEA monitoring and verification in exchange for multilateral sanctions relief. The Iranian nuclear deal is a major achievement but remains vulnerable to hardliners in the United States and Iran, the possibility of more undisclosed secret desert facilities being built, noncompliance on alleged weaponization activities, and Israeli spoilers. It has put nuclear weapons a good distance away but not out of reach of the Islamic Republic. Given that Iran has pursued nuclear weapons in the recent past, it is worth exploring what the ALF model would predict regarding Iranian foreign policy if Tehran were able to develop nuclear weapons.

Before the nuclear deal, Iran was estimated to be between two to five months away from enriching enough weapons-grade uranium for one or more nuclear weapons.[48] Iran's military is large, but its conventional weapons are obsolete for military engagements with the United States. Tehran could not defeat the American military if US forces were sent to defend the Gulf States from Iranian aggression. Israel also has superior conventional ground, sea, air, and space capabilities.[49] The future development of nuclear weapons by Iran may be motivated by its desire for deterrence from threats from the US and its regional allies as well as national pride and international status. But Supreme Leader Khamenei, a senior Revolutionary Guard commander with custodianship over the nuclear arsenal, or any of their associates may desire to revise important parts of the regional status quo. Iran has long desired to reduce American, Israeli, and Saudi influence in the region, or at least increase the economic and political cost of this influence. Iran has many options to accomplish this: by supporting violence by operatives or proxies such as Hezbollah and Hamas against US troops in Iraq and Afghanistan; conducting provocative naval maneuvers in the Persian Gulf; threatening Saudi oil infrastructure; undermining US-brokered Israeli-Palestinian peace talks; or via the subversion of regimes in conservative Sunni neighbors.[50] Iranian leaders may authorize any one of these policies after developing nuclear weapons. Because they would be hard to deter short of the use of force, many have argued that an Iranian nuclear bomb would be a serious threat and would undermine US extended deterrence commitments to Israel, Saudi Arabia, Egypt, and the smaller conservative Sunni states. Dangerous Iranian lessons of nuclear assertion may be sufficient for a crisis or war without Israeli attacks or computer hackers.[51] Gary Samore, President Obama's former coordinator for arms control and weapons of mass destruction, stated in October 2010 that stopping Iran's nuclear program was his "number one job" because Iranian nuclear weapons would have an "utterly catastrophic effect" in the region.[52] Matthew Kroenig has argued that the regional consequences of an Iranian bomb would be so costly that the United States should attack and attempt to destroy Iranian nuclear facilities.[53]

The ALF model would expect Iranian leaders to learn about nuclear assertion from their own cognitively accessible successes with nuclear weapons development rather than from the historical record. If they are able to develop nuclear weapons they will be likely to initially authorize an assertive foreign policy. Like Khrushchev, Musharraf, and others before them, they would likely attribute desired outcomes to nuclear assertion and write off any failures to bad luck or insincerity. But Iranian nuclear assertion will sooner or later cause Khamenei and his associates to stumble into a nuclear crisis with the United States or Israel. The historical record suggests that if Iran's regional adversaries respond with assertive policies, sooner or later Iranian leaders will experience fear of imminent nuclear escalation that will cause a more restrained regional foreign policy. Thus, James Lindsay and Ray Takeyh claim, a nuclear Iran would be most dangerous "at first, when it would likely be at its most reckless." But, "like other nuclear aspirants before them, the guardians of the theocracy might discover that nuclear bombs are simply not good for diplomatic leverage or strategic aggrandizement."[54] The ALF model would suggest that an Iranian bomb would initially be dangerous. But it would not be as costly as Kroenig and others predict, because Iranian leaders would authorize an assertive foreign policy in the short term but experience fear of imminent nuclear war and authorize a restrained foreign policy over the long run.

One might argue that if Iran develops nuclear weapons and the ALF model is correct, the best policy would be for Washington and Israel (or both) to authorize assertive foreign policies designed to instigate a nuclear crisis with Iran shortly after it develops nuclear weapons; this would allegedly cause the desired effect of fear immediately rather than having to endure a few nuclear crisis–filled years. But this would be a mistake for two reasons. First, gaining the desired effect of fear in a nuclear crisis is based on a leader's belief that he or she has some control over whether nuclear escalation occurs. Thus Khrushchev stated in his memoirs that at the climax of the Cuban Missile Crisis, "We thought we would still be able to influence the extremely tense situation in such a way as to prevent war."[55] If a leader experiences fear of imminent nuclear war and believes that he has no control over it, he may attempt to strike first with nuclear weapons to increase the costs to his adversary or to gamble for resurrection. If the United States starts a nuclear crisis with Iran, Khamenei may accurately believe that he has no control over the crisis. He may believe that Washington's ultimate goal is regime change, and he would be unlikely to authorize a restrained foreign policy under such conditions.

Second, starting a crisis with a newly nuclear Iran would likely convince Khamenei and his associates that Washington and its allies have hostile aims on the regime. Thirty years of mistrust combined with George W. Bush's 2003 invasion of Iraq and his "axis of evil" speech may have convinced Khamenei and his associates that the ultimate US goal toward Iran is regime change. An assertive US policy may actually cause the kind of Iranian revisionism that it is designed to prevent. If Iran develops nuclear weapons and engages in nuclear assertion, Washington and its allies should authorize an assertive foreign policy that either prevents Iran from realizing any revisions to the regional status quo or that threatens to take the initiative to Iran in such a way that Khamenei and his associates believe that they cannot revise the status quo, have some control over nuclear escalation, and would still be in power after the crisis. The ALF model predicts that if Iranian leaders develop nuclear weapons, throw their weight around the region, experience fear of imminent nuclear war, and believe that they have some control over whether nuclear escalation occurs, they will likely authorize restrained foreign policies like other experienced nuclear powers have done before them.

Some scholars optimistically hope that the United States "might be able to 'teach' a nuclear state about how to behave as a nuclear power, carefully communicating information about the limits of nuclear possession for coercive purposes."[56] One possibly optimistic example is India in 1990. Indian leaders did not authorize an assertive foreign policy, and the plethora of confidence-building measures that occurred in the late 1990s caused Vajpayee to effectively learn that nuclear weapons were "tools for peace." But such claims underestimate the chronic mistrust between the United States and its potential nuclear adversaries and the psychological pressure for those adversaries to initially believe that nuclear assertion will pay off.

There are at least two reasons to be pessimistic about future leaders of new nuclear powers learning such "safe" lessons. One is that India was relatively satisfied with the status quo. But the leaders of Pakistan's military learned a very different set of lessons from the tacit cooperation of the late 1990s. Insofar as future nuclear powers like North Korea and Iran are more likely to resemble Pakistan than India in their dissatisfaction with the status quo and chronic mistrust of Washington, confidence-building measures are unlikely to cause them to learn that restrained foreign policies are better than assertive ones. Indeed, their leaders will likely conclude that their nuclear weapons caused the concessions. Moreover, the Indian leader's naïve optimism was shattered within twelve months by the Pakistani military operation at Kargil. It is more than likely that if a South Korean leader develops nuclear weapons and initially authorizes a restrained foreign policy toward the North, North

Korea will authorize nuclear assertion. Seoul would in turn learn from Pyongyang's behavior that nuclear assertion is possible and perhaps effective, and it would persist with assertive behavior until the rival leaders on the Korean Peninsula reach the nuclear brink. When it comes to leader learning about nuclear coercion, there is no substitute for direct experience.

Future Research

This analysis is a first attempt at developing a rigorous and dynamic understanding of how leaders approach the fundamental trade-off of nuclear assertion that nuclear weapons present. It provides a new explanation for the foreign policies of new and experienced nuclear powers. It shows that nuclear proliferation tends to be dangerous when leaders learn that nuclear assertion is safe, and proliferation tends to be safe when leaders learn that nuclear assertion is dangerous. Much more research must be done to augment these findings. Such research could address the British and French cases and address whether having a nuclear-armed ally causes more restrained forms of emboldened assertiveness. It would be useful to have data on Israeli and South African decision-making to further corroborate the effect of availability and fear on these leaders' foreign policies. More data on the beliefs of Brezhnev and his associates regarding nuclear assertion during the 1960s and Indian leaders' beliefs and experiences of fear in May 2002 would also be highly probative for hypotheses on the transmission of lessons learned from nuclear crises. As more data becomes available, future research can build on the findings presented here.

Moreover, while the distinction between assertive and restrained foreign policies is broad enough to capture the logical and empirical differences between the two distinct orientations that a leader can have toward a status quo, it does not address the many types of explicit and implicit forms of assertion and restraint that leaders can authorize. Understanding the drivers of this variation would provide a fuller understanding of how nuclear proliferation causes regional conflict and cooperation. Further research could also unpack which advances in nuclear capability tend to cause which levels of emboldenment.

A further issue involves addressing how allies of new nuclear powers make nuclear proliferation dangerous when the new nuclear power has authorized an assertive or even restrained foreign policy. After Khrushchev and Musharraf had experienced fear and toned down their nuclear assertion, Castro and several Islamic insurgent groups attempted to bring their former patrons back to the nuclear brink. Castro pushed hard to keep Soviet personnel and equipment stationed in Cuba, and several insurgent groups likely attacked targets inside India to exacerbate Indo-Pakistani tensions. Research could examine how new nuclear powers have addressed and overcome these challenges and how allies of new nuclear powers have become emboldened to authorize dangerous policies, especially as new evidence on the relationship between the Pakistani government, the Pakistani Army, and ISI and different insurgent groups becomes available. Finally, while this review has shown that the experience of fear tempers leaders' acceptance of risk, future research should examine if anger increases their willingness to take risks, as experimental research suggests. Soviet foreign minister Andrei Gromyko partly attributed the Soviet invasion of Afghanistan to Brezhnev's highly emotional response to Afghan general secretary Nur Taraki's murder: "It was too much for Brezhnev to bear. He was simply beside himself."[57] Research might also address whether anger moderates the effect of fear on new nuclear power foreign policy.

Political scientists and international relations scholars should pay more attention to the effect of experience with technologies, strategies, and institutions on leaders' policies and the effect of variation on the policies of others. This interaction should influence the onset, escalation, and resolution of interstate and intrastate conflict. Jack Snyder and Edward Mansfield have shown that a state's experience with democracy strongly influences its propensity to initiate international conflict.[58] Michael Horowitz and Allan Stam show that, at least in democracies, leaders with military experience but not combat experience are more likely to initiate wars than leaders with combat experience.[59] Other research has shown that experience tends to reduce the propensity of US presidents to engage in international conflict.[60] The ALF model also suggests that if leaders in interstate conflicts, civil wars, or with terrorist groups have acquired new technologies or resources, they may learn that assertive strategies will ameliorate security challenges and cause sustained changes to their status quo.

We should not expect people to learn about the coercive limits of different resources from systematic or even attentive assessments of the historical record. Rather, we should expect dangerous challenges to the status quo until the experience of fear of imminent conflict or destruction causes learning about the dangers and limits of the coercive tool or strategy. Inexperience with particular distributions of economic or military power could cause states to overestimate their ability to influence the status quo.[61] It is possible that inexperience with different levels of economic interdependence causes conflict but that the experience of fear reduces the danger. China's recent economic growth and economic interdependence with the United States may have emboldened Beijing to unsuccessfully challenge Washington's acceptance of China's monetary policy.[62] This pattern need not be confined to international and instrastate security affairs, but it might also be useful in explaining cycles of instability and stability in any strategic interaction involving competition over scarce and unevenly distributed resources, diffuse or weak authority structures, and the possibility of very costly outcomes. The experience of fear of destructive or even highly undesirable outcomes could cause actors to accept intolerable status quos, transform competitive rivalries, and constitute the foundation of long-term cooperation.

Conclusion

Scholars and policymakers have tended to argue that nuclear proliferation is either stabilizing or destabilizing through selective readings of the historical record without addressing the conditions when each obtains. But the historical record of new nuclear powers is consistent with key insights from decades of psychological research and shows that nuclear weapons have had a more complex impact on state foreign policy, regional conflict, and stability. New nuclear powers tend to be conflict prone, but experienced nuclear powers do not. Fear stands at the heart of the transformative effect that nuclear weapons have had on international politics.

Nuclear proliferation is dangerous when leaders learn that nuclear assertion is safe, but it is safe when they learn that nuclear assertion is dangerous. The psychology of availability and fear explains why some, usually
new, nuclear powers are more conflict prone than other, often more
experienced, nuclear powers. Deterring new nuclear powers tends to be
difficult because their leaders have not experienced fear of imminent
nuclear war, but deterrence is easier once they have. This analysis explains
why new nuclear powers seem not to learn from earlier cases despite high
incentives to do so. It explains why some leaders of new nuclear powers
push so hard to revise unfavorable security arrangements but then seem
to accept them after little has changed.

Inexperience with nuclear weapons tends to cause dangerous assertive
policies that are central to international security, and the examples herein
show what it is about experience with nuclear weapons that moderates
foreign policies, and offers theoretically grounded and empirically supported explanations of key turning points in the nuclear age. This history
suggests policy prescriptions to reduce the dangers imposed by the limitations of the human brain and the destructive potential of nuclear
weapons today. The finding that new nuclear powers are dangerously
conflict prone but that fear of imminent nuclear war will cause restrained
foreign policy points to the limits of scholarship in influencing foreign
policy. It implies that leaders—with John Kennedy an exception to the
rule—do not learn from history or scholarship. Rather, they must stumble into their own nuclear crisis to reduce the dangers of nuclear weapons. The Indians and Pakistanis did not learn enough from the Cold
War to save themselves from a dangerous cycle of instability and stability,
and North Korean leaders are similarly likely to learn little from past
events in South Asia. There is sadly little basis to be confident that new
nuclear powers can be taught about the trade-offs of nuclear assertion,
short of their own direct experience at the nuclear brink.

However, the good news is that the United States and its allies don't
need to do much to ensure that menacing new nuclear powers behave
like most experienced nuclear powers today; they simply need to come
to terms with the effect of fear. Given the perils of loss of control that
are associated with the inherently weak states that are likely to develop
nuclear weapons in the twenty-first century, the nuclear nonproliferation
community would do well to come to terms with this fact. Washington

will not need to do much to bring an emboldened nuclear North Korea or Iran to the brink. If anything, President Trump and his successors must find ways to credibly commit to *not* attack states like North Korea.

Correctly understanding the sources of continuity and change in key foreign policies made by earlier nuclear powers during the Cold War and after provides a strong basis for effectively managing future nuclear powers such as North Korea and Iran. If Iran and North Korea develop nuclear weapons and plunge their regions into conflict and war, Washington, Seoul, and Tel Aviv need to strike a balance that lies between working to ensure that new nuclear powers experience fear of imminent nuclear war and assuring them that they have some control over whether nuclear escalation occurs and their regime survives.

The "to deter or assert" question has been the critical dilemma facing nuclear powers since 1945 and has determined whether nuclear rivalries have been plunged into dangerous conflict and war or trust building, diplomacy, and tacit cooperation. How leaders have approached the dilemma of nuclear assertion has profoundly influenced international relations. The psychology of availability and fear stands at the heart of the grand strategies and foreign policies that have determined whether the spread of nuclear weapons has been a force for war or peace. Significant opportunities lie within the dangerous crises that the spread of nuclear weapons inevitably present.

Notes

1. Gaddis, *United States and the End of the Cold War*, 110.
2. Sagan, *Limits of Safety*, 266.
3. Kapur, *Dangerous Deterrent*; and Sagan and Waltz, *Spread of Nuclear Weapons*, 210.
4. Mueller, *Atomic Obsession*.
5. Gartzke and Jo, "Bargaining, Nuclear Proliferation."
6. Horowitz, "Spread of Nuclear Weapons."
7. Heikal, *Sphinx and Commissar*, 98.
8. Betts, "Universal Deterrence," 60.
9. Kydd, *Trust and Mistrust*, 19.
10. On Indian nuclear policy in the 1990s, see Kampani, "New Delhi's Long Nuclear Journey."
11. For a similar argument, see Minozzi, "Endogenous Beliefs."

12. Narang, *Nuclear Strategy*, 303–4, italics in original.

13. Ibid., 304, italics in original.

14. Horowitz, "Spread of Nuclear Weapons."

15. Gavin, *Nuclear Statecraft*, 59.

16. Narang, *Nuclear Strategy*.

17. Gibler, Territorial Peace.

18. Skitka, Bauman, and Mullen, "Political Tolerance," 754; and Huddy, Khatid, and Capelos, "Trends."

19. Khrushchev, *Memoirs*, 3:340.

20. Sagan, *Limits of Safety*, 207–9, 249.

21. Breslauer and Tetlock, "Introduction," 6–8.

22. Sagan and Waltz, *Spread of Nuclear Weapons*, 81.

23. Ibid., 48–67.

24. Cited in Gavin, *Nuclear Statecraft*, 120.

25. For an exception that models small audience costs, see Tarer and Leventoglu, "Limited Audience Costs."

26. Snyder and Borghard, "Cost of Empty Threats"; and Trachtenberg, "Audience Costs."

27. Mark Landler, "North Korea Nuclear Threat Cited by James Clapper, Intelligence Chief," *New York Times*, February 9, 2006.

28. John Grady, "PACOM Commander Harris: North Korea Greatest Day-to-Day Threat," *USNI News*, October 12, 2015.

29. "More Nuclear Tests, Urges North Korean Leader Kim Jong Un," *Guardian*, March 11, 2016.

30. Sam LaGrone, "U.S. Official: North Korean Submarine Is Missing, Presumed Sunk," *USNI News*, March 11, 2016.

31. Kim Jong-un, "New Year Address," *Korean Central News Agency*, January 1, 2015, http://www.kcna.co.jp/index-e.htm.

32. Joel S. Wit and Sun Young Ahn, *North Korea's Nuclear Futures: Technology and Strategy*, North Korea's Nuclear Futures Series, US-Korea Institute at SAIS, February 2015, http://uskoreainstitute.org/wp-content/uploads/2016/02/NKNF_NK-Nuclear-Futures.pdf; and David Albright and Christina Walrond, "North Korea's Estimated Stocks of Plutonium and Weapon-Grade Uranium," Institute for Science and International Security Report, August 16, 2012, http://isis-online.org/uploads/isis-reports/documents/dprk_fissile_material_production_16Aug2012.pdf.

33. See, for example, David Albright, "North Korean Miniaturization," *38 North*, February 13, 2013, http://38north.org/2013/02/albright021313/; and International Institute for Strategic Studies, *North Korean Security Challenges: A Net Assessment*, July 21, 2011.

34. See Jeffrey Lewis, "North Korea's Nuclear Weapons: The Great Miniaturization Debate," *38 North*, February 5, 2015, http://38north.org/2015/02/jlewis020515/.

35. Gates, "Media Roundtable"; and Choe Sang-Hun, "North Korea Threatens to Attack U.S. with Lighter and Smaller Nukes," *New York Times,* March 5, 2013.

36. Dennis C. Blair, *Annual Threat Assessment of the U.S. Intelligence Community* (February 2, 2010), 13–14; and International Institute for Strategic Studies, *The Military Balance* (London: IISS, 2011).

37. Cited in Cha, *Impossible State,* 213.

38. James Kirchick, "I Smuggled Posters for 'The Interview' into North Korea," *Daily Beast,* January 21, 2015, http://www.thedailybeast.com/articles /2015/01/20/i-smuggled-poster-for-the-interview-into-north-korea.html#.

39. Chris McGreal, "North Korea Defiant over Nuclear Tests as Obama Promises Swift Action," *Guardian,* February 13, 2013.

40. Cha, *Impossible State,* 237.

41. Richard Dudley, "US Reinforcing Pacific Defenses to Counter North Korean Threats," *Defense Update,* April 6, 2013, http://defense-update.com /20130406_us-reinforcing-pacific-defenses-to-counter-north-korean-threats .html.

42. "Park Pledges Strong Defense to Render N. Korean Nukes Useless," *Yonhap News Agency,* October 1, 2013, http://english.yonhapnews.co.kr/national /2013/10/01/29/0301000000AEN20131001003351315F.html?utm_source =NAPSNet&utm_campaign=8ad1a776edWeekly_Report_October _3_201310_2_2013&utm_medium=email&utm_term=0_f1452487e1 -8ad1a776ed-39601577; and Lee Chi-Dong, "Korean, U.S. Presidential Aides to Discuss OPCON, Missile Defense," *Yonhap News Agency,* October 23, 2013.

43. Steve Herman, "US, South Korea Announce New Counter-Attack Plan," *Voice of America,* March 25, 2013, http://www.voanews.com/content/us -south-korea-announce-new-counter-attack-plan/1627869.html.

44. James Hardy, "South Korea Takes Hard Line on North's Incessant Belligerence," *IHS Janes,* November 30, 2010.

45. "Seoul Vows 'Stern' Response to North Korean Provocation," *Chosun Ilbo Online,* March 7, 2013.

46. Kwanwoo Jun, "U.S., South Korea Sign Pact on Deterrence against North," *Wall Street Journal,* October 2, 2013, http://www.wsj.com/articles /SB10001424052702304906704579110891808197868.

47. See Denmark, "Proactive Deterrence."

48. The estimate increases to fourteen months if Iran relies only on natural unenriched uranium. See David Albright and Andrea Stricker, "Iranian Breakout Study Drastically Overestimates Time to Nuclear Weapon," Institute for Science and International Security Report, June 17, 2014, http://isisonline.org/uploads /isisreports/documents/critique_of_Iran_breakout_estimates_17June2014-final .pdf (link no longer available); and William C. Witt et al., "Iran's Evolving Breakout Potential," ISIS *Report,* October 8, 2012, http://www.isisnucleariran .org/assets/pdf/Irans_Evolving_Breakout_Potential_8October2012.pdf.

49. Cordesman, *Iran, the Gulf, and Strategic Competition*; and Fitzpatrick and Elleman, *Iran's Ballistic Missile Capabilities*.

50. Kapur, "Ten Years of Instability," 94; Sagan, "How to Keep the Bomb from Iran," 53; Chubin, "Iran's Risk Taking"; Cordesman, *Iran's Evolving Threat*; Byman, "Iran, Terrorism, and Weapons of Mass Destruction"; and Talmadge, "Closing Time."

51. See William J. Broad, John Markoff, and David E. Sanger, "Israeli Test on Worm Called Crucial in Iran Nuclear Delay," *New York Times*, January 15, 2011; Lake, "Operation Sabotage"; and Raas and Long, "Osirak Redux?"

52. David E. Sanger, "Obama Set to Offer Stricter Nuclear Deal to Iran," *New York Times*, October 27, 2010.

53. Kroenig, "Time to Attack Iran."

54. Lindsay and Takeyh, "After Iran Gets the Bomb," 37–38.

55. Khrushchev, *Memoirs*, 3:338.

56. Gerson, *Sino-Soviet Border Conflict*, v.

57. Cited in Lebow and Stein, *We All Lost the Cold War*, 243.

58. Mansfield and Snyder, "Democratization and the Danger of War"; Mansfield and Snyder, "Democratic Transitions."

59. Horowitz and Stam, "How Prior Military Experience Influences."

60. Potter, "Does Experience Matter?"

61. Johnson, *Overconfidence and War*.

62. Drezner, "Bad Debts."

BIBLIOGRAPHY

Primary Sources

Cold War International History Project Digital Archive, Woodrow Wilson International Center for Scholars
Cold War International History Project Bulletin, Woodrow Wilson International Center for Scholars
Department of State Bulletin, Office of Public Communication, Bureau of Public Affairs
Digital National Security Archive, George Washington University
Foreign Relations of the United States, US Department of State
George H. W. Bush Presidential Library and Museum
John F. Kennedy Presidential Library and Museum
Kremlin Decision-Making Project, Miller Center of Public Affairs

Secondary Sources

Albright, David, and Andrea Stricker. "Iranian Breakout Study Drastically Overestimates Time to Nuclear Weapon." Institute for Science and International Security Report, June 17, 2014, http://isisonline.org/uploads /isisreports/documents/critique_of_Iran_breakout_estimates_17June2014 -final.pdf.
Albright, David, and Christina Walrond. "North Korea's Estimated Stocks of Plutonium and Weapon-Grade Uranium." Institute for Science and International Security Report, August 16, 2012, http://isis-online.org/uploads /isis-reports/documents/dprk_fissile_material_production_16Aug2012.pdf.
Alford, Mimi. *Once upon a Secret: My Affair with President John F. Kennedy and Its Aftermath.* New York: Random House, 2012.
Allison, Graham, and Philip Zelikow. *Essence of Decision: Explaining the Cuban Missile Crisis.* New York: Longman, 1999.
Ambrose, Stephen E. *Nixon: The Education of a Politician, 1913–1962.* New York: Simon and Schuster, 1987.
Arkin, R., H. Cooper, and T. Kolditz. "A Statistical Review of the Literature concerning the Self-Serving Attribution Bias in Interpersonal Influence Situations." *Journal of Personality* 48 (1980): 435–48.

Art, Robert J. "Coercive Diplomacy: What Do We Know?" In *The United States and Coercive Diplomacy*, edited by Robert J. Art and Patrick M. Cronin, 359–420. Washington, DC: United States Institute of Peace Press, 2003.

Bacon, Edwin, and Mark Sandle, eds. *Brezhnev Reconsidered.* New York: Palgrave Macmillan, 2002.

Basrur, Rajesh. "The Lessons of Kargil as Learned by India." In Lavoy, *Asymmetric Warfare in South Asia*, 311–32.

———. *Minimum Deterrence and India's Nuclear Security.* Stanford, CA: Stanford University Press, 2006.

Bass, Gary J. *The Blood Telegram: Nixon, Kissinger, and a Forgotten Genocide.* New York: Alfred A. Knopf, 2013.

Beardsley, Kyle, and Victor Asal. "Winning with the Bomb." *Journal of Conflict Resolution* 53, no. 2 (2009): 278–301.

Bechara, Antoine, and Antonio R. Damasio. "The Somatic Marker Hypothesis: A Neural Theory of Economic Decision." *Games and Economic Behavior* 52 (2005): 336–72.

Beck, Nathaniel. "Is Causal Process Observation an Oxymoron?" *Political Analysis* 14, no. 3 (Summer 2006): 347–52.

Becker, Ernest. *The Denial of Death.* New York: Free Press, 1973.

Bernstein, Barton. "Understanding Decisionmaking, U.S. Foreign Policy, and the Cuban Missile Crisis: A Review Essay." *International Security* 25, no. 1 (Summer 2000): 134–64.

Beschloss, Michael. *The Crisis Years: Kennedy and Khrushchev, 1960–1963.* New York: HarperCollins, 1991.

Betts, Richard K. *Nuclear Blackmail and Nuclear Balance.* Washington, DC: Brookings Institution, 1987.

———. "Universal Deterrence or Conceptual Collapse? Liberal Pessimism and Utopian Realism." In *The Coming Crisis: Nuclear Proliferation, U.S. Interests, and World Order*, edited by Victor Utgoff, 51–85. Cambridge, MA: MIT Press, 2000.

Biddle, Tami Davis. *Rhetoric and Reality in Air Warfare: The Evolution of British and American Ideas about Strategic Bombing, 1914–1945.* Princeton, NJ: Princeton University Press, 2002.

Blair, Bruce G. *The Logic of Accidental Nuclear War.* Washington, DC: Brookings Institution Press, 1993.

———. "Nuclear Inadvertence: Theory and Evidence." *Security Studies* 3, no. 3 (Spring 1994): 494–500.

Blair, Dennis C. *Annual Threat Assessment of the U.S. Intelligence Community.* February 2, 2010. Accessed at: file:///D:/Users/MQ20154517/Downloads/ADA514221.pdf.

Blight, James G., Bruce J. Allyn, and David A. Welch. *Cuba on the Brink: Castro, the Missile Crisis, and the Soviet Collapse.* New York: Pantheon, 1993.

Blight, James G., and David A. Welch. *On the Brink: Americans and Soviets Reexamine the Cuban Missile Crisis*. New York: Hill and Wang, 1989.

Bloomfield, Lincoln, Walter C. Clemens Jr., and Franklyn Griffiths. *Khrushchev and the Arms Race: Soviet Interests in Arms Control and Disarmament, 1954–1962*. Cambridge, MA: MIT Press, 1966.

Brader, Ted. "Striking a Responsive Chord: How Political Ads Motivate and Persuade Voters by Appealing to Emotions." *American Journal of Political Science* 49, no. 2 (2005): 388–405.

Brader, Ted, and George E. Marcus. "Emotion and Political Psychology." In *The Oxford Handbook of Political Psychology*. 2nd ed. Edited by Leonie Huddy, David O. Sears, and Jack S. Levy, 165–204. New York: Oxford University Press, 2013.

Brady, Henry E., and David Collier, eds. *Rethinking Social Inquiry: Diverse Tools, Shared Standards*. Plymouth, UK: Rowman and Littlefield, 2010.

Brandon, Henry. *The Retreat of American Power*. Garden City, NY: Doubleday, 1973.

Breslauer, George W., and Philip E. Tetlock. "Introduction." In *Learning in US and Soviet Foreign Policy*, edited by George W. Breslauer and Philip E. Tetlock, 3–19. Boulder, CO: Westview, 1991.

Brodie, Bernard. *Strategy in the Missile Age*. Princeton, NJ: Princeton University Press, 1959.

Bueno de Mesquita, Bruce, and David Lalman. *War and Reason*. New Haven, CT: Yale University Press, 1992.

Bueno de Mesquita, Bruce, and William H. Riker. "An Assessment of the Merits of Selective Nuclear Proliferation." *Journal of Conflict Resolution* 26, no. 2 (June 1982): 283–306.

Bundy, McGeorge. *Danger and Survival: Choices about the Bomb in the First Fifty Years*. New York: Random House, 1988.

Burlatsky, Fedor. *Khrushchev and the First Russian Spring: The Era of Khrushchev through the Eyes of His Adviser*. Translated by Daphne Skillen. New York: Scribner, 1988.

Burr, William. "Sino-American Relations, 1969: The Sino-Soviet Border War and Steps Toward Rapprochement." *Cold War History* 1, no. 3 (2001): 73–112.

Burr, William, and Jeffrey Kimball. "Nixon's Secret Nuclear Alert: Vietnam War Diplomacy and the Joint Chiefs of Staff Readiness Test, October 1969." *Cold War History* 3 (January 2003): 113–56.

Burr, William, and Jeffrey T. Richelson. "Whether to 'Strangle the Baby in the Cradle': The United States and the Chinese Nuclear Program, 1960–64." *International Security* 25, no. 3 (2000): 54–99.

Byman, Daniel. "Iran, Terrorism, and Weapons of Mass Destruction." *Studies in Conflict and Terrorism* 31 (2008): 169–81.

Byman, Daniel, and Kenneth M. Pollack. "Let Us Now Praise Great Men: Bringing the Statesman Back In." *International Security* 25, no. 4 (Spring 2001): 107–46.

Cha, Victor. *The Impossible State: North Korea, Past and Future.* New York: HarperCollins, 2013.

Chang, Lawrence, and Peter Kornbluh, eds. *The Cuban Missile Crisis, 1962: A National Security Archive Documents Reader.* New York: New Press, 1992.

Chari, P. R., Pervaiz Iqbal Cheema, and Stephen P. Cohen. *Four Crises and a Peace Process: American Engagement in South Asia,* Washington, DC: Brookings Institution Press, 2007.

Chiozza, Giacomo, and H. E. Goemans. *Leaders and International Conflict.* New York: Cambridge University Press, 2011.

Chubin, Shahram. "Iran's Risk-Taking in Perspective." Proliferation Papers of the Institut Français des Relations Internationales Security Studies Centre, 2008.

Clinton, Bill. *My Life.* New York: Vintage, 2004.

Clore, Gerald L., and Karen Gasper. "Feeling Is Believing: Some Affective Influences on Belief." In *Emotions and Beliefs: How Feelings Influence Thoughts,* edited by Nico H. Frijda, Antony S. R. Manstead, and Sacha Bem, 10–44. Cambridge: Cambridge University Press, 2000.

Cohen, Eliot A., and John Gooch. *Military Misfortunes: The Anatomy of Failure in War.* New York: Free Press, 1990.

Cohen, Michael D. "How Nuclear South Asia Is Like Cold War Europe: The Stability-Instability Paradox Revisited." *Nonproliferation Review* 20, no. 2 (2013): 433–51.

———. "Live and Learn: Availability Biases and Beliefs about Military Power," *Foreign Policy Analysis,* forthcoming.

Cohen, Stephen P. *India: Emerging Power.* Washington, DC: Brookings Institution Press, 2001.

Coll, Steve. "The Back Channel: India and Pakistan's Secret Kashmir Talks." *New Yorker,* March 2, 2009, http://www.newyorker.com/reporting/2009/03/02/090302fa_fact_coll.

———. "The Stand-Off: How Jihadi Groups Helped Provoke the Twenty-First Century's First Nuclear Crisis." *New Yorker,* February 13, 2006.

Collins, A. M., and E. F. Loftus. "A Spreading-Activation Theory of Semantic Processing." *Psychological Review* 82 (1975): 407–28.

Cordesman, Anthony. *Iran's Evolving Threat.* Washington, DC: Center for Strategic and International Studies, 2010.

———. Iran, the Gulf, and Strategic Competition: The Conventional Balance. Washington, DC: Center for Strategic and International Studies, August 2010.

Cousins, Norman. *The Improbable Triumvirate: John F. Kennedy, Pope John, Nikita Khrushchev.* New York: Norton, 1972.

Crail, Peter, Daniel Horner, and Daryl G. Kimball. "Pursuing the Prague Agenda: An Interview with White House Coordinator Gary Samore." *Arms Control Today,* May 2011, http://www.armscontrol.org/act/2011_05 /Samore.

Crescenzi, Mark J. C. "Reputation and Interstate Conflict." *American Journal of Political Science* 51, no. 2 (April 2007): 382–96.

Croco, Sarah E. "The Decider's Dilemma: Leader Culpability, War Outcomes, and Domestic Punishment." *American Political Science Review* 105, no. 3 (2011): 457–77.

Dallek, Robert. *An Unfinished Life: John F. Kennedy, 1917–1963.* New York: Little Brown, 2004.

Damasio, Antonio R. *Descartes' Error: Emotion, Reason, and the Human Brain.* New York: Putnam, 2004.

Denmark, Abraham M. "Proactive Deterrence: The Challenge of Escalation Control on the Korean Peninsula." Academic Paper Series of the Korea Economic Institute. December 2011.

DiCicco, Jonathan M. "Fear, Loathing, and Cracks in Reagan's Mirror Images: Able Archer 83 and an American First Step Toward Rapprochement in the Cold War." *Foreign Policy Analysis* 7 (2011): 253–74.

DiGiandomenico, S., R. Masi, D. Cassandrini, M. El-Hachem, R. DeVito, C. Bruno, and F. M. Santorelli. "Lipoid Proteinosis: Case Report and Review of the Literature." *Acta Otorhinolaryngol Ital* 26 (2006): 162–67.

Dingman, Roger. "Atomic Diplomacy during the Korean War." *International Security* 13, no. 3 (1988): 50–91.

Dobbs, Michael. *One Minute to Midnight: Kennedy, Khrushchev, and Castro on the Brink of Nuclear War.* New York: Knopf, 2008.

Dobrynin, Anatoly. *In Confidence: Moscow's Ambassador to America's Six Cold War Presidents.* New York: Times Books, 1995.

Drezner, Daniel W. "Bad Debts: Assessing China's Financial Influence in Great Power Politics." *International Security* 34, no. 2 (2009): 7–45.

Eden, Lynn, and Steven Miller, eds. *Nuclear Arguments: Understanding the Strategic Nuclear Arms and Arms Control Debates.* Ithaca, NY: Cornell University Press, 1989.

Elliott, A. J., and P. G. Devine. "On the Motivational Nature of Cognitive Dissonance: Dissonance as Psychological Discomfort." *Journal of Personality and Social Psychology* 67 (1994): 382–94.

Elster, Jon. *Alchemies of the Mind: Rationality and the Emotions.* Cambridge, UK: Cambridge University Press, 1999.

Enthoven, Alain C., and K. Wayne Smith. *How Much Is Enough? Shaping the Defense Program, 1961–1969.* New York: Harper and Row, 1971.

Evangelista, Matthew. "Stalin's Postwar Army Reappraised." *International Security* 7, no. 3 (Winter 1982–83): 110–38.

Fair, C. Christine. *Fighting to the End: The Pakistan Army's Way of War.* New York: Oxford University Press, 2014.

Fearon, James D. "Domestic Political Audiences and the Escalation of International Disputes." *American Political Science Review* 88, no. 3 (September 1994): 577–92.

———. "Selection Effects and Deterrence." *International Interactions* 28 (2002): 5–29.

———. "Signaling versus the Balance of Power and Interests: An Empirical Test of a Crisis Bargaining Model." *Journal of Conflict Resolution* 38, no. 2 (1994): 236–69.

Feaver, Peter D. *Guarding the Guardians: Civilian Control of Nuclear Weapons in the United States.* Ithaca, NY: Cornell University Press, 1993.

———. "Neooptimists and the Enduring Problem of Nuclear Proliferation." *Security Studies* 6, no. 4 (Summer 1997): 126–36.

———. "Optimists, Pessimists, and Theories of Nuclear Proliferation Management." *Security Studies* 4, no. 4 (1995): 754–72.

———. "The Politics of Inadvertence." *Security Studies* 3, no. 3 (Spring 1994): 501–8.

Feaver, Peter, and Emerson Niou. "Managing Nuclear Proliferation: Condemn, Strike, or Assist?" *International Studies Quarterly* 40 (1996): 209–34.

Feinstein, Justin S., Ralph Adolphs, Antonio Damasio, and Daniel Tranel. "The Human Amygdala and the Induction and Experience of Fear." *Current Biology* 21, no. 1 (2011): 34–38.

Festinger, Leon. *A Theory of Cognitive Dissonance.* Stanford, CA: Stanford University Press, 1957.

Filson, Darren, and Suzanne Werner. "A Bargaining Model of War and Peace." *American Journal of Political Science* 46 (2002): 819–38.

Finucane, Melissa L., Ali Alhakami, Paul Slovic, and Stephen M. Johnson. "The Affect Heuristic in Judgments of Risks and Benefits." *Journal of Behavioral Decision Making* 13 (2000): 1–17.

Fischhoff, Baruch, Roxana M. Gonzalez, Jennifer S. Lerner, and Deborah A. Small. "Evolving Judgments of Terror Risks: Foresight, Hindsight, and Emotion." *Journal of Experimental Psychology: Applied* 11 (2005): 124–39.

Fiske, Susan T., and Shelley E. Taylor. *Social Cognition: From Brains to Culture.* New York: McGraw-Hill, 2008.

Fitzpatrick, Mark, and Michael Elleman. *Iran's Ballistic Missile Capabilities: A Net Assessment.* International Institute for Strategic Studies, London, 2010.

Flanagan, Stephen J. *NATO's Conventional Defenses.* Cambridge, MA: Ballinger, 1988.

Foot, Rosemary. "Nuclear Coercion and the Ending of the Korean Conflict." *International Security* 13, no. 3 (1988): 92–112.

Fravel, M. Taylor. *Strong Borders, Secure Nation: Cooperation and Conflict in China's Territorial Disputes*. Princeton, NJ: Princeton University Press, 2008.

Fravel, M. Taylor, and Evan S. Medeiros. "China's Search for Assured Retaliation: The Evolution of Chinese Nuclear Strategy and Force Structure." *International Security* 35, no. 2 (2010): 48–87.

Freedman, Lawrence. *The Evolution of Nuclear Strategy*. 3rd ed. New York: Palgrave Macmillan, 2003.

———. *Kennedy's Wars: Berlin, Cuba, Laos, and Vietnam*. New York: Oxford University Press, 2002.

Frijda, Nico H., Anthony S. R. Manstead, and Agneta H. Fischer. "Feelings and Emotions: Where Do We Stand?" In Manstead, Frijda, and Fischer, *Feelings and Emotions*, 455–67.

Fuhrmann, Matthew, and Todd S. Sechser. "Signaling Alliance Commitments: Hand-Tying and Sunk Costs in Extended Nuclear Deterrence." *American Journal of Political Science* (forthcoming).

Fursenko, Aleksandr, and Timothy Naftali. *Khrushchev's Cold War*. New York: Norton, 2007.

———. *One Hell of a Gamble: Khrushchev, Castro, and Kennedy, 1958–1964*. New York: Norton, 1998.

Gaddis, John Lewis. "The Long Peace." *International Security* 10, no. 4 (1986): 99–142.

———. *Strategies of Containment: A Critical Appraisal of American National Security Policy during the Cold War*. New York: Oxford University Press, 2005.

———. *The United States and the End of the Cold War: Implications, Reconsiderations, Provocations*. Oxford, UK: Oxford University Press, 1992.

Ganguly, Sumit. "Nuclear Stability in South Asia." *International Security* 33, no. 2 (2008): 45–70.

———. *The Crisis in Kashmir: Portents of War, Hopes for Peace*. New York: Cambridge University Press, 1997.

Ganguly, Sumit, and Devin T. Hagerty. *Fearful Symmetry: India-Pakistan Crises in the Shadow of Nuclear Weapons*. Seattle: University of Washington Press, 2005.

Ganguly, Sumit, and Michael R. Kraig. "The 2001–2002 Indo-Pakistani Crisis: Exposing the Limits of Coercive Diplomacy." *Security Studies* 14, no. 2 (2005): 290–324.

Garthoff, Raymond L. *Détente and Confrontation: American-Soviet Relations from Nixon to Reagan*, rev. ed. Washington, DC: Brookings Institution Press, 1994.

Gartzke, Erik, and Dong Joon Jo. "Bargaining, Nuclear Proliferation, and Interstate Disputes." *Journal of Conflict Resolution* 53, no. 2 (2009): 209–33.

Gavin, Francis J. "Blasts from the Past: Proliferation Lessons from the 1960s." *International Security* 29, no. 3 (Winter 2004–5): 100–135.

———. *Nuclear Statecraft: History and Strategy in America's Atomic Age*. Ithaca, NY: Cornell University Press, 2012.

Gearson, John, and Kori Schake. *The Berlin Wall Crisis: Perspectives on Cold War Alliances.* New York: Palgrave Macmillan, 2002.

Gelman, Harry. *The Soviet Far East Buildup and Soviet Risk-Taking against China.* Santa Monica, CA: RAND, 1982.

George, Alexander L., and Andrew Bennett. *Case Studies and Theory Development in the Social Sciences.* Cambridge, MA: MIT Press, 2005.

George, Alexander, and William E. Simons. "Findings and Conclusions." In George and Simons, *Limits of Coercive Diplomacy,* 267–94.

George, Alexander L., and William E. Simons, eds. *The Limits of Coercive Diplomacy.* 2nd ed. Boulder, CO: Westview, 1994.

George, Alexander L., and Richard Smoke. *Deterrence in American Foreign Policy.* New York: Columbia University Press, 1974.

Gerson, Michael S. *The Sino-Soviet Border Conflict: Deterrence, Escalation, and the Threat of Nuclear War in 1969.* Arlington, VA: Center for Naval Analyses, 2010.

Gibler, Douglas M. *The Territorial Peace: Borders, State Development, and International Conflict.* New York: Cambridge University Press, 2014.

Gigerenzer, G., J. Czerlinski, and L. Martignon. "How Good Are Fast and Frugal Heuristics?" In Gilovich, Griffin, and Kahneman, *Heuristics and Biases,* 559–81.

Gilovich, Thomas D., and Dale W. Griffin. "Judgment and Decision Making." In *Handbook of Social Psychology: Volume 1.* 5th ed. Edited by Susan T. Fiske, Daniel T. Gilbert, and Gardner Lindzey, 542–88. New York: Wiley, 2010.

Gilovich, Thomas D., Dale W. Griffin, and D. Kahneman, eds. *Heuristics and Biases: The Psychology of Intuitive Judgment.* New York: Cambridge University Press, 2002.

Giner-Sorolla, Roger, and Angela T. Maitner. "Angry at the Unjust, Scared of the Powerful: Emotional Responses to Terrorist Threat." *Personality and Social Psychology Bulletin* 39, no. 8 (August 2013): 1069–82.

Glaser, Charles L. *Analyzing Strategic Nuclear Policy.* Princeton, NJ: Princeton University Press, 1990.

———. *Rational Theory of International Politics: The Logic of Competition and Cooperation.* Princeton, NJ: Princeton University Press, 2010.

Gobarev, Viktor M. "Soviet Policy toward China: Developing Nuclear Weapons, 1949–1969." *Journal of Slavic Military Studies* 12, no. 4 (1999): 37–47.

Goemans, Hein E., and Mark Fey. "Risky but Rational: War as an Institutionally Induced Gamble." *Journal of Politics* 71, no. 1 (January 2009): 35–54.

Goldgeier, James M. "Psychology and Security." *Security Studies* 6 (1997): 137–66.

Goldstein, Lyle. *Preventive Attack and Weapons of Mass Destruction: A Comparative Historical Analysis.* Stanford, CA: Stanford University Press, 2006.

———. "Return to Zhenbao Island: Who Started Shooting and Why It Matters." *China Quarterly* 168 (2001): 985–97.

Greenberg, J., S. Solomon, and T. Pyszczynski. "Terror Management Theory of Self-Esteem and Cultural Worldviews: Empirical Assessments and Conceptual Refinements." *Advances in Experimental Social Psychology* 29 (1997): 61–139.

Gribkov, Anatoli I. "The View from Moscow and Havana." In *Operation ANADYR: U.S. and Soviet Generals Recount the Cuban Missile Crisis*, edited by Alfred Friendly Jr., 3–76. Chicago: Edition Q, 1994.

Grynaviski, Eric. *Constructive Illusions: Misperceiving the Origins of International Cooperation*. Ithaca, NY: Cornell University Press, 2014.

Guisinger, Alexandra, and Alastair Smith. "Honest Threats: The Interaction of Reputation and Political Institutions in International Crises." *Journal of Conflict Resolution* 46, no. 2 (2002): 175–200.

Gurtov, Melvin, and Byong-Moo Hwang. *China under Threat: The Politics of Strategy and Diplomacy*. Baltimore: Johns Hopkins University Press, 1980.

Guthman, Edwin O., and Jeffrey Shulman, eds. *Robert Kennedy in His Own Words: The Unpublished Recollections of the Kennedy Years*. New York: Bantam, 1988.

Hagerty, Devin T. *The Consequences of Nuclear Proliferation: Lessons from South Asia*. Cambridge, MA: MIT Press, 1998.

Haldeman, H. R. *The Ends of Power*. New York: Times Books, 1978.

Halperin, Morton H. *Nuclear Fallacy: Dispelling the Myth of Nuclear Strategy*. Cambridge, MA: Ballinger, 1987.

Haqqani, Husain. *Pakistan: Between Mosque and Military*. Washington, DC: Carnegie Endowment for International Peace, 2005.

Harrison, Hope M. *Driving the Soviets Up the Wall: Soviet–East German Relations, 1953–1961*. Princeton, NJ: Princeton University Press, 2003.

Hatemi, Peter K., Rose McDermott, Lindon J. Eaves, Kenneth S. Kendler, and Michael C. Neale. "Fear as a Disposition and an Emotional State: A Genetic and Environmental Approach to Out-Group Political Preferences." *American Journal of Political Science* 57, no. 2 (April 2013): 279–93.

Heikal, Mohamed. *Sphinx and Commissar*. London: Collins, 1978.

Hermann, Margaret G., Thomas Preston, Baghat Korany, and Timothy Shaw. "Who Leads Matters: The Effects of Powerful Individuals." *International Studies Review* 3, no. 2 (2001): 83–131.

Holsti, Ole R. "Crisis Decision Making." In *Behavior, Society, and Nuclear War*, Vol. 1, edited by Philip E. Tetlock, Jo Husbands, Robert Jervis, Paul C. Stern, and Charles Tilly, 8–84. New York: Oxford University Press, 1989.

Hopf, Ted. *Peripheral Visions: Deterrence Theory and American Foreign Policy in the Third World, 1965–1990*. Ann Arbor: University of Michigan Press, 1995.

Horelick, Arnold. "The Cuban Missile Crisis: An Analysis of Soviet Calculations and Behavior." *World Politics* 16 (April 1964): 363–89.

Horelick, Arnold, and Myron Rush. *Strategic Power and Soviet Foreign Policy*. Chicago: University of Chicago Press, 1966.

Horowitz, Michael. "The Spread of Nuclear Weapons and International Conflict: Does Experience Matter?" *Journal of Conflict Resolution* 53, no. 2 (2009): 234–57.

Horowitz, Michael C., and Allan C. Stam. "How Prior Military Experience Influences the Future Militarized Behavior of Leaders." *International Organization* 68, no. 3 (June 2014): 527–59.

Hoyt, Timothy D. "Pakistan's Nuclear Posture: Thinking about the Unthinkable?" In *Strategy in the Second Nuclear Age,* edited by Toshi Yoshihara and James R. Holmes, 181–200. Washington, DC: Georgetown University Press, 2012.

Huddy, Leonie, Stanley Feldman, Charles Taber, and Gallya Lahav. "Threat, Anxiety, and Support of Antiterrorism Policies." *American Journal of Political Science* 49, no. 3 (July 2005): 593–608.

Huddy, L., N. Khatid, and T. Capelos. "Trends: Reactions to the Terrorism Attacks of September 11, 2001." *Public Opinion Quarterly* 66 (2002): 418–50.

Hussain, Zahid. *Frontline Pakistan: The Struggle with Militant Islam.* New York: Columbia University Press, 2008.

Hymans, Jacques. *Achieving Nuclear Ambitions: Scientists, Politicians, and Proliferation.* New York: Cambridge University Press, 2012.

———. *The Psychology of Nuclear Proliferation: Identity, Emotions, and Foreign Policy.* Cambridge, UK: Cambridge University Press, 2006.

Institute for Conflict Management. South Asia Terrorism Portal. http://www
.satp.org/satporgtp/countries/india/states/jandk/data_sheets/annual
_casualties.htm.

International Institute for Strategic Studies. *The Military Balance.* London: IISS, 2011.

———. *North Korean Security Challenges: A Net Assessment,* July 21, 2011.

Israelyan, Victor. *Inside the Kremlin during the Yom Kippur War.* University Park: Penn State University Press, 1995.

Jalal, Ayesha. *Democracy and Authoritarianism in South Asia.* New York: Cambridge University Press, 1995.

———. *The State of Martial Rule: The Origins of Pakistan's Political Economy of Defence.* New York: Cambridge University Press, 1990.

James, William. "What Is an Emotion?" *Mind* 9, no. 34 (1884): 188–205.

Jervis, Robert. "Cooperation under the Security Dilemma." *World Politics* 30, no. 2 (January 1978): 167–214.

———. "Do Leaders Matter and How Would We Know?" *Security Studies* 22, no. 2 (2013): 153–79.

———. "Kargil, Deterrence, and International Relations Theory." In Lavoy, *Asymmetric Warfare,* 377–97.

———. *The Meaning of the Nuclear Revolution: Statecraft and the Prospect of Armageddon.* Ithaca, NY: Cornell University Press, 1989.

———. "Perceiving and Coping with Threat." In Jervis, Lebow, and Stein, *Psychology and Deterrence*, 13–33.

———. *Perception and Misperception in International Politics*. Princeton, NJ: Princeton University Press, 1976.

———. "Understanding Beliefs." *Political Psychology* 27, no. 5 (2006): 641–63.

———. "Unipolarity: A Structural Perspective." *World Politics* 61, no. 1 (2009): 188–213.

Jervis, Robert, Richard Ned Lebow, and Janice Stein, eds. *Psychology and Deterrence*. Baltimore: Johns Hopkins University Press, 1985.

Jian, Chen. "China and the First Indo-China War, 1950–54." *China Quarterly* 133 (March 1993): 85–110.

Johnson, Dominic D. P. *Overconfidence and War: The Havoc and Glory of Positive Illusions*. Cambridge, MA: Harvard University Press, 2004.

Johnson, Dominic D. P., and Dominic Tierney. "The Rubicon Theory of War: How the Path to Conflict Reaches the Point of No Return." *International Security* 36, no. 1 (Summer 2011): 7–40.

Jones, Rodney W., Mark G. McDonough, with Toby F. Dalton and Gregory D. Koblentz. *Tracking Nuclear Proliferation: A Guide in Maps and Charts*. Washington, DC: Carnegie Endowment for International Peace, 1998.

Kahneman, Daniel. "New Challenges to the Rationality Assumption." In *Choices, Values, and Frames*, edited by Daniel Kahneman, and Amos Tversky, 758–74. New York: Russell Sage, 2000.

———. *Thinking, Fast and Slow*. New York: Farrar, Straus and Giroux, 2011.

Kahneman, Daniel, Paul Slovic, and Amos Tversky, eds. *Judgment under Uncertainty: Heuristics and Biases*. Cambridge, UK: Cambridge University Press, 1982.

Kahneman, Daniel, and Amos Tversky. "Judgment under Uncertainty: Heuristics and Biases." In Kahneman, Slovic, and Tversky, *Judgment under Uncertainty*, 3–20.

Kampani, Gaurav. "New Delhi's Long Nuclear Journey: How Secrecy and Institutional Roadblocks Delayed India's Weaponization." *International Security* 38, no. 4 (2014): 79–114.

Kapur, S. Paul. "Revisionist Ambitions, Capabilities, and Nuclear Instability: Why Nuclear South Asia Is Not Like Cold War Europe." In *Inside Nuclear South Asia*, edited by Scott D. Sagan, 184–218. Stanford, CA: Stanford University Press, 2009.

———. "Ten Years of Instability in Nuclear South Asia." *International Security* 33, no. 2 (2008): 71–94.

———. *Dangerous Deterrent: Nuclear Weapons Proliferation and Conflict in South Asia*. Stanford, CA: Stanford University Press, 2007.

———. "India and Pakistan's Unstable Peace: Why Nuclear South Asia Is Not Like Cold War Europe." *International Security* 30 (2005): 127–52.

Kapur, S. Paul, and Sumit Ganguly. "The Jihad Paradox: Pakistan and Islamist Militancy in South Asia." *International Security* 37, no. 1 (Summer 2012): 111–41.

Karabell, Zachary. *Parting the Desert: The Creation of the Suez Canal.* New York: Knopf, 2003.

Kargil Review Committee. *From Surprise to Reckoning.* New Delhi: Sage, 1999.

Karl, David J. "Proliferation Pessimism and Emerging Nuclear Powers." *International Security* 21, no. 3 (Winter 1996–97): 87–119.

Keefer, Edward. "President Dwight D. Eisenhower and the End of the Korean War." *Diplomatic History* 10, no. 3 (1986): 267–89.

Kempe, Frederick. *Berlin 1961.* New York: Putnam, 2011.

Kendler, K. S., J. Myers, and C. A. Prescott. "The Etiology of Phobias: An Evaluation of the Stress-Diathesis Model." *Archives of General Psychiatry* 59, no. 3 (2002): 242–48.

Kennedy, Andrew. *The International Ambitions of Mao and Nehru: National Efficacy Beliefs and the Making of Foreign Policy.* New York: Cambridge University Press, 2012.

Kennedy, Robert F. *Thirteen Days: A Memoir of the Cuban Missile Crisis.* New York: Norton, 1969.

Khan, Feroz Hassan. *Eating Grass: The Making of the Pakistan Bomb.* Stanford, CA: Stanford University Press, 2012.

Khan, Feroz Hassan, and Peter R. Lavoy. "Pakistan: The Dilemma of Nuclear Deterrence." In *The Long Shadow: Nuclear Weapons and Security in Twenty-First Century Asia,* edited by Muthiah Alagappa, 215–40. Stanford, CA: Stanford University Press, 2008.

Khan, Feroz Hassan, Peter R. Lavoy, and Christopher Clary. "Pakistan's Motivations and Calculations for the Kargil Conflict." In Lavoy, *Asymmetric Warfare in South Asia,* 64–91.

Khong, Yuen Foong. *Analogies at War: Korea, Munich, Dien Bien Phu, and the Vietnam Decisions of 1965.* Princeton, NJ: Princeton University Press, 1992.

Khrushchev, Nikita. *Memoirs of Nikita Khrushchev.* Edited by Sergei Khrushchev. Vol. 2: *Reformer, 1945–1964.* University Park: Penn State University Press, 2006.

———. *Memoirs of Nikita Khrushchev.* Edited by Sergei Khrushchev. Vol. 3: *Statesman, 1953–1964.* University Park: Penn State University Press, 2007.

Khrushchev, Sergei. *Khrushchev on Khrushchev: An Inside Account of the Man and His Era.* Boston: Little, Brown, 1990.

———. *Nikita Khrushchev and the Creation of a Superpower.* Translated by Shirley Benson. University Park: Penn State University Press, 2000.

Kilgour, D. Marc. "Domestic Political Structure and War Behavior: A Game-Theoretic Approach." *Journal of Conflict Resolution* 35 (1991): 266–84.

Kim Jong-un. "New Year Address." *Korean Central News Agency.* January 1, 2015. http://www.kcna.co.jp/index-e.htm.

Kimball, Jeffrey. *The Vietnam War Files: Uncovering the Secret History of Nixon-Era Strategy.* Lawrence: University Press of Kansas, 2003.

Kissinger, Henry. *White House Years.* Boston: Little, Brown, 1979.

Knopf, Jeffrey W. "The Concept of Nuclear Learning." *The Non-Proliferation Review* 19, no. 1 (2012): 79–93.

Koenigs, M., E. D. Huey, V. Raymont, B. Cheon, J. Solomon, E. M. Wassermann, and J. Grafman. "Focal Brain Damage Protects against Post-Traumatic Stress Disorder in Combat Veterans." *Nature Neuroscience* 11 (2008): 232–37.

Kroenig, Matthew. "Exporting the Bomb: Why States Provide Sensitive Nuclear Assistance." *American Political Science Review* 103, no. 1 (February 2009): 113–33.

———. "Nuclear Superiority and the Balance of Resolve: Explaining Nuclear Crisis Outcomes." *International Organization* 67, no. 1 (January 2013): 141–71.

———. "Time to Attack Iran: Why a Strike Is the Least Bad Option." *Foreign Affairs,* January–February 2012, 76–86.

Kuisong, Yang. "The Sino-Soviet Border Clash of 1969: From Zhenbao Island to Sino-American Rapprochement." *Cold War History* 1 (August 2000): 21–51.

Kunz, Diane. *The Economic Diplomacy of the Suez Crisis.* Chapel Hill: University of North Carolina Press, 1991.

Kydd, Andrew H. *Trust and Mistrust in International Relations.* Princeton, NJ: Princeton University Press, 2005.

Ladwig, Walter C., III. "A Cold Start for Hot Wars? The Indian Army's New Limited War Doctrine." *International Security* 32, no. 3 (2008): 158–90.

Lake, Eli. "Operation Sabotage: Our Secret War against Iran." *New Republic* 241, no. 12 (July 22, 2010): 16–17.

Larson, Deborah Welch. *Origins of Containment: A Psychological Explanation.* Princeton, NJ: Princeton University Press, 1985.

Lavoy, Peter R., ed. *Asymmetric Warfare in South Asia: The Causes and Consequences of the Kargil Conflict.* New York: Cambridge University Press, 2009.

———. "The Strategic Consequences of Nuclear Proliferation." *Security Studies* 4, no. 4 (Summer 1995): 695–753.

Lazarus, Richard S. "On the Primacy of Affect." *American Psychologist* 39, no. 2 (1984): 124–29.

Lebow, Richard Ned, and Janice Gross Stein. *We All Lost the Cold War.* Princeton, NJ: Princeton University Press, 1994.

LeDoux, Joseph. "Emotion: Clues from the Brain." *Annual Review of Psychology* 46 (1995): 209–30.

———. *The Emotional Brain.* New York: Simon and Schuster, 1996.

LeDoux, Joseph, and Jacek Debiek. "Fear and the Brain." *Social Research* (December 2004): 807–18.

Lee, Chan Jean, and Eduardo Andrade. "Fear, Social Projection, and Financial Decision Making." *Journal of Marketing Research* 48 (2011): 121–29.

Leffler, Melvyn P., and Odd Arne Westad, eds. *The Cambridge History of the Cold War*. Vol. 2, *Crises and Détente*. New York: Cambridge University Press, 2010.

Leng, Russell J. *Bargaining and Learning in Recurring Crises: The Soviet-American, Egyptian-Israeli, and Indo-Pakistani Rivalries*. Ann Arbor: University of Michigan Press, 2000.

———. "Realpolitik and Learning in the India-Pakistan Rivalry." In *The India-Pakistan Conflict: An Enduring Rivalry*, edited by T. V. Paul, 103–27. New York: Cambridge University Press, 2005.

Lerner, Jennifer, Roxana M. Gonzalez, Deborah A. Small, and Baruch Fischhoff. "Effects of Fear and Anger on Perceived Risks of Terrorism: A National Field Experiment." *Psychological Science* 14 (2003): 144–50.

Lerner, Jennifer S., and Dacher Keltner. "Beyond Valence: Toward a Model of Emotion-Specific Influences on Judgment and Choice." *Cognition and Emotion* 14 (2000): 473–93.

———. "Fear, Anger, and Risk." *Journal of Personality and Social Psychology* 81, no. 1 (2001): 146–59.

Lerner, Jennifer S., Deborah A. Small, and George Loewenstein. "Heart Strings and Purse Strings: Carryover Effects of Emotions on Economic Decisions." *Psychological Science* 15, no. 5 (May 2004): 337–41.

Levy, Jack S. "Learning and Foreign Policy: Sweeping a Conceptual Minefield." *International Organization* 48, no. 2 (1994): 279–312.

———. "Political Psychology and Foreign Policy." In *The Oxford Handbook of Political Psychology*, edited by David O. Sears, Leonie Huddy, and Robert Jervis, 253–84. New York: Oxford University Press, 2003.

———. "Prospect Theory, Rational Choice, and International Relations." *International Studies Quarterly* 41, no. 1 (March 1997): 87–112.

Lewis, John Wilson, and Xue Litai. *Imagined Enemies: China Prepares for Uncertain War*. Stanford, CA: Stanford University Press, 2006.

Lewis, Michael, Jeannette M. Haviland-Jones, and Lisa Feldman Barrett, eds. *Handbook of Emotions*. 3rd ed. New York: Guilford, 2008.

Linden, Carl A. *Khrushchev and the Soviet Leadership, 1957–1964*. Baltimore: Johns Hopkins University Press, 1966.

Lindsay, James M., and Ray Takeyh. "After Iran Gets the Bomb: Containment and Its Complications." *Foreign Affairs*, March–April 2010, 33–50.

Lobell, Steven E., Norrin M. Ripsman, and Jeffrey W. Taliaferro, eds. *Neoclassical Realism, the State, and Foreign Policy*. New York: Cambridge University Press, 2009.

Logevall, Fredrik. *Embers of War: The Fall of an Empire and the Making of America's Vietnam*. New York: Random House, 2012.

Losch, Mary E., and John T. Cacioppo. "Cognitive Dissonance May Enhance Sympathetic Tonus, but Attitudes Are Changed to Reduce Negative Effect

Rather Than Arousal." *Journal of Experimental Social Psychology* 26, no. 4 (July 1990): 289–304.

Luthi, Lorenz M. *The Sino-Soviet Split: Cold War in the Communist World.* Princeton, NJ: Princeton University Press, 2008.

MacFarquhar, Roderick, and Michael Schoenhals. *Mao's Last Revolution.* Cambridge, MA: Harvard University Press, 2008.

MacLeod, C., and L. Campbell. "Memory Accessibility and Probability Judgment: An Experimental Evaluation of the Availability Heuristic." *Journal of Personality and Social Psychology* 63 (1992): 890–902.

Maliniak, Daniel, Susan Peterson, Ryan Powers, and Michael J. Tierney. "Snap Poll: How Likely Is War with Russia in the Next Ten Years?" foreignpolicy .com, January 28, 2015.

Malik, V. P. *Kargil: From Surprise to Victory.* Noida UP: HarperCollins India, 2006.

———. "Lessons from Kargil." *Bharat Rakshak Monitor* 4, no. 6 (May–June 2002), www.bharat-rakshak.com/MONITOR/ISSUE4-6/malik.html.

Manis, M., J. Shedler, J. Jonides, and T. E. Nelson. "Availability Heuristic in Judgments of Set Size and Frequency of Occurrence." *Journal of Personality and Social Psychology* 65 (1993): 448–57.

Mansfield, Edward D., and Jack Snyder. "Democratic Transitions, Institutional Strength and War." *International Organization* 56, no. 2 (2002): 297–337.

———. "Democratization and the Danger of War." *International Security* 20, no. 1 (1995): 5–38.

Manstead, Anthony S. R., Nico Frijda, and Agneta Fischer, eds. *Feelings and Emotions: The Amsterdam Symposium.* Cambridge, UK: Cambridge University Press, 2004.

Marcus, George E., W. Russell Neuman, and Michael MacKuen. *Affective Intelligence and Political Judgment.* Chicago: University of Chicago Press, 2000.

Marcus, George E., J. L. Sullivan, E. Theiss-Morse, and S. L. Wood. *With Malice toward Some: How People Make Civil Liberties Judgments.* New York: Cambridge University Press, 1995.

Markman, Keith, Igor Gavanski, Stephen Sherman, and Matthew McCullen. "The Impact of Perceived Control on the Imagination of Better and Worse Possible Worlds." *Personality and Social Psychology Bulletin* 21, no. 6 (1995): 588–95.

Maxwell, Neville. "The Chinese Account of the 1969 Fighting at Chenpao." *China Quarterly,* October–December 1973, 730–39.

May, Ernest R., and Philip D. Zelikow, eds. *The Kennedy Tapes: Inside the White House during the Cuban Missile Crisis.* New York: W. W. Norton, 2002.

McAllister, James, and Diane Labrosse, eds. "What We Talk about When We Talk Nuclear Weapons." *H-Diplo/International Security Studies Forum.* https://issforum.org/forums/2-what-we-talk-about-when-we-talk-about -nuclear-weapons.

McDermott, Rose. "Emotions and War: An Evolutionary Model of Motivation." In *Handbook of War Studies 3*, edited by Manus Midlarsky, 30–61. Ann Arbor: University of Michigan Press, 2009.

——. "The Feeling of Rationality: The Meaning of Neuroscientific Advances for Political Science." *Perspectives on Politics* 2, no. 4 (December 2004): 691–706.

——. *Political Psychology in International Relations.* Ann Arbor: University of Michigan Press, 2004.

——. *Presidential Leadership, Illness, and Decision Making.* New York: Cambridge University Press, 2008.

——. *Risk Taking in International Politics: Prospect Theory in American Foreign Policy.* Ann Arbor: University of Michigan Press, 1998.

Mearsheimer, John J. "The Case for a Ukrainian Nuclear Deterrent." *Foreign Affairs* 72, no. 3 (Summer 1993): 50–66.

——. "Numbers, Strategy, and the European Balance." *International Security* 12, no. 4 (Spring 1988): 174–85.

——. *The Tragedy of Great Power Politics.* New York: Norton, 2003.

Mercer, Jonathan. "Emotion and Strategy in the Korean War." *International Organization* 67, no. 2 (2013): 221–52.

——. "Emotional Beliefs." *International Organization* 64, no. 1 (Winter 2010): 1–31.

——. *Reputation and International Politics.* Ithaca, NY: Cornell University Press, 1996.

Meyerle, Jerry, Ken Gause, and Afshon Ostovar. "Nuclear Weapons and Coercive Escalation in Regional Conflicts: Lessons from North Korea and Pakistan." CNA, November 2014, https://www.cna.org/CNA_files/PDF/DRM-2014-U-008209-Final2.pdf.

Mikoyan, Anastas. *Tak Bylo.* Moscow: Vagrius, 1994.

Mikoyan, Sergo. *The Soviet Cuban Missile Crisis: Castro, Mikoyan, Kennedy, Khrushchev, and the Missiles of November.* Edited by Svetlana Savranskaya. Stanford, CA: Stanford University Press, 2012.

Miller, D., and M. Ross. "Self-Serving Biases in the Attribution of Causality: Fact or Fiction?" *Psychological Bulletin* 82 (1975): 213–25.

Miller, Steven E. "The Case against a Ukrainian Nuclear Deterrent." *Foreign Affairs* 73, no. 3 (Summer 1993): 67–80.

Minozzi, William. "Endogenous Beliefs in Models of Politics." *American Journal of Political Science* 57, no. 3 (2013): 566–81.

Mintz, Alex, and Karl DeRouen Jr. *Understanding Foreign Policy Decision Making.* New York: Cambridge University Press, 2010.

Mistry, Dinshaw. "Complexity of Deterrence among New Nuclear States: The India-Pakistan Case." In Paul, Morgan, and Wirtz, *Complex Deterrence*, 183–203.

Montgomery, Alexander H., and Scott D. Sagan. "The Perils of Predicting Proliferation." *Journal of Conflict Resolution* 53, no. 2 (2009): 320–28.

Morgan, Patrick. *Deterrence Now.* New York: Cambridge University Press, 2003.

Morris, J. S., A. Öhman, and R. J. Dolan. "Conscious and Unconscious Emotional Learning in the Human Amygdala." *Nature* 393, no. 6684 (1998): 467–70.

Morrow, James D. "Capabilities, Uncertainty, and Resolve: A Limited Information Model of Crisis Bargaining." *American Journal of Political Science* 33 (1989): 941–72.

Mueller, John E. *Atomic Obsession: Nuclear Alarmism from Hiroshima to Al-Qaeda.* New York: Oxford University Press, 2009.

Mullen, B., and C. A. Riordan. "Self-Serving Attributions for Performance in Naturalistic Settings: A Meta-Analytic Review." *Journal of Applied Social Psychology* 18 (1988): 3–22.

Musharraf, Pervez. *In the Line of Fire: A Memoir.* New York: Free Press, 2006.

Nalebuff, Barry. "Brinkmanship and Nuclear Deterrence: The Neutrality of Escalation." *Conflict Management and Peace Science* 9 (1986): 19–30.

Narang, Vipin. *Nuclear Strategy in the Modern Era.* Princeton, NJ: Princeton University Press, 2014.

Nash, Philip. "Bear Any Burden? John F. Kennedy and Nuclear Weapons." In *Cold War Statesmen Confront the Bomb: Nuclear Diplomacy since 1945,* edited by John Lewis Gaddis, Philip Gordon, Ernest May, and Jonathan Rosenberg, 124–39. New York: Oxford University Press, 1999.

———. *The Other Missiles of October: Eisenhower, Kennedy, and the Jupiters, 1957–1963.* Chapel Hill: University of North Carolina Press, 1997.

Nathan, James A., ed. *The Cuban Missile Crisis Revisited.* New York: St. Martin's, 1992.

Nawaz, Shuja. *Crossed Swords: Pakistan, Its Army, and the Wars Within.* New York: Oxford University Press, 2008.

Nayak, Polly, and Michael Krepon. "U.S. Crisis Management in South Asia's Twin Peaks Crisis." Henry L. Stimson Center Report 57 (September 2006).

Neale, Michael C., and David W. Fulker. "A Bivariate Path Analysis of Fear Data on Twins and Their Parents." *Acta Geneticae Medicae et Gemellologiae* 33, no. 2 (1984): 273–86.

Nisbett, R. E., and L. D. Ross. *Human Inference: Strategies and Shortcomings of Social Judgment.* Upper Saddle River, NJ: Prentice Hall, 1980.

Nixon, Richard. *The Memoirs of Richard Nixon.* New York: Simon and Schuster, 1978.

———. *No More Vietnams.* New York: Arbor House, 1985.

Norris, Robert, and Hans Kristensen. "Nuclear Notebook: Pakistan's Nuclear Forces 2011." *Bulletin of the Atomic Scientists* 67, no. 4 (July-August 2011): 91–99, http://bos.sagepub.com/content/67/4/91.full.pdf+html.

Nussbaum, Martha C. *Upheavals of Thought: The Intelligence of Emotions*. Cambridge, UK: Cambridge University Press, 2001.

O'Brien, Michael. *Kennedy: A Biography*. New York: St. Martin's, 2005.

O'Donnell, Kenneth P., David F. Powers, and Joe McCarthy. *Johnny, We Hardly Knew Ye: Memories of John Fitzgerald Kennedy*. Boston: Little, Brown, 1983.

Öhman, Arne. "Fear and Anxiety: Overlaps and Dissociations." In Lewis, Haviland-Jones, and Barrett, *Handbook of Emotions*, 709–29.

Öhman, Arne, and Susan Mineka. "Fears, Phobias, and Preparedness: Toward an Evolved Module of Fear and Fear Learning." *Psychological Review* 108, no. 3 (2001): 483–522.

Öhman, Arne, and Stefan Wiens. "The Concept of an Evolved Fear Module and Cognitive Theories of Anxiety." In Manstead, Frijda, and Fischer, *Feelings and Emotions*, 58–80.

Pape, Robert A. *Bombing to Win: Air Power and Coercion in War*. Ithaca, NY: Cornell University Press, 1995.

Parrott, Bruce. *Politics and Technology in the Soviet Union*. Cambridge, MA: MIT Press, 1983.

Paul, T. V. *Power versus Prudence: Why Nations Forgo Nuclear Weapons*. Montreal: McGill-Queen's University Press, 2000.

Paul, T. V., Patrick Morgan, and James Wirtz, eds. *Complex Deterrence: Strategy in the Global Age*. Chicago: University of Chicago Press, 2009.

Perkovich, George. *India's Nuclear Bomb: The Impact on Global Proliferation*. Berkeley: University of California Press, 1999.

Peterson, John. *The Cuban Missile Crisis: A Political Perspective after Forty Years*. Video excerpt from The Cuban Missile Crisis: A Political Perspective after Forty Years Conference, Havana, Cuba, October 11–13, 2002. Posted by National Security Archive, October 24, 2012, https://www.youtube.com/watch?v=AII2KNH18Jc&feature=youtu.be.

Pitman, Roger K., and Scott P. Orr. "Psychophysiology of Emotional and Memory Networks in Posttraumatic Stress Disorder." In *Brain and Memory: Modulation and Mediation of Neuroplasticity*, edited by James L. McGaugh, Norman Weinberger, and Gary Lynch, 75–83. New York: Oxford University Press, 1995.

Pleshakov, Constantine. "Studying Soviet Strategies and Decision-making in the Cold War Years." In *Reviewing the Cold War: Approaches, Interpretations, Theory*, edited by Odd Arne Westad, 232–41. London: Frank Cass, 2000.

Podvig, Pavel, ed. *Russian Strategic Nuclear Forces*. Cambridge, MA: MIT Press, 2001.

Posen, Barry. *Inadvertent Escalation: Conventional War and Nuclear Risks*. Ithaca, NY: Cornell University Press, 1991.

———. "Is NATO Decisively Outnumbered?" *International Security* 12, no. 4 (Spring 1988): 186–202.

———. "Measuring the European Conventional Balance: Coping with Complexity in Threat Assessment." *International Security* 9, no. 3 (Winter 1984–85): 47–88.

Post, Jerrold M. *Leaders and Their Followers in a Dangerous World: The Psychology of Political Behavior.* Ithaca, NY: Cornell University Press, 2004.

Potter, Phillip. "Does Experience Matter? American Presidential Experience, Age, and International Conflict." *Journal of Conflict Resolution* 51, no. 3 (2007): 351–79.

Powaski, Ronald E. *The Cold War: The United States and the Soviet Union, 1917–1991.* Oxford, UK: Oxford University Press, 1998.

Powell, Robert. "Bargaining and Learning While Fighting." *American Journal of Political Science* 48, no. 2 (April 2004): 344–61.

———. "Crisis Bargaining, Escalation and MAD." *American Political Science Review* 81, no. 3 (1987): 717–36.

———. "Nuclear Brinksmanship with Two-Sided Incomplete Information." *American Political Science Review* 82, no. 1 (1988): 155–78.

———. *Nuclear Deterrence Theory: The Search for Credibility.* New York: Cambridge University Press, 1990.

Press, Daryl G. *Calculating Credibility: How Leaders Assess Military Threats.* Ithaca, NY: Cornell University Press, 2005.

Pyszczynski, T., J. Greenberg, and S. Solomon. "Why Do We Need What We Need? A Terror Management Perspective on the Roots of Human Social Motivation." *Psychological Inquiry* 8 (1997): 1–20.

Qadir, Shaukat. "An Analysis of the Kargil Conflict 1999." *RUSI Journal* 147, no. 2 (2002): 24–30.

Raas, Whitney, and Austin Long. "Osirak Redux? Assessing Israeli Capabilities to Destroy Iranian Nuclear Facilities." *International Security* 31, no. 4 (2007): 7–33.

Raghavan, V. R. "Limited War and Nuclear Escalation in South Asia." *Non-Proliferation Review* 8, no. 3 (2001): 82–98.

———. *Siachen: Conflict without End.* Delhi: Viking, 2002.

Randolph, Stephen P. *Powerful and Brutal Weapons: Nixon, Kissinger, and the Easter Offensive.* Cambridge, MA: Harvard University Press, 2007.

Rashid, Ahmed. *Descent into Chaos: The United States and the Failure of Nation Building in Pakistan, Afghanistan, and Central Asia.* New York: Penguin, 2008.

Reagan, Ronald. *An American Life.* New York: Simon and Schuster, 1990.

Reeves, Richard. *President Kennedy: Profile of Power.* New York: Simon and Schuster, 1993.

Reiter, Dan. *Crucible of Beliefs: Learning, Alliances, and World Wars.* Ithaca, NY: Cornell University Press, 1996.

Richter, James. *Khrushchev's Double Bind: International Pressures and Domestic Coalition Politics.* Baltimore: Johns Hopkins University Press, 1994.

Riedel, Bruce. *American Diplomacy and the 1999 Kargil Summit at Blair House.* Center for the Advanced Study of India, University of Pennsylvania, Philadelphia, 2002.

Robinson, Thomas. "China Confronts the Soviet Union: Warfare and Diplomacy on China's Inner Asian Frontiers." In *The Cambridge History of China—The People's Republic.* Vol. 15, part 2, *Revolutions within the Chinese Revolution, 1966–1982,* edited by Roderick MacFarquhar and John K. Fairbank, 218–302. Cambridge, UK: Cambridge University Press, 1991.

———. "The Sino-Soviet Border Conflict." In *Diplomacy of Power: Soviet Armed Forces as a Political Instrument,* edited by Stephen Kaplan, 265–313. Washington, DC: Brookings Institution Press, 1981.

———. "The Sino-Soviet Border Dispute: Background, Development, and the March 1969 Clashes." *American Political Science Review,* December 1972: 1187–89.

Rosen, Stephen P. *War and Human Nature.* Princeton, NJ: Princeton University Press, 2007.

Ross, Michael, and Fiore Sicoly. "Egocentric Biases in Availability and Attribution." *Journal of Personality and Social Psychology* 37 (1979): 322–37.

Rothman, A. J., and C. D. Hardin. "Differential Use of the Availability Heuristic in Social Judgment." *Personality and Social Psychology Bulletin* 23 (1997): 123–28.

Rusk, Dean. *As I Saw It.* New York: W. W. Norton, 1990.

Sagan, Scott D. "How to Keep the Bomb from Iran." *Foreign Affairs* 85, no. 5 (September–October 2006): 45–59.

———. *The Limits of Safety: Organizations, Accidents, and Nuclear Weapons.* Princeton, NJ: Princeton University Press, 1993.

———. "More Will Be Worse." In Sagan and Waltz, *Spread of Nuclear Weapons,* 41–81.

———. *Moving Targets: Nuclear Strategy and National Security.* Princeton, NJ: Princeton University Press, 1989.

———. "The Reasons to Worry." In Sagan and Waltz, *Spread of Nuclear Weapons,* 200–214.

———. "Why Do States Build Nuclear Weapons? Three Models in Search of the Bomb." *International Security* 21, no. 3 (Winter 1996–97): 54–86.

Sagan, Scott D., and Jeremi Suri. "The Madman Nuclear Alert: Secrecy, Signaling, and Safety in October 1969." *International Security* 27, no. 4 (2003): 150–83.

Sagan, Scott D., and Kenneth N. Waltz, eds. *The Spread of Nuclear Weapons: An Enduring Debate.* 3rd ed. New York: Norton, 2013.

Salinger, Pierre. *With Kennedy.* Garden City, NY: Doubleday, 1966.

Sanderson, W. C., R. M. Rapee, and D. H. Barlow. "Panic Induction via Inhalation of 5.5% CO_2 Enriched Air: A Single Subject Analysis of

Psychological and Physiological Effects." *Behaviour Research and Therapy* 26, no. 4 (1988): 333–35.

Saunders, Elizabeth N. *Leaders at War: How Presidents Shape Military Interventions.* Ithaca, NY: Cornell University Press, 2011.

Schecter, Jerrold L., ed. *Khrushchev Remembers: The Glasnost Tapes.* Boston: Little, Brown, 1990.

Schecter, Jerrold L., and Peter A. Deriabin. *The Spy Who Saved the World: How a Soviet Colonel Changed the Course of the Cold War.* New York: Scribner, 1992.

Schelling, Thomas. *Arms and Influence.* New Haven, CT: Yale University Press, 1966.

———. *The Strategy of Conflict.* Cambridge, MA: Harvard University Press, 1960.

Schlesinger, Arthur, Jr. *A Thousand Days: John F. Kennedy in the White House.* New York: Houghton Mifflin, 2002.

———. *Robert Kennedy and His Times.* New York: Random House, 1978.

Schultz, Kenneth. "Domestic Opposition and Signaling in International Crises." *American Political Science Review* 92, no. 4 (1998): 829–44.

Schwarz, Norbert, Fritz Strack, Herbert Bless, Gisela Klumpp, Helga Rittenauer-Schatka, and Annette Simons. "Ease of Retrieval as Information: Another Look at the Availability Heuristic." *Journal of Personality and Social Psychology* 61 (1991): 195–202.

Scobell, Andrew. *China's Use of Military Force: Beyond the Great Wall and the Long March.* New York: Cambridge University Press, 2003.

Scott, Sophie K., Andrew W. Young, Andrew J. Calder, Deborah J. Hellawell, John P. Aggleton, and Michael Johnsons. "Impaired Auditory Recognition of Fear and Anger Following Bilateral Amygdala Lesions." *Nature* 385 (1997): 254–57.

Seaborg, Glenn T. *Kennedy, Khrushchev and the Test Ban.* Berkeley: University of California Press, 1981.

Sechser, Todd S. "Militarized Compellent Threats, 1918–2001." *Conflict Management and Peace Science* 28, no. 4 (2011): 377–401.

Sechser, Todd S., and Matthew Fuhrmann. "Crisis Bargaining and Nuclear Blackmail." *International Organization* 67, no. 1 (January 2013): 173–95.

Seng, Jordan. "Less Is More: Command and Control Advantages of Minor Nuclear States." *Security Studies* 6, no. 4 (Summer 1997): 50–92.

Shah, Aqil. *The Army and Democracy: Military Politics in Pakistan.* Cambridge, MA: Harvard University Press, 2014.

Shaikh, Farzana. *Making Sense of Pakistan.* New York: Columbia University Press, 2009.

Shevchenko, Arkady. *Breaking with Moscow.* New York: Knopf, 1985.

Short, Philip. *Mao: A Life.* New York: Henry Holt, 2000.

Simon, Herbert A. "A Behavioral Model of Rational Choice." *Quarterly Journal of Economics* 69, no. 1 (1955): 99–118.

Siniver, Asaf. "The Nixon Administration and the Cienfuegos Crisis of 1970: Crisis-Management of a Non-Crisis?" *Review of International Studies* 34 (2008): 69–88.

Skitka, Linda, Christopher Bauman, Nicholas Aramovich, and G. Scott Morganet. "Confrontational and Preventative Policy Responses to Terrorism: Anger Wants a Fight and Fear Wants 'Them' to Go Away." *Basic and Applied Social Psychology* 28, no. 4 (2006): 375–84.

Skitka, Linda J., Christopher. Bauman, and Elizabeth Mullen. "Political Tolerance and Coming to Psychological Closure Following the September 11, 2001, Terrorist Attacks: An Integrative Approach." *Personality and Social Psychology Bulletin* 30, no. 6 (2004): 743–56.

Skovgaard Poulsen, Lauge N., and Emma Aisbett. "When the Claim Hits: Bilateral Investment Treaties and Bounded Rational Learning." *World Politics* 65, no. 2 (2013): 273–313.

Slantchev, Branislav. "Feigning Weakness." *International Organization* 64, no. 3 (2010): 357–88.

———. "Military Coercion in Interstate Crises." *American Political Science Review* 99, no. 4 (2005): 533–47.

———. "The Power to Hurt: Costly Conflict with Completely Informed States." *American Political Science Review* 47 (2002): 1–11.

———. "The Principle of Convergence in Wartime Negotiations." *American Political Science Review* 97, no. 4 (November 2003): 621–32.

Slovic, Paul, and Ali Alhakami. "A Psychological Study of the Inverse Relationship between Perceived Risk and Perceived Benefit." *Risk Analysis* 14, no. 6 (December 1994): 1085–96.

Slusser, Robert M. *The Berlin Crisis of 1961: Soviet-American Relations and the Struggle for Power in the Kremlin, June-November 1961.* Baltimore: Johns Hopkins University Press, 1973.

Smith, Alastair. "Fighting Battles, Winning Wars." *Journal of Conflict Resolution* 42 (June 1998): 301–20.

———. "International Crises and Domestic Politics." *American Political Science Review* 92, no. 3 (September 1998): 623–38.

Smith, Alastair, and Allan C. Stam. "Bargaining and the Nature of War." *Journal of Conflict Resolution* 48, no. 6 (2004): 783–813.

Smith, Craig A., and Phoebe C. Ellsworth. "Patterns of Cognitive Appraisal in Emotion." *Journal of Personality and Social Psychology* 48 (1985): 813–38.

Smoke, Richard. *National Security and the Nuclear Dilemma: An Introduction to the American Experience in the Cold War.* New York: McGraw-Hill, 1993.

Smyser, W. R. *Kennedy and the Berlin Wall.* Lanham, MD: Rowman and Littlefield, 2009.

Snyder, Glenn H. "The Balance of Power and the Balance of Terror." In *The Balance of Power*, edited by Paul Seabury, 184–201. San Francisco: Chandler, 1965.

Snyder, Glenn H., and Paul Diesing. *Conflict among Nations: Bargaining, Decision Making, and System Structure in International Crises*. Princeton, NJ: Princeton University Press, 1977.

Snyder, Jack, and Erica D. Borghard. "The Cost of Empty Threats: A Penny, Not a Pound." *American Political Science Review* 105, no. 3 (August 2011): 437–56.

Solingen, Etel. *Nuclear Logics: Contrasting Paths in East Asia and the Middle East*. Princeton, NJ: Princeton University Press, 2007.

Sood, V. K., and Pravin Sawhney. *Operation Parakram: The War Unfinished*. New Delhi: Sage, 2003.

Sorensen, Theodore C. *Counselor: A Life at the Edge of History*. New York: HarperCollins, 2008.

———. *Kennedy*. New York: Harper and Row, 1965.

Stein, Janice Gross. "Political Learning and Political Psychology: A Question of Norms." In *Political Psychology*, edited by Kristen Renwick Monroe, 107–15. Hillsdale, NJ: Lawrence Erlbaum Associates, 2002.

———. "Rational Deterrence against 'Irrational Adversaries?' No Common Knowledge." In Paul, Morgan, and Wirtz, *Complex Deterrence*, 58–82.

Sutter, Robert. *China Watch: Toward Sino-American Reconciliation*. Baltimore: Johns Hopkins University Press, 1978.

Talbot, Ian. *Pakistan: A Modern History*. New Delhi: Oxford University Press, 1999.

Talbott, Strobe. *Engaging India: Diplomacy, Democracy, and the Bomb*. Washington, DC: Brookings Institution Press, 2004.

———. *Khrushchev Remembers*. Boston: Little, Brown, 1970.

Talmadge, Caitlin. "Closing Time: Assessing the Iranian Threat to the Strait of Hormuz." *International Security* 33, no. 1 (2008): 82–117.

Tang, Shiping. "Fear in International Politics: Two Positions." *International Studies Review* 10 (2008): 451–71.

Tarer, Ahmer, and Bahar Leventoglu. "Limited Audience Costs in International Crises." *Journal of Conflict Resolution* 57, no. 6 (2013): 1065–89.

Taubman, William. *Khrushchev: The Man and His Era*. New York: Norton, 2003.

Taylor, Frederick. *The Berlin Wall: A World Divided, 1961–1989*. New York: HarperCollins, 2007.

Taylor, Maxwell D. *Swords and Ploughshares*. New York: W. W. Norton, 1972.

Tellis, Ashley, C. Christine Fair, and Jamison Jo Medby. *Limited Conflicts under the Nuclear Umbrella: Indian and Pakistani Lessons from the Kargil Crisis*. Santa Monica, CA: RAND, 2002.

Tellis, Ashley, Angel Rabasa, Robert Blackwill, Pater Chalk, Kim Cragin, C. Christine Fair, Brian Jackson, Brian Michael Jenkins, Seth Jones, and Nathaniel Shestak. "The Lessons of Mumbai." RAND Occasional Paper, 2009.

Thompson, William J. *Khrushchev: A Political Life*. New York: St. Martin's Griffin, 1997.

Tomz, Michael. "Domestic Audience Costs in International Relations: An Experimental Approach." *International Organization* 61 (Fall 2007): 821–40.

———. *Reputation and International Cooperation: Sovereign Debt across Three Centuries*. Princeton, NJ: Princeton University Press, 2007.

Tooby, John, and Leda Cosmides. "The Evolutionary Psychology of the Emotions and Their Relationship to Internal Regulatory Variables." In Lewis, Haviland-Jones, and Barrett, *Handbook of Emotions*, 114–37.

Trachtenberg, Marc. "Audience Costs: An Historical Analysis." *Security Studies* 21, no. 1 (2012): 3–42.

———. *A Constructed Peace: The Making of the European Settlement, 1945–1963*. Princeton, NJ: Princeton University Press, 1999.

———. *History and Strategy*. Princeton, NJ: Princeton University Press, 1991.

Trager, Robert F. "Diplomatic Calculus in Anarchy: How Communication Matters." *American Political Science Review* 104, no. 2 (2010): 347–68.

Trager, Robert F., and Lynn Vavreck. "The Political Costs of Crisis Bargaining." *American Journal of Political Science* 55, no. 3 (2011): 526–45.

Troyanovsky, Oleg. "The Making of Soviet Foreign Policy." In *Nikita Khrushchev*, edited by William Taubman, Sergei Khrushchev, and Abbott Gleason, 209–41. New Haven, CT: Yale University Press, 2000.

Tuchman, Barbara W. *The Guns of August*. New York: Macmillan, 1962.

Tyler, Patrick. *A Great Wall, Six Presidents, and China: An Investigative History*. New York: Public Affairs, 1999.

Vastfjäll, Daniel, Ellen Peters, and Paul Slovic. "Affect, Risk Perception, and Future Optimism after the Tsunami Disaster." *Judgment and Decision Making* 3, no. 1 (2008): 64–72.

Volkogonov, Dmitri. *Autopsy for an Empire: The Seven Leaders Who Built the Soviet Regime*. New York: Free Press, 1998.

Wagner, R. Harrison. "Bargaining and War." *American Journal of Political Science* 44 (July 2000): 469–84.

———. "Nuclear Deterrence, Counterforce Strategies, and the Incentive to Strike First." *American Political Science Review* 85, no. 3 (1991): 727–49.

———. "Uncertainty, Rational Learning, and Bargaining in the Cuban Missile Crisis." In *Models of Strategic Choice in Politics*, edited by Peter C. Ordeshook, 177–205. Ann Arbor: University of Michigan Press, 1989.

Waltz, Kenneth. *Man, the State, and War*. New York: Columbia University Press, 1959.

"More May Be Better." In Sagan and Waltz, *Spread of Nuclear Weapons*, 3–40.

———. "Reflections on Theory of International Politics: A Response to My Critics." In *Neorealism and Its Critics*, edited by Robert O. Keohane, 322–46. New York: Columbia University Press, 1986.

———. "The Spread of Nuclear Weapons: More May be Better." Adelphi Papers 171. London: International Institute for Strategic Studies, 1981.

———. *Theory of International Politics*. New York: McGraw-Hill, 1979.

———. "Waltz Responds to Sagan." In *The Spread of Nuclear Weapons: A Debate Renewed*, edited by Kenneth N. Waltz and Scott D. Sagan, 125–54. New York: Norton, 2003.

Wanke, M., N. Schwarz, and H. Bless. "The Availability Heuristic Revisited: Experienced Ease of Retrieval in Mundane Frequency Estimates." *Acta Psychologica* 89 (1995): 83–90.

Weeks, Jessica L. P. *Dictators at War and Peace*. Ithaca, NY: Cornell University Press, 2014.

Wich, Richard. *Sino-Soviet Crisis Politics: A Study of Political Change and Communication*. Cambridge, MA: Harvard University Press, 1980.

Wirsing, Robert G. *India, Pakistan, and the Kashmir Dispute: On Regional Conflict and Its Resolution*. New York: St. Martin's, 1998.

Wit, Joel S., and Sun Young Ahn. *North Korea's Nuclear Futures: Technology and Strategy*. US-Korea Institute at SAIS, February 2015, http://uskoreainstitute .org/wp-content/uploads/2016/02/NKNF_NK-Nuclear-Futures.pdf.

Witt, William C., Christina Walrond, David Albright, and Houston Wood. "Iran's Evolving Breakout Potential." ISIS Report, October 8, 2012, http:// www.isisnucleariran.org/assets/pdf/Irans_Evolving_Breakout_Potential _8October2012.pdf.

Yarhi-Milo, Keren. *Knowing the Adversary: Leaders, Intelligence, and Assessment of Intentions in International Relations*. Princeton, NJ: Princeton University Press, 2014.

Zajonc, Robert B. "On the Primacy of Affect." *American Psychologist* 39, no. 2 (1984): 117–23.

Zaloga, Steven. *The Kremlin's Nuclear Sword: The Rise and Fall of Russia's Strategic Nuclear Forces, 1945–2000*. Washington, DC: Smithsonian Institute Press, 2002.

Zubok, Vladislav. *A Failed Empire: The Soviet Union in the Cold War from Stalin to Gorbachev*. Chapel Hill: University of North Carolina Press, 2007.

Zubok, Vladislav M., and Constantine Pleshakov. *Inside the Kremlin's Cold War: From Stalin to Khrushchev*. Cambridge, MA: Harvard University Press, 1996.

INDEX

Figures and tables are denoted by f and t following the page number.

Indian Parliament attacks and, 126, 138–39; Islamic insurgent groups and, 232; Jammu army base attacks and, 126, 139–40; Lahore declaration and, 169; leader learning and, 124, 149–51, 150t; Line of Control for, 131, 139, 140, 172; May 2002 crisis, 141–44, 145; Mumbai attacks and, 147–49, 151; non-military solutions to, 136–37; nuclear deterrence and, 130, 133, 136, 148, 151; progress in, 216; rational-signaling model and, 124, 130, 135–37, 150, 150t, 170, 171, 172–73, 173t; Saltoro Mountain region and, 132; Siachen glacier sector and, 131, 133, 137; superpower model and, 124; 2001-2002 crisis, 123, 138–46, 147, 215; United States and, 134–35, 136, 137, 140–41, 146; Waltzian learning model and, 124, 125, 128, 130, 149–50, 150t, 170, 171, 172, 173t, 210. See also Kargil War; Kashmir insurgency

inferential shorcuts, 31

information processing, 7–8, 30, 31, 60

intercontinental ballistic missiles. See ICBM

interdependence, economic, 233

international relations: ALF model and, 14; availability heuristic and, 12; control and, 7; dilemma of nuclear assertion and, 235; emotion in, 44–45; fear in, 9; future research on, 232; psychological approaches to, 30; rational-choice model and, 58, 66; stabilization of, 205–7

Inter-Services Intelligence (ISI), 131, 147, 151

interstate conflict: fear and, 44; future research on, 232–33; Jervis on, 54; new nuclear powers and, 2, 7; probability of, 5, 6; promotion or prevention of, 205–6; rational-choice model and, 57

interwar years, strategic bombing during, 51–52

Iran, 227–31; ALF model and, 213, 227, 228–30; assertive foreign policy against, 229–30; fear of imminent nuclear war and, 24, 228–29; Joint Comprehensive Plan of Action, 227; lack of allies for, 16; nuclear assertion and, 24, 228–30; nuclear weapons development by, 227–28, 235, 237n38; restrained foreign policy by, 229; a shield for, 205; Soviet pressure on, 32, 89; threat posed by, 2, 228

Iraq, 216, 220, 229

Iraq coup (1958), 89–91, 107

ISI (Inter-Services Intelligence), 131, 147, 151

Islamic homeland, Pakistan as, 126–27

Islamic insurgent groups, 232

isolationism, 47

Israel: Arab-Israeli War and, 174, 178–79; conventional military forces of, 227; Iran and, 228; lack of information on, 19; as a new nuclear power, 5; Suez Crisis and, 84–86; superpower patron for, 15; Yom Kippur War (1973), 5

Jagow, Gottlieb von, 38

Jaish-e-Mohammad, 172

James, William, 51

Jammu army base attacks (2002), 126, 139–40

Japan, 38

ABOUT THE AUTHOR

Michael D. Cohen is senior lecturer in the Department of Security Studies and Criminology at Macquarie University in Australia. He was previously assistant professor in the Department of Political Science at the University of Southern Denmark and in 2014–2015 was a visiting scholar at the Arnold A. Saltzman Institute of War and Peace Studies at Columbia University. He is coeditor (with Sung Chull Kim) of the volume *North Korea and Nuclear Weapons*. His research has been funded by the Lyndon Baines Johnson Foundation, the Simons Foundation, and the Nordic International Studies Association and published in journals such as *International Security, Foreign Policy Analysis, International Relations of the Asia-Pacific, Non-Proliferation Review,* and *Strategic Studies Quarterly.*